THE ACTOR AT WORK

NINTH EDITION

THE ACTOR AT WORK

ROBERT BENEDETTI

Boston   New York   San Francisco
Mexico City   Montreal   Toronto   London   Madrid   Munich   Paris
Hong Kong   Singapore   Tokyo   Cape Town   Sydney

Series Editor: Molly Taylor
Series Editorial Assistant: Michael Kish
Marketing Manager: Mandee Eckersley
Senior Production Editor: Annette Pagliaro
Editorial Production Service: Omegatype Typography, Inc.
Composition Buyer: Linda Cox
Manufacturing Buyer: JoAnne Sweeney
Cover Administrator: Kristina Mose-Libon
Electronic Composition: Omegatype Typography, Inc.

For related titles and support materials, visit our online catalog at www.ablongman.com.

Library of Congress Cataloging-in-Publication Data

Benedetti, Robert L.
    The actor at work / Robert Benedetti.—9th ed.
      p. cm.
    Includes bibliographical references and index.
    ISBN 0-205-41850-3
     1. Acting. I. Title.
  PN2061.B39 2004
  792.02'8--dc22
                        2003070189

Printed in the United States of America
10 9 8 7 6 5 4 3   09 08 07 06

Photo Credits: Photographs on pages 11, 12, 15, 37, 53, and 173 are courtesy of Robert Benedetti.

This edition is dedicated to the memory of my mother,
Lola Benedetti.

CONTENTS

PART III   CHARACTERIZATION   109

LIST OF EXERCISES

PREFACE

It is now thirty-four years since Oscar Brockett first encouraged me to write *The Actor at Work*. Each of the previous eight editions reflected my growing understanding of the acting process, and in each I benefited from the input of my students, fellow teachers, and the fine professional actors with whom I've worked in finding clearer, simpler, and more useful descriptions of that process. This ninth edition continues that evolution.

Some fifteen years ago, with the help of my friend Ted Danson, I began a new career as a film and television producer and have been lucky enough to win several Emmys and a Peabody Award. The seventh and eighth editions of *The Actor at Work* reflected my growing experience with acting for the camera, and that is continued here, including references to a sample scene from the television show *Cheers*. However, acting for the camera deserves separate study, and I have since written a book called *ACTION! Acting for Film and Television*. This uses the same philosophy of acting contained in *The Actor at Work* but adapts it to the specific requirements of the camera.

The Actor at Work was always intended to present a fairly complete view of the acting process, one addressed to the student intending to enter the acting profession. I recently decided that a simpler, more introductory text was also needed, so a few years ago I wrote *The Actor in You: Sixteen Simple Steps to Understanding the Art of Acting*. This book also uses the same approach presented in *The Actor at Work* but condenses it and presents it in a form accessible to beginners and nonmajors. It has served a useful purpose and is already in its second edition.

I want to thank the folks at Allyn and Bacon for their continued support of these and the other books of mine they have recently published, *From Concept to Screen: An Overview of Film and Television Production* and *Creative Postproduction: Editing, Sound, Effects, and Music for Film and Video*.

Thanks also to the reviewers of this edition, Rick D. Anderson, Kirkwood Community College; Bill Gelber, Texas Tech University; and Lori Horvik, North Dakota State University.

THE ACTOR AT WORK

PART I

PREPARING YOURSELF

Buddhists describe the process of personal growth as the "threefold way." It begins with preparing the *ground,* in the way a gardener cultivates the soil to make it ready to accept the seed. Next a *path* is opened, as when the gardener plants the seed and waters the young plant. Finally, the *fruition* follows naturally, as when the gardener perfects the plant by pruning and tending, always with respect for its own nature.

We will use this idea of the threefold way of *ground, path,* and *fruition* to organize our study of acting. The first part of this book begins with *you,* your body, voice, thoughts, and feelings. You are the "ground," the instrument, of your work as an actor.

The second part opens the "path," which is the concept of *action.* Here we will explore your ability to experience the needs and thoughts of the character within his or her circumstances and to experience for yourself the things the character does to try to satisfy those needs.

The "fruition" of this process makes up the third part of the book, the *characterization.* Building on what you discovered in action, you develop an artistically heightened creation that serves the purposes for which the role was created.

The final part details *the working process* by which most plays and films are created.

At the back of the book, you will find a new Glossary of Acting Terminology and an Acting Checklist.

THE EXERCISES AND READINGS

Each lesson in this book contains exercises. They are a program of self-discovery and self-development and are arranged roughly according to a natural acquisition of skills and insights. The experiences provided by the exercises are essential to a true understanding (in the muscles as well as in the mind) of what this book is about. These exercises have no "right" outcome, so just follow the instructions and see what happens!

In addition to the exercises, later lessons contain examples taken from sample scenes included in Appendix A at the back of this book. Included is a scene from

Luis Valdez's *Zoot Suit* and a scene from the television show *Cheers* by Tom Reeder. I often refer to other plays, especially Tennessee Williams's *The Glass Menagerie,* Arthur Miller's *Death of a Salesman,* Samuel Beckett's *Endgame,* Tennessee Williams's *A Streetcar Named Desire,* and Bertolt Brecht's *Mother Courage.* You will benefit more from my examples if you read at least some of these plays in their entirety, especially *Death of a Salesman* and *The Glass Menagerie.*

THE ACTOR IN YOU

You are already an actor. You "play a role" every time you present yourself in a social situation. In various circumstances and in various relationships, you pursue your needs by behaving in certain ways, doing things to other people, and reacting to the things they do to you. It is this interaction with your world, this give and take of acting and reacting, that shapes and expresses your personality, your *character*, in everyday life.

In his book *The Presentation of Self in Everyday Life,* social psychologist Erving Goffman observed:

> It does take deep skill, long training, and psychological capacity to become a good stage actor. But...almost anyone can quickly learn a script well enough to give a charitable audience some sense of realness.... Scripts even in the hands of unpracticed players can come to life because life itself is a dramatically enacted thing.... In short, we all act better than we know how.[1]

The fact that you are "acting" most of the time does not mean that you are insincere: behaving in ways that achieve your objectives is a natural and necessary way of coping with life. You often adapt your social behavior to the demands of your situation automatically and unconsciously. In fact, you play several characters every day—student, son or daughter, friend, employee—each with its own appropriate behavior, speech, thought, and feelings: your own little repertory company!

This fact was noticed years ago by the psychologist William James, who said that our personalities are actually composites of many social roles; he called these roles our various "me"s. Behind the "me"s, of course, there is one consciousness, which he called our "I." But our "I" is not rigid and is expressed through all of our "me"s, even though some of them may be quite different from one another.

We may even experience situations in which two or more of our "me"s come into conflict with one another. If you're busy being "buddy" with your friends, or "lover" with that special other, the arrival of parents or a boss may cause an uncomfortable conflict between your role as "buddy" or "lover" and your role as "child" or "employee."

As you become aware of this, you also notice that your sense of "I" tends to flow into whichever "me" you are being. As an actor, you will still have your "I," but you will learn to let it flow into the new "me" of each character you play, some of which may be very different from any of the roles you have experienced in life. And of course, the qualities of these new "me"s are determined not by you but by the writer, who has created a new world in which this new "me" lives. *One of the actor's most important skills is to allow his or her "I" to flow fully and freely into this new "me" of the character and its world while still maintaining an awareness of the artistic purposes for which this new "me" was created.*

The art of acting, then, is based on everyday life principles. In many important ways, you already know how to act!

EXERCISE 1.1: THE ACTOR IN YOU

For the next few days, observe your own behavior and that of those around you. Make note of the ways in which you present yourself differently in various circumstances.

1. Notice changes in your behavior.
2. Notice changes in your manner of speaking and choice of words.
3. Be aware of your choice of clothing and the "props" you use to help present yourself.
4. Most of all, note the changes in the way you think and feel as you inhabit your various "me"s.

Notice how you naturally tend to "become" each of the roles that you present.

THE SKILLS OF THE ACTOR

Although acting is based on everyday life skills, acting for the stage or camera demands that these everyday abilities be heightened, purified, and brought within the control of a purposeful discipline. As Brian Bates of the Royal Academy of Dramatic Art says in his book *The Way of the Actor:*

> Almost everything that actors do can be identified with things we do in less dramatic form, in everyday life. But in order to express the concentrated truths which are the life-stuff of drama, and to project convincing performances before large audiences, and the piercing eye of the film and television camera, the actor must develop depths of self-knowledge and powers of expression far beyond those with which most of us are familiar.[2]

The development of your everyday acting skills into the greater power of artistic technique is the aim of this book. You will work on three kinds of skills as you develop your acting techniques: physical, conceptual, and spiritual. The physical skills develop your body and voice as expressive instruments. The conceptual skills enable you to analyze plays and scenes and to recognize how the characters you perform function within their plays. The spiritual skills involve your ability to relax, to be centered, to observe and focus, to be aware on several levels at once, and—most important—to experience transformation, to "become" the character.

Your task, then, is to recognize, focus, and strengthen the natural actor you already are. Only you can do this, but the ideas and exercises in this book can provide insights and experiences to help you fulfill your natural talents.

OBSERVATION

In addition to the physical skills of body and voice, the conceptual skills of analysis, and the spiritual skills leading to transformation, there is another skill that many actors say is essential to artistry on stage or in front of the camera, and that is the skill of *observation*. As Brian Bates says, "Actors have been keen observers for centuries, for without this keen attention to others, performances are limited to the prison of one's own personal life."[3]

The purpose of observation for the actor is not merely the duplication of the physical and vocal appearances and mannerisms of other people; that is mere mimicry. As skillful as some imitators are at re-creating others, few imitators are also good actors. Acting requires the creation of a transformed personality that, however much it may be inspired by the observation of someone else, also lives within a specific world and fulfills a specific function as determined by the story being told. The actor's characterization, unlike the imitator's performance, is never an end unto itself and is always at the service of a higher purpose.

Moreover, the actor observes in order to understand how human behavior operates *in context*. All our behavior, and especially emotional behavior (as we will explore later) is profoundly tied to our situation, even when we are alone and even in those rare instances when our behavior is directed inward.

Actors, then, are acute observers of life, but not merely of its surface qualities. Rather, the actor observes in order to understand the vocabulary of human behavior and the underlying principles that give our expression its emotional and spiritual meaning. This vocabulary and grammar of behavior are then used by the actor in creating characters who are extensions beyond the actor's self.

EXERCISE 1.2: LIFE STUDY

Notice behavior of other people that seems especially expressive of their emotional and spiritual state.

1. What are the physical and vocal qualities that are especially expressive?
2. How do these qualities operate in context?
3. How do they reveal emotion and personality?

Nearly all explorers keep *journals*, daily records of their journeys. Acting students likewise may benefit from keeping a daily record of their experiences and discoveries as they journey into the realm of acting. The simple act of recording one's experiences can help to organize and focus them in useful ways, and looking back on one's journal can reveal meaningful patterns and inspire fresh insights. Try it and see if it's right for you.

ACTING AND YOUR PERSONAL GROWTH

The development of the actor's self-knowledge and power of expression is an unending process of personal as well as artistic growth. It is exactly this opportunity for ongoing personal growth that attracts many people to the profession of acting. Even if you do not commit to the profession, your study of the acting process can enrich you in many ways. Brian Bates, who is both an acting teacher and a psychologist, lists some of the ways in which the study of acting can contribute to personal growth:

> Finding our inner identity. Changing ourselves. Realizing and integrating our life experience. Seeing life freshly and with insight into others. Becoming aware of the powers of our mind. Risking and commitment. Learning how to concentrate our lives into the present, and the secrets of presence and charisma. Extending our sense of who we are, and achieving liberation from restricted concepts of what a person is.[4]

In all these ways, the study of acting, even if it does not lead to actual performance, is a meaningful journey of personal discovery and expansion.

For those who have made acting not only a career but also a way of life (and this includes all our greatest actors), it is clear that acting addresses needs that are far deeper than the desire for attention or material success. These actors often speak of the release that playing a role gives them from what Sir Alec Guinness called "my dreary old life"; acting gives them permission to have experiences they would never dare have in real life. Patrick Stewart, best known as Captain Picard on *Star Trek: The Next Generation* (and who is also a great Shakespearean actor), says, "What first attracted me to acting was the fantasy world of the theater into which I could escape from the much less pleasant world of my childhood."[5] For others, the special position of the actor compensates for a sense of personal unworthiness. Whatever the needs may be, those with the deepest needs seem to have the best chance for a professional life, for acting is a difficult way to earn a living and only very deep needs provide sufficient motivation to sustain a career.

DISCIPLINE

Before you begin in earnest your journey into acting, think about the one skill that will make all others possible: *discipline.*

Real discipline is not a matter of following someone else's rules: in the best sense it is *your acceptance of the responsibility for your own development through systematic effort.* You accept this responsibility not to please someone else, not to earn a grade or a good review or a job, but because you choose to become all that you can be.

Discipline is rooted in your respect for yourself, as well as your respect for your fellow workers, for your work, and for the world you serve through that work. Poor discipline is really a way of saying, "I'm not worth it" or "What I do doesn't matter." Discipline comes naturally if you acknowledge your own value, the importance and seriousness of your work, and the great need for your work in the world.

Discipline also involves regularity. Your work, especially on technical skills, must be a daily affair. Stanislavski, looking back late in his life, had this to say:

> Let someone explain to me why the violinist who plays in an orchestra on the tenth violin must daily perform hour-long exercises or lose his power to play? Why does the dancer work daily over every muscle in his body? Why do the painter, the sculptor, the writer practice their art each day and count that day lost when they do not work? And why may the dramatic artist do nothing, spend his day in coffee houses and hope for the gift [of inspiration] in the evening? Enough. Is this an art when its priests speak like amateurs? There is no art that does not demand virtuosity.[6]

Patience and a sense of striving together—being able to accept momentary failure for the sake of long-range success—are the attitudes that you must nurture. The pressures of our educational system and of professional acting work against these attitudes, as does the normal desire of all of us to be "successful" right now. Resist your desire for immediate success and instead begin to enjoy the journey, the exploration itself.

Take the long view: enjoy your freedom as a student to explore a variety of approaches and experiences. Most of your explorations will lead up blind alleys, but it is better to suffer momentary failures now than to commit yourself to an approach or an attitude that may limit you later. Your discipline is dedicated to the whole of your career. As playwright David Mamet says:

> Those of you who are called to strive to bring a new theatre, the theatre of your generation, to the stage, are set down for a very exciting life.
>
> You will be pulling against an increasingly strong current, and as you do so, you will reap the great and priceless reward of knowing yourself a truly mature man or woman—if, in the midst of the panic which surrounds you, which calls itself common sense, or commercial viability, you are doing your job simply and well.
>
> If you are going to work in the true theatre, that job is a great job in this time of final decay; that job is to bring to your fellows, through the medium of your understanding and skill, the possibility of communion with what is essential in us all: that we are born to die, that we strive and fail, that we live in ignorance of why we were placed here, and, that, in the midst of this we need to love and be loved, but we are afraid.[7]

SUMMARY

You are already an actor. You "play a role" every time you present yourself or adjust your behavior to achieve some desired goal. As an art, however, acting requires that these everyday abilities be heightened and purified. The development of your every-day acting skills into the greater power of artistic technique is the aim of this book. Your task is to recognize, focus, and strengthen the natural actor you already are.

Actors learn to observe human behavior in order to understand the vocabulary and underlying principles of our expressiveness. Some actors record their observations and experiences in journals that trace their journeys of artistic discovery.

Even if you do not commit to the profession, your study of the acting process can help you to grow in many ways. For many actors, acting addresses needs far deeper than the desire for attention or material success. Whatever your reasons, they motivate you to take this journey of personal discovery and expansion.

One skill makes all others possible: discipline. Real discipline is not a matter of following someone else's rules; it is *your acceptance of the responsibility for your own development through systematic effort.* Discipline comes naturally if you acknowledge your own value and the importance of your work and the great need for it in the world.

THE CREATIVE STATE

In the process of growing up, you may have begun to lose some of the natural playfulness, wholeness, and openness you enjoyed as a child. There may be some aspects of your body and voice and some forms of expression that you no longer permit yourself to use, at least not in public. As you begin your work as an actor, you will begin to rediscover some of the freedom, unself-consciousness, and ability for fantasy that you enjoyed as a child, when "making believe" was a natural process. You can recapture it best when you are *relaxed, playful,* and *nonjudgmental.* Some psychologists call this *the creative state,* and they say it happens when your internal "parent" allows your inner "child" to come out and play.

The first and most important step toward this creative state is reducing tension and excessive effort and learning to relax.

TENSION AND EXCESSIVE EFFORT

For most of us, acting arouses anxiety. This can be both pleasurable (as in the quest for creative discovery) and painful (as in the fear of failure). In either case, this anxiety can make your muscles tense and disrupt your breathing and thinking. It also interferes with your ability to react; it "freezes" you and reduces your creativity. For all these reasons, tension is the greatest enemy of the creative state.

When you find yourself scared or stuck, you may attempt to compensate by trying harder, by putting more effort into the work, and by trying to force your way through it. Unfortunately, this is exactly the wrong thing to do. It only increases your tension and further reduces your freedom of creative response. Student actors commonly make the mistake of trying too hard, and the harder they try, the worse they get. This is because excessive effort makes you self-aware, obscures your own experience of your work, and reduces your control.

Think of trying to open a drawer that is stuck: if you just tug at it with all your might, chances are that it will let loose all at once and go flying out, spilling the contents. Because you were using excessive force, you failed to feel the exact moment when the drawer loosened. You weren't experiencing the drawer anymore; you were instead experiencing only *your own effort.*

Unfortunately, many actors are driven to excessive effort by their fear of failure or their desire to please their audience. They feel unworthy of the audience's attention unless they do something extraordinary to earn it; the option of doing nothing, of simply allowing themselves to "be there," is terrifying. They feel naked, exposed, and become desperate to do something, anything! As a result, they have difficulty experiencing what is really happening on stage and instead experience only their own effort. This feeling of effort can become their mistaken idea of the way it feels to act.

Here is the secret that will make miracles happen for you as an actor: acting is mostly a matter of *letting go*—letting go of too much effort, letting go of chronic physical tension, letting go of a false voice, letting go of your preconceptions about the work, letting go of fear, and most of all, letting go of who you already are so that you can become someone new. The first step in letting go is to stop forcing yourself into unnatural thought, feeling, or behavior.

RESTFUL ALERTNESS

When we speak of relaxation for the actor, we do not mean it in the ordinary sense of reduced energy or slackness. Rather, we mean that all unnecessary tensions have been removed; the remaining energy has been purposefully focused, and awareness is acute. The kind of relaxation you want is a state in which you are *most ready to react,* like a cat in front of a mousehole. Tensions that would inhibit movement are gone, and you are in a state of balance, which leaves you free to react in any way required.

The best description of the relaxed actor's state is what meditators call "restful alertness." You are already capable of restful alertness. You don't need to do anything to achieve it; you only need to become still enough to experience it. You can do this right now, through a simple meditation.

EXERCISE 2.1: A MEDITATION

Sit comfortably in your chair, both feet flat on the floor, back and neck straight but not rigid, and hands resting on your thighs. Your head is floating comfortably above your neck, your energy flowing from deep within your body out the top of your head. You feel your weight in the chair; your breath is even and deep. We call this *chair alignment* (see Figure 2.1).

Look at a spot on the floor eight feet in front of you. Focus your awareness on your breath flowing in and out of your nose. Allow any thoughts that come up to play across your consciousness, then simply return your awareness to your breath. Nothing is to be resisted. If you like, close your eyes. Sit for as long as you are comfortable. Whatever experience you have is correct.

Your meditation was focused on your breath for a very good reason: the breath is life. The word *psychology* means "study of the soul," and the word for soul, *psyche,*

FIGURE 2.1   Chair Alignment

originally meant "vital breath." A common superstition is that the expiring breath of a dying person is the soul leaving the body.

Your breath constantly reflects your relationship to your world. It is through the breath that you literally bring the outside world into your body and then expel it again; the way you feel about your world is expressed in the way you breathe it in and breathe it out. This is why your natural voice, which is profoundly affected by your breath, is so expressive of your inner state. You can see sobbing, laughing, gasping, sighing, and all the other forms of breathing as the reflections of your relationship to your world. Unfortunately, television has turned many of us into "talking heads," breaking our natural connection between upper and lower body, causing us to lose touch with our natural breathing and, therefore, with our natural voice and emotional wholeness.

EXPERIENCING WHOLENESS

However physically and emotionally fragmented many people are in real life, a believable and artistically complete performance on stage or before the camera demands total involvement. All the parts of your body, your voice, and your mind need to work together. This integration is a natural state. Even if you learned habits of movement or voice that made you "dis-integrated" and awkward as you grew up, you can easily rediscover your natural integration and wholeness.

The trick is not to *do* anything but to *stop doing* whatever it is you do that distorts your natural wholeness and responsiveness. Trust that the natural wisdom of your body and mind will take over if you let them.

FIGURE 2.2   Floor Alignment

EXERCISE 2.2: PLAYING CAT

Lie on the floor comfortably in a surrounding that is not too distracting. Stretch out face up, hands at your sides. Put yourself at rest by yawning and stretching.

> To see yawning and stretching at their luxurious best, watch a cat just awakening from a siesta. It arches its back, extends to the utmost its legs, feet, and toes, drops its jaw, and all the while balloons itself up with air. Once it has swelled until it occupies its very maximum of space, it permits itself slowly to collapse—and then is ready for new business.[1]

Act like a cat. Stretch, arch your back, extend all your limbs to their utmost, drop your jaw, wiggle your arms and hands, and breathe deeply (not once but many times), each time taking in more and more air. When a real yawn comes, encourage it, let the full natural sound of the yawn pour out.

Settle back with your knees raised enough to make the small of your back touch the floor. Place your toes, heels, hip joints, and shoulders on two imaginary parallel lines. We call this *floor alignment:* the head is level (place a small pad under it); the waistline is also level; the knees are raised to avoid any strain on the lower back. This alignment will be used in later exercises (see Figure 2.2).

As you rediscover your own relaxed wholeness, you will realize that you are, by your very nature, connected to your world. Your sense of a separate "I" bounded by your physical body is a limited understanding of your place in nature. Your ideas of an "inner" and an "outer" world are only different attitudes toward experience; the world is one world, which we merely experience as "inner" and "outer." We are in it, and it is in us. Your breath itself reveals this, as potter and poet Mary Caroline Richards points out:

> The innerness of the so-called outer world is nowhere so evident as in the life of our body. The air we breathe one moment will be breathed by someone else the next and has been breathed by someone else before. We exist as respiring, pulsating organisms within a sea of life-serving beings. As we become able to hold this more and more steadily in our consciousness, we experience relatedness at an elemental level. We see that it is not a matter of trying to be related, but rather of living consciously into the actuality of being related. As we yield ourselves to the living presence of this relatedness, we find that life begins to possess an ease and a freedom and a naturalness that fill our hearts with joy.[2]

EXERCISE 2.3: JUST BREATHING

In either chair or floor alignment, take some time to experience your breath in the way that's just been described. Feel the world, the ocean of air, moving into you and out of you. Feel your connection to it and to everyone else in your space.

RELAXATION

The ability to relax can be learned. Psychologists speak of a "relaxation response" that develops with repetition just like any other skill. The following exercise is the classic in the field of relaxation. Though you can quickly learn it yourself, it is useful for your teacher or a partner to lead at first. If necessary, a tape recording of these instructions with the necessary pauses can be useful.

EXERCISE 2.4: PHASIC RELAXATION

Begin in floor alignment. Breath is again the focus of your awareness: Imagine that each inhalation is a warm, fresh, energy-filled fluid flowing into your body. Each exhalation carries away with it tension and inhibition, like a refreshing wave. Breathe deeply and easily in a slow, natural, regular rhythm; don't "act" your breathing or artificially exaggerate it.

Each successive breath is sent into a different part of the body, awakening that area. As the breath flows into a new area, let the muscles there contract as much as they can; then, as the breath flows out, the muscles release and the breath carries all the tension away with it, leaving the area refreshed and at ease. *Exhaling is letting go.*

The sequence of breaths moves from the top of the body downward, and the regular rhythm of your breathing should make the muscular contractions and relaxations flow smoothly down the body like a slow wave. Allow only one area at a time to be involved.

1. *The forehead and scalp,* furrowing the brow, then releasing it; the eyes are at rest, closed, and turned slightly downward;
2. *The jaw,* clenching it, then letting it fall easily downward until the teeth are about one-half inch apart;
3. *The tongue,* extending it, then letting it lie easily in the mouth;
4. *The front of the neck,* extending the chin down to touch the chest, stretching the back of the neck—then rolling the head easily back down;
5. *The back of the neck,* rolling the top of the head under to touch the floor, stretching the front of the neck—then rolling the head slowly down and lengthening the neck;
6. *The upper chest,* swelling outward in all directions so that the shoulders are widened—then easily subsiding, feeling the shoulder blades spread and melt into the floor, wider than before;
7. *The arms and hands,* becoming stiff and straight like steel rods; the hands clenching into fists, then easily uncurling and melting into the floor;
8. *The pit of the stomach,* clenching, becoming a small, hard ball—then, with a sigh, releasing;
9. *The buttocks,* clenching, then releasing and widening so that the hips are wider than before;
10. *The knees,* stiffening as the legs straighten, the feet being pushed downward by this action—then releasing the legs and feeling them melt into the floor;
11. *The toes,* reaching up to touch the eyes (but the heels remain on the floor)—then releasing and falling into a natural position;
12. *The heels and the shoulder blades,* simultaneously pushing downward into the floor so that the whole body lifts in a long arch—then, with a sigh, you slowly fall, the body lengthening as it relaxes, melting deep into the floor.

Now take ten deep, slow, regular breaths, and with each breath move more deeply into relaxation, remaining alert and refreshed. The flow of breath is a continuous cycle of energy that is stored comfortably in the body; with each breath this store of energy is increased. If a yawn comes to you, enjoy it fully; vocalize the exhalation, letting the sound of the yawn pour out.

As you repeat this exercise on successive days, you can begin to give yourself the instructions silently, reminding yourself of the specific activities in each phase. Keep a steady rhythm that follows the tempo of deep, relaxed breathing. Gradually the action of the exercise will become natural, and you will no longer need to think of the instructions. Your full awareness is given to the flow of contractions and relaxations that follow the breath as it travels down the body like a wave, awakening, refreshing, and relaxing it, making you ready for work.

You can use this exercise as an easy, quick preparation for all future work. Over time, it will help chronic bundles of tension within your body to break up and dissolve.

THE HERE AND NOW

Did you notice that relaxation allowed you to immerse yourself in the present instant, in the *here and now?* It is now that you exist and now that you can act. In everyday life you rarely achieve complete contact with the present: you prefer to create a sense of comfortable continuity by blurring the lines that separate the present from the past and future. The past, in memory, and the future, in expectation, can be controlled by your consciousness; but the present can be met only on its own terms. Although you can never specifically isolate it, you can put yourself in touch with the unending flow of the present. As the psychologist Frederick Perls put it:

> The wish to seize the present and pin it down—to mount it, as it were, like a butterfly in a case—is doomed to failure. Actuality forever changes. In healthy persons, the feeling of actuality is steady and continuous but, like the view from a train window, the scenery is always different.[3]

When you act, you must work in the here and now. Even though your character may be lost in memory, consumed with desire for the future or dreaming of being far away, you perform all this in the here and now.

EXERCISE 2.5: BEING THERE

Take turns sitting in front of the group. Place yourself in sitting alignment, restful alertness, and simply "be there." Let go of your need to do something until you are quite still. Keep your eyes open and your senses alert.

FIGURE 2.3   Standing Alignment

Fully experience stillness both as actor and as audience; support one another with quiet attention. See how interesting the simple, unadorned presence of a human being can be!

When you are comfortable "being there" while sitting, repeat the exercise while standing. Stand with your toes directly below your shoulders, your arms hanging comfortably at your sides, your waist level, and your head floating easily atop your neck, as if lifted gently upward and slightly forward. Feel your weight flowing into the ground. This is *standing alignment* (see Figure 2.3).

SUMMARY

Your work as an actor requires that you rediscover the natural integration of mind and body that you enjoyed as a child at play. It is this relaxed, nonjudgmental condition that we call "the creative state." The first step in recapturing it is *to relax by reducing tension and excessive effort.* Acting, like all creative activity, arouses anxiety, which disrupts your breathing and raises the level of your bodily tension. In turn, this tension "freezes" you and reduces your creativity. When you find yourself "stuck" in this way, you may attempt to compensate by trying harder. This, however, only *increases* your tension and further reduces your freedom of creative response; excessive effort makes you self-aware.

Unfortunately, many actors are prone to excessive effort; they feel unworthy of the audience's attention unless they *do* something extraordinary to earn it.

The kind of relaxation best for you as an actor is a state in which you are most ready to react, the state meditators call "restful alertness." The breath is deeply involved with relaxation because it constantly reflects your relationship to your world. Our cultural disintegration, unfortunately, has caused many of us to lose touch with our natural breathing.

Relaxation in the sense of simply "being there," ready to react, allows you to immerse yourself in the present instant, in a state of restful alertness, in the *here and now.*

CENTERING AND MOVING

Incarnation: bodying forth. Is this not our whole concern? The bodying forth of our sense of life?... We body forth our ideals in personal acts, either alone or with others in society. We body forth felt experience in a poem's image and sound. We body forth our inner residence in the architecture of our homes and common buildings. We body forth our struggles and our revelations in the space of theatre. That is what form is: the bodying forth...[1]

This thought is from a book called *Centering* by Mary Caroline Richards, a poet and potter. As a potter she knows how the centering of the clay on the wheel is essential to creation of a pot, for only from perfectly centered clay can the motion of the wheel and the potter's hands bring the pot's shape freely and naturally toward its ultimate form. As a poet she also knows how the experiences of one's life must touch a personal center before they can, in turn, flow outward and be embodied in the form of a poem. As an actor you must also center yourself so that your energy, like the clay, flows outward into the new form of yourself demanded by your role.

The idea of a personal center is not just a metaphor; it has a tangible physical dimension. Finding and activating your bodily center are necessary first steps in laying a foundation for good stage movement and voice; the sense of center can integrate your responses and give you strength by involving your total organism in your actions.

Developing your physical center is also a way of developing a psychological and spiritual centeredness as well, because at this deep level your energy exists simultaneously in physical and psychological forms; movement, feeling, thought, and the beginnings of sound all intermingle here. This deep *psychophysical* energy is the raw material of the acting process; like the potter's clay, you must gather it, make it responsive, and center it so that it can be shaped easily into new forms.

As you work on a role, this psychophysical energy flows outward into new forms of behavior demanded by your character's actions and the style of the play. As this happens, you begin to experience yourself anew. As you come to experience this new form of yourself more fully, you begin to enter into a new state of being, which in turn summons new energies from you; this is the creative cycle of the acting process.

This lesson explores the physical dimension of centering. Part III shows how its psychological dimension can be a primary tool of characterization. Here is an exercise to help you localize a specific sense of your physical center.

EXERCISE 3.1: FINDING CENTER

Place yourself in standing alignment, clear your mind, and witness your body as it performs the following activities:

1. Move either foot out to the side about two feet; rock from foot to foot, feeling your center of gravity moving from side to side. Quickly make your rocking smaller and smaller, like a bowling pin that almost falls down; come to rest on center.
2. Move either foot forward about two feet; find your center with front-to-back motions as described above.
3. Move your center around rotationally, exploring the limits of various stances. Feel the weight of your body flowing into the ground and out of your center through the legs.
4. Point into your body at the spot that you feel is your center; don't be concerned about where it "ought" to be; sense where it really is.
5. Explore how your center is involved in moving and speaking.

As you become aware of your center over a period of days, you notice that it moves within the body as your mood changes; frequently, your center rises upward when you are in an excited or fearful state or downward in states of well-being or determination. You notice, too, that different people have different characteristic centers and that the locations of their centers are very appropriate to their personalities. Such diversity can be found in people who have a "lot of guts," who "follow their nose," "lead with their chins," are "all heart," "drag their feet," "have their heads in the clouds," and so on.

This sense of centeredness is, for the actor, rooted in a literal, specific recognition of a physical center from which all impulses to move or make sound flow outward and into the external world.

THE PURE CENTER AND THE VOICE

The martial arts teach a "pure" sense of center, which is the natural biomechanical center of an undistorted body. This "ideal" center is deep within the body, in an area roughly three finger-widths below your navel. It is here that the breath (and therefore the voice) originates, as do all large motions of the body. This area is the literal center of gravity of your body, as shown by Leonardo da Vinci's famous drawing (Figure 3.1).

You must develop a sense of your pure center, for it is from this center that your deepest impulses spring. If you are operating instead from some higher center

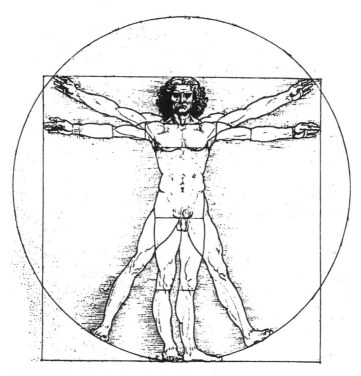

FIGURE 3.1   The Bodily Center According to Leonardo

(such as the chest, or even the head), you inevitably look and sound "stiff" and "superficial"; the movements and sounds you produce are not deeply motivated or complete because they do not originate from the true center of your being, and your voice in particular does not have the fullness and expressiveness required for good stage speech.

The committed worker is often the noisy one—humming, singing, laughing, or grunting; all action usually flows into the world through sound as well as motion. The student of karate learns this—the outward flow of energy from our deepest center naturally carries the breath, and hence the voice, with it. Unfortunately, we sometimes inhibit this natural flow of sound because our upbringing has taught us to restrain our natural impulse to move, breathe, and create sound. The following exercise gives you an experience of the breath flowing from your center, carrying sound and motion with it.

EXERCISE 3.2: MOVING AND SOUNDING FROM CENTER

Align and center yourself as in the previous exercise.

1. As you breathe easily and slowly, become aware of the breath rising and falling in the body from the center.

2. As the breath travels outward, make sound lightly. Do not disturb the breath; just allow it to vibrate. This is your voice: your vibrating breath carrying energy from your center into the outside world.
3. Reach effortlessly with your vibrating breath into the world around you. Put yourself, at random, into new positions and experience the vibrating breath flowing through each. What changes are there in the voice?
4. As you continue to produce sound, feel the vibrations of that sound spreading into every part of your body: out of the neck into the head and chest, into the back, the stomach, the buttocks, into the arms and hands, into the legs and feet, and into the scalp. Feel the sound radiating from every part of your body! With a light fingertip touch, check every surface of your body. Are there "dead spots" that are not participating in the sound?

Examine your experience during sounding: Were there parts of your body that did not join in the vibration? Did you have a new sense of the capacity of your entire body to join in the act of sounding? Did you feel more in touch with yourself and with the space around you, as if your sound were literally reaching outside yourself in a tangible way? Are you now more alert, refreshed, and relaxed?

You have begun to experience how vocal and physical qualities are integral with one another, because the breath, body, and voice are all integral with one another. As you begin to gain freedom and ease in one, you enhance the other, enhancing, too, a quality of mind important to your work, for your consciousness is itself a partner in this same wholeness.

THE ACTOR'S USE OF CENTER

Just as we experienced relaxation as a readiness to react, so our aim in aligning and centering the body is to put ourselves in the most responsive physiovocal condition. The "pure" center is an undistorted condition from which we begin our work so that we may develop in any direction required by a role.

Although we *begin* from a pure center, however, we certainly do not *end* there. We are not interested in "correct" posture or voice for performance, for the actor has no "correct" voice or posture until they are determined by the demands of the role. Each character you play has his or her own center, which functions as the source of that character's breathing, motion, and sound. You begin from as undistorted or "neutral" a base as you can, exploring and testing the particular qualities, the particular distortions that comprise the personality of the character and are therefore useful in creating the role.

However, you can never eradicate *all* your personal idiosyncrasies, nor should you; they give your work special and individual qualities that enable you, when at your best, to bring special insights and qualities to the roles you play. But your personal misalignments, inhibitions, and unconscious mannerisms—such as regional dialect, unnatural posture or breathing, or repetitive gestures—must be brought within the control of your conscious artistic discipline or they may forever limit the roles and qualities you can play.

Note that we wish not to eliminate these personal habits and qualities but rather to bring them within our control. We actors shouldn't throw anything away; any quality, mannerism, way of speaking, or experience might be needed someday! But we must hold all these in such a way that *we control them instead of them controlling us.*

In Part III you will explore the use of the center as a tool of characterization, but for now, explore this concept in a general way.

EXERCISE 3.3: SHIFTING CENTER

Repeat the previous exercise and move and sound from center, but this time allow your sense of center to shift within your body. Move and sound from your *head,* then your *chest,* then your *stomach,* then from your *genitals.* Allow yourself to "become" each of these centers. Have you ever felt any of these centers before? Do any remind you of someone you know?

GROUNDING

As you begin to sense your physical center more acutely, also begin to feel the way your energy interacts with gravity. Your energy flows not only upward and outward but also downward into the ground as well. There is also energy coming up into your center from the earth. We can speak, therefore, not only of being "centered" but also of being "grounded." Here is an exercise that will help you to experience grounding.

EXERCISE 3.4: GROUNDING

In standing alignment, briefly repeat the rocking motions in Exercise 3.1. Establish again a strong sense of your center, wherever it happens to be today.

Now imagine yourself standing on a mirror. Below you is your other self with its own center; imagine a bond between your center and that in your mirror image. This imaginary bond of energy is like a root, giving you stability, strength, and nourishment.

As your energy flows into your root, it also flows upward so that your rootedness permits you to stand taller, to be stronger. As you move, your rootedness moves with you; you "detach" your rooted center, and at your destination you "plant" or ground yourself again. Try it. Select a destination, lift your rooted center, move to the destination, and *plant* yourself there.

As our species evolved, we gradually became more and more erect, standing within the field of gravity. (This adaptation is far from complete; our common lower back problems may be due partly to an incomplete adaptation to standing erect.) Your relationship to gravity is continuous; even when lying down, you are making constant adjustments within the field of gravity.

The way in which you experience gravity, like your breathing, is a fundamental expression of your relationship to your world. Some days, it seems that we have the "weight of the world" on our shoulders. At such times, we speak of feeling "down," and at the saddest times we say we have a "heavy heart." On the other hand, sometimes we feel "light as a feather," "floating on cloud nine," or "lighthearted."

A person's attitude toward gravity can be seen in his or her posture. Arthur Miller opens his great play *Death of a Salesman* with Willy Loman crossing the stage, his back bent under the weight of his sample case. Willy's sense of defeat and his hopelessness are directly expressed in the way he is losing his fight with gravity.

We also seem to receive strength from gravity when we feel at one with it; at such times we speak of "knowing where we stand" or "holding our ground." One of the qualities of some classical heroes (Oedipus or Electra, for example) is their oneness with the earth and the way the power of nature flows up through the earth and into them. Perhaps for this reason, I have noticed that it is impossible to play a strong character if the feet are kept too close together. Not only do strong characters need a wide, stable base, but they also need to be open to receive the flow of energy that is coming upward from the earth.

YOUR CHANGING RELATIONSHIP TO GRAVITY

You experienced in the previous exercise how your relationship to gravity can be expressed by the idea of your "root." Your own characteristic relationship to gravity, the one that is "normal" or "usual" for you, is, like your breath and your center, a profound expression of your dominant relationship to your world. But just as your breathing changes and your center may shift upward or downward as your emotional state changes, so your relationship to gravity changes as well. We see signs of such changes in ourselves and others all the time. Our everyday language reflects this: we speak of the happy person as "lighthearted" or "on cloud nine," whereas the depressed person is a "drag" or a "downer."

Consider the tremendous expressiveness of a person's walk. The walk reflects a person's relationship toward gravity, perhaps the most fundamental relationship we have with our world. An insecure person, with a weak sense of self-identity, tends to be unstable, to "walk on eggshells." We speak of such a person as a "pushover," someone who "won't stand on his two feet." The opposite extreme is the "pushy" person who carries his or her weight on the balls of the feet and whose energy flows up the back into the aggressive stance of a fighter. Pushy people walk as if they were punishing the floor and expected everything to get out of the way. It is not surprising that Sir Alec Guinness said that he knew he had found the essential ingredients of a character when he had found the correct walk, because our walk is the most active expression of our relationship to gravity.

This will be explored in greater detail in Part III, but for now, be aware that there are four main relationships to gravity that can be expressed by different qualities of your root. The first is the one you experienced in the previous exercise, a *variable* root, which is lifted for movement and planted when you come to rest, as appropriate to your needs. This is the most responsive and well-adjusted way of relating to gravity.

The second is one in which you are so "weighed down" by gravity, so "heavy-hearted," that your root remains planted even when you are trying to move, as if you were plowing a furrow through the ground. You can feel so "down," in fact, that you may have to work against the pull of gravity to move at all. This quality can extend to all your movements, as if you were pushing your way through space. This kind of movement is called *molding*.

The third is one in which your root remains unplanted so that you are light and easily moved, even when you are still, as if you were *floating*. The fourth is the lightest of all, as if your root has been pulled upward through the top of your head and you are being lifted by it so that your feet have to reach down to touch the ground. This is called *flying*.

Notice that all these forms of movement can have positive or negative qualities, depending on the context. Molding can feel dejected or defeated, or it can feel determined and resolute. Floating can feel lighthearted and carefree, or it can feel confused and vulnerable. Flying can feel euphoric or effervescent, or it can feel lost and scattered.

In the dance world, these different modes of movement were called *effort-shape* by the great movement theorist Rudolph Laban. Here is an exercise to explore them.

EXERCISE 3.5: MOLDING, FLOATING, AND FLYING

1. As in Exercise 3.4, establish your sense of your root. Use it in a *variable* way, lifting it to move, then planting it at your destination.
2. Now move to a destination without lifting the root; *plow* yourself there. Don't act this out; simply experience moving with this image and feel what it is like to *plow*. Extend this feeling so that you are pushing your way through the air itself, as if you are *molding* space as you move through it.
3. Now lift your root and leave it dangling all the time, whether moving or still: *float*. Again, give yourself time to experience *floating*.
4. Now imagine the root being drawn upward, still attached at your center but now lifting your center upward and out of the top of your head. Move with the sense that you have to reach down to touch the floor: you are *flying*.

As you see, there is a distinct difference between the experiences of *molding, floating,* and *flying,* though each state offers numerous possibilities. The particular emotional quality of any one of these states can be determined only by *context,* and our bodily expression cannot be understood according to any sort of fixed vocabulary.

PHRASING MOVEMENT

In the last exercise you began to move through space by "lifting" your rooted center, moving, then "planting" your rooted center again at your destination. Review this experience; did it give you a heightened sense of clarity and purposefulness in your movements? The exercise made you more aware of the *shape* of your movements, the fact that each had a beginning, middle, and end. Just as our thoughts are shaped into words and sentences that are eventually reflected in the way we speak, so our movement on stage needs to be organized and shaped into clear phraseology.

EXERCISE 3.6: PHRASING MOVEMENT

As in Exercise 3.4, begin by "seeing" your own rooted center in relationship to your mirror image beneath the floor. Now make a movement by following each of these steps:

1. Select your destination: locate a specific spot with your eyes and let your face turn toward it so that your movement "follows your nose."
2. Begin to move by *lifting* the root; exaggerate this motion at first.
3. Carry your root to your destination and "land" there.
4. As you land, "spear" your root into the floor to complete your movement.
5. Repeat this action several times, paying special attention to the sense of beginning, middle, and end to each movement phrase.
6. Now begin to play with variations of this cycle, extending them beyond realistic movement. For instance, try lifting the root slowly and heavily, then drag it to the destination and *dump* it there so that it "plops" into the ground. Or make your lift light and high, moving *away* from your destination, then *throw* your root toward your destination and *fly* there, landing with a light jump. These are the kinds of "stylized" movements associated with *commedia dell'arte*.

Virtually any quality of movement can be created by using these and other variables. On stage, your performance is partly a dance, which, without appearing to be dance-like, is nevertheless composed, intensified, and purified through repeated testing and rehearsal (even if this process is rarely a conscious one). Your aim here is *not* to self-consciously control your movements but rather to begin to experience the almost limitless range of movement qualities of which you are capable: this is one of the "palettes" from which you will "paint" as an actor, and you want to be sure that you have a wide choice of colors available to you.

SUMMARY

A potter knows how the centering of the clay on the wheel is essential to the creation of a pot; the actor must also be centered so that his or her energy, like the clay, flows outward into the new form of the role. This idea of a personal center is not just a metaphor; it has a tangible physical dimension. Finding and activating your bodily center are necessary first steps in laying a foundation for good stage movement and voice.

Developing your physical center is also a way of developing a psychological and spiritual centeredness, because at this deep level your energy exists simultaneously in physical and psychological forms. The center moves within the body as your mood changes; also, different people have different characteristic centers that are appropriate to their personalities.

The center functions in relationship to gravity, and the way in which you experience gravity, like your breathing, is a fundamental expression of your relationship to your world.

There is an "ideal" center deep within the body, roughly three finger-widths below your navel. The breath (and therefore the voice) originates here, as do all large motions of the body and all your deepest impulses. The "pure" center is an undistorted condition from which we begin our work so that we may develop in any direction required by the role, but there is no "correct" voice or posture for the actor until they are determined by the demands of a role.

Our energy moves as a *cycle* that flows from our center outward toward the world *and back again.* It also flows downward into the ground, and energy also comes up into our center from the earth. We can speak, therefore, not only of being "centered" but also of being "grounded."

Various kinds of energy states produce different experiences. There is a distinct difference between *molding, floating,* and *flying.* These different qualities of energy express different conditions, though the particular emotional quality of any one of these states can be determined only by *context.* Our movement on stage expresses these qualities in a natural way, though perhaps with an expanded and purified palette and with a clarity of phraseology as appropriate to the desired style of performance.

GESTURE

When you have an impulse, feeling, or idea, it arouses an energy at your deep center that naturally flows outward, reaching the outer world in many forms: words, sounds, motions, or postures. Broadly speaking, any such external sign of a feeling or thought may be called a *gesture*.

In fact, the word *express* literally means "to move outward." When you have a feeling or idea, it is natural to externalize it, to "move it outward" through gesture and speech. Although this expressive behavior communicates your feelings and ideas to others, it is also an automatic part of your thought process that goes on even when you are alone. Watch people driving alone on the highway, for instance; you can see some amazingly animated conversations.

This lesson examines gestures of the body; Lesson 5 explores gestures of the voice, which are both verbal (the speaking of words) and nonverbal (the many sounds we make other than words).

COMMUNICATING THROUGH GESTURE

Our culture uses a large vocabulary of body gestures to augment and often to substitute for verbal communication. Although our verbal language communicates fairly precise meanings, our gestural language provides information about feelings with greater expressiveness than words alone. Simply put, words can best say *what we mean* and gestures can best tell *how we feel* about what we mean.

Psychologists have for years been interested in body language, and this area of study has been given the name "Kinesics" by Raymond Birdwhistell. His basic premises are of interest to you as an actor:

1. body gestures are socially learned;
2. so that most gestures must be interpreted in context;
3. some gestures, however, develop roughly standardized meanings within our culture.

Here is a brief example of nonverbal expression at work in real life as recorded by Birdwhistell.

26

(The situation is that a guest of honor at a party arrives forty-five minutes late. Three couples besides the host and hostess had been waiting. The doorbell rings.)

Hostess: Oh! We were afraid you weren't coming; but good.

(As the hostess opened the door to admit her guest, she smiled a closed-toothed smile. As she began speaking she drew her hands, drawn into loose fists, up between her breasts. Opening her eyes very wide, she then closed them slowly and held them closed for several words. As she began to speak, she dropped her head to one side and then moved it toward the guest in a slow sweep. She then pursed her lips momentarily before continuing to speak, nodded, shut her eyes again, and spread her arms, indicating that he should enter.)

Guest: I'm very sorry; got held up you know, calls and all that.

(He looked at her fixedly; shook his head, and spread his arms with his hands held open. He then began to shuffle his feet and raise one hand, turning it slightly outward. He nodded, raised his other hand, and turned it palm-side up as he continued his vocalization. Then he dropped both hands and held the palms forward, to the side and away from his thighs. He continued his shuffling.)

Hostess: Put your wraps here. People are dying to meet you. I've told them all about you.

(She smiled at him, lips pulled back from clenched teeth, then, as she indicated where he should put his coat, she dropped her face momentarily into an expressionless pose. She smiled toothily again, clucked and slowly shut, opened, and shut her eyes again as she pointed to the guests with her lips. She then swept her head from one side to the other. As she said the word "all" she moved her head in a sweep up and down from one side to the other, shut her eyes slowly again, pursed her lips, and grasped the guest's lapel.)

Guest: You have! Well, I don't know.... Yes.... No.... I'd love to meet them.

(The guest hunched his shoulders, which pulled his lapel out of the hostess' grasp. He held his coat with both hands, frowned, and then blinked rapidly as he slipped the coat off. He continued to hold tightly to his coat.)[1]

As you reconstruct this scene in your mind's eye, it is obvious that the nonverbal behavior is very eloquent; you get a great deal of specific information from the gestures. The "logic of the body" has, within our culture, provided some gestures with conventionalized meanings: the clenching of the teeth beneath the smile, the making of fists, the shuffling of feet all tend to have similar meanings when they appear in similar situations.

Moreover, many of the gestures tend to express feelings that run *counter* to the surface meaning of the words being spoken. This is an extremely important aspect of nonverbal expression: it often "counterpoints" or even contradicts our verbal expression and "safely" expresses feelings that would otherwise be impolite or embarrassing. For example, while the guest and the hostess are being very polite to one another, what is going on physically is that she is grabbing him and pulling him into the room against his will. To the very end, he continues to clutch his coat as a way of saying, "I want to run away!" even while his words are saying, "I'd love to meet them."

In acting terms, these nonverbal gestures are conveying a *subtext,* feelings running beneath the surface of the dialogue that are different from those being expressed on the surface of the scene. (Subtext is examined in greater detail in Part II.)

Though most of us read "body language" on an almost unconscious level all the time, the actor needs to heighten this skill through observation and analysis. You need to become an expert, like the famous fictional detective Sherlock Holmes:

> He had risen from his chair and was standing between the parted blinds, gazing down into the dull neutral-tinted London street.... On the pavement opposite there stood a large woman with a heavy fur boa around her neck, and a large curling red feather in a broad-brimmed hat which was tilted in a coquettish Duchess of Devonshire fashion over her ear. From under this great panoply she peeped up in a nervous, hesitating fashion at our window, while her body oscillated backward and forward, and her fingers fidgeted with her glove buttons. Suddenly, with a plunge as of the swimmer who leaves the bank, she hurled across the road and we heard the sharp clang of the bell. "I have seen these symptoms before," said Holmes, throwing his cigarette into the fire. "Oscillation upon the pavement always means an *affair de coeur.* She would like advice, but is not sure that the matter is not too delicate for communication. And yet even here we may discriminate. When a woman has been seriously wronged by a man she no longer oscillates, and the usual symptom is a broken bell wire. Here we may take it that there is a love matter, but that the maiden is not so much angered as perplexed, or grieved. But here she comes in person to resolve our doubts."[2]

In his book *The Silent Language*, Edward Hall says that Sherlock Holmes "made explicit a highly complex process which many of us go through without knowing that we are involved. Those of us who keep our eyes open can read volumes into what we see going on around us."[3]

EXERCISE 4.1: THE SCIENCE OF DEDUCTION

1. Through observation over the next few days, find for yourself a brief real-life scene and record it in the same way as the hostess–guest scene.
2. Analyze it as if you were Sherlock Holmes. Re-create as completely as you can the reasons for the behavior of the characters and create a personality profile for each.
3. With a partner, re-create the scene for the group. Let everyone develop his or her own ideas about the subtext, then compare your accounts to see what

similar deductions you have made. What areas were the most commonly agreed upon, and what evidence was the most persuasive? Be specific: Why did you draw the conclusions you reached from each bit of evidence?

Although the scientific study of body language is fairly new, our interest in it is very old. One of the first studies of the "silent language" (which may have been influential on the style of acting of its time) was John Bulwer's *Chirologia and Chironomia*, written in 1644. The book calls itself a study of "the Speaking Motions, and Discoursing Gestures, the patheticalle motions of the minde." The book discussed and illustrated an enormous number of feelings as expressed by nonverbal gestures (see Figure 4.1). Similar attempts to categorize physical gestures for the performer were made throughout the seventeenth, eighteenth, and nineteenth centuries. Even a few modern systems of acting use, in a very modified form, a formalized approach to the physical expression of emotion by locating "emotional centers" in the body, an idea borrowed from Asian acting and medicine.

THE GENESIS OF GESTURE

As we have seen, some of our body gestures have developed a common meaning within similar situations, forming a gestural subvocabulary. This is because these gestures have a common origin.

Some of these gestures derive their meaning from the structure of the body itself. For example, a man hitching up his pants is usually asserting his masculinity, because this action refers attention to his genitals. Likewise, a woman covering her cheeks with her hands is probably expressing embarrassment, and her gesture is a substitute blush as the hands rise to the face in the same way that the blood would have risen to the cheeks in a real blush.

Other gestures are leftovers of animal behavior that we would have used at an earlier, more primitive stage of our evolution as a species. These vestiges of animal behavior live on as symbolic activity long after the action has ceased to be practical. This idea was developed by Charles Darwin as part of his theory of evolution in *The Expression of the Emotions in Man and Animals*. Darwin's ideas are expanded here by Robert S. Breen:

> Consider the expressive value of behavior that was once in our human history adaptive, but is no longer so except in a vestigial sense—for example, the baring of teeth in the preparation for attack or defense. In primitive experience, the use of the teeth for tearing and rending an enemy was common enough, and a very effective means of adapting to an environmental necessity. Today, the use of teeth in this primitive fashion is rare, but the baring of the teeth is still very much with us. In an attitude of pugnacity, men will frequently clench their teeth and draw back their lips to expose their teeth. This action is a reinstatement of the primitive pattern of biting, though there is no real intention of using the teeth in such a fashion. The "tough guy" talks through his teeth because he is habituated to an attitude of aggressiveness. When he bares his teeth, it is a

FIGURE 4.1 From *Chirologia and Chironomia*, 1644

warning to all who see him that he is prepared to attack or to defend himself. His speech is characterized by a nasality because his oral cavity is closed, and his breath escapes primarily through his nose. Lip action in speech is curtailed because the jaw is held so close to the upper jaw that there is little room between the lips for even their normal activity. Restriction of the lip action results in the tough guy's talking out of the corner of his mouth.

When we see a person bare his clenched teeth, curl his lip, narrow his eyes, deepen his breathing, etc., we conclude that he is angry. These are the signs of attack in our ancestors which have become for us *social symbols expressive of an emotional state* known as *anger*.[4]

EXERCISE 4.2: ANIMAL GESTURES

Select a strongly physical action directed toward another, such as intimidation, seduction, rejection, or approval. Adopt the characteristics of an ape or prehistoric human performing the same function. When you have begun to experience the activity on a purely physical, "animalistic" level, begin gradually to "civilize" the behavior. If you begin by grabbing at your partner and pulling him or her toward you, let the grabbing turn into a beckoning finger or a beckoning gesture of the head. Let the activity itself lead you as it gradually becomes less and less practical and more and more "symbolic."

Using the hostess–guest scene, or your own scene, work with a partner to develop the scene as it might have happened between two animals.

You will probably notice that the "animalized" version of your scene brought the subtext to the surface, because the purposeful suppression of feelings is an exclusively human ability. You also noticed that the animal version involved a great deal more overt movement of the lower body than its civilized offspring. Consider, however, that all these same "animal" impulses are at work in you even when you are engaging in highly civilized behavior. They are felt as muscular arousal even though they may not result in observable movement, and they affect your voice and movement quality no matter how polite and symbolic you are being.

IMPLIED GESTURES IN THE TEXT

When performing scripted material, the writer has provided the words you are to speak. You must develop the many nonverbal aspects of your performance—the physical gestures, postures, vocal inflections, and facial expressions. In doing this, you may find some guidance in the script, either in stage directions or by implications in the highly physical language that is the mark of a good dramatist.

EXERCISE 4.3: IMPLIED GESTURES IN THE TEXT

The following speech from Shakespeare's *King Lear* suggests many gestures. Read it aloud and feel the strong, specific gestures it arouses in you.

Behold yond simpering dame, whose face between her forks presages snow, that minces virtue, and does shake the head to hear of pleasure's name: The fitchew nor the soiled horse goes to't with a more riotous appetite. Down from the waist they are centaurs, though women all above. But to the girdle do the gods inherit, beneath is all the fiend's. There's hell, there's darkness, there is the sulfurous pit: burning, scalding, stench, consumption. Fie, fie, fie! pah, pah! Give me an ounce of civet, good apothecary, to sweeten my imagination. There's money for thee.

Now perform an "animalization" of the speech; see how far you can go, allowing the impulses for gesture to return to their deepest animal origins in biting, hitting, spitting, vomiting, embracing, and so on. Allow the words themselves to "regress" into the sounds of these activities.

SUMMARY

Any external sign of a feeling or thought may be called a gesture. When you have a feeling or idea, it is natural to express it, to "move it outward" through gesture and speech. This is an automatic part of your thought process that goes on even when you are alone.

Words can best say *what we mean,* and gestures can best tell *how we feel* about what we mean. Gestures are socially learned, though the "logic of the body" has provided some gestures with conventionalized meanings in similar situations.

Gestures sometimes express feelings that run *counter* to the surface meaning of the words being spoken. In acting terms, these nonverbal gestures are conveying a *subtext.* Though most of us read "body language" on an almost unconscious level all the time, the actor needs to heighten this skill through observation and analysis.

Some gestures derive their meaning from the structure of the body itself. Others are vestiges of animal behavior; when we see a person with clenched teeth, curled lips, narrowed eyes, and deepened breathing, we know that these were signs of attack in our ancestors, which have become for us *social symbols expressive of an emotional state* known as *anger.*

When you perform scripted material, the playwright may have provided gestures in the stage directions. Gestures are also implied in the highly physical language that is the mark of a good playwright.

■ ■ ■ ■ ■ ▬▬▬▬▬▬▬▬▬▬▬▬▬▬▬▬▬▬▬

VOICE

The emphasis our culture places on words as a way of communicating information sometimes makes us forget that the voice, apart from the speaking of words, also expresses feelings and attitudes far more effectively than can words alone.

Articulated speech is a learned ability, but vocal gesture is instinctive. Perhaps for this reason, vocal sounds are universal in appeal. As Margaret Schlauch puts it in *The Gift of Language:*

> A cry, a tonal inflection, a gesture, are means of communication far more universal than language as we understand it. They are, in fact, universal enough to be conveyed to animals as well as other human beings.[1]

In this lesson, you begin exploring the wide range of vocal behavior that surrounds and supports the speaking of words. Some theorists believe that these nonverbal sounds are, in fact, the source from which our spoken language evolved. In any case, they express those deep feelings that are "beyond speaking of."

THE VOICE AND EMOTION

Your voice is involved with your most basic bodily functions because it is produced by so many deep muscles and organs. As linguist Edward Sapir points out, "There are properly speaking no organs of speech. There are only organs that are incidentally useful in the production of speech sounds."[2] For this reason, your voice is called an "overlaid function," a sort of double duty performed by organs and muscles that evolved originally for other, more basic activities: the diaphragm and lungs for breathing; the larynx for swallowing; the tongue, the teeth, and the lips for chewing; the palate and tongue for tasting. In fact, the network of muscles that produce the voice are so complex and far reaching that they ultimately involve the entire body.

As said in Lesson 4, your natural impulse is to externalize your feelings and that these externalizations are part and parcel of your emotions. Because the voice is produced by the deep muscles that are the seat of emotion, your voice is completely integrated with your emotional life. As Sapir puts it:

The sound of pain or the sound of joy does not, as such, indicate the emotion, it does not stand aloof, as it were, and announce that such and such an emotion is being felt. What it does is to serve as a more or less automatic overflow of the emotional energy: in a sense, it is part and parcel of the emotion itself.[3]

Because the voice is produced by the same muscles and organs that are central to our emotional life, the sounds we make are directly expressive of our inner life. We can even say that the voice is the way we "turn ourselves inside out." It is no accident that the Latin root of the word *personality* is *per sona,* "through sound."

THE SOURCE OF THE VOICE

Of the vast range of sounds of which our bodies are capable, only a limited number are utilized for speech. For one thing, all the sounds of our language are "*ex*piratory," produced by outgoing breath. "*In*spiratory" sounds in our culture are used only as nonverbal gestures, as in a gasp (though some of the other languages in the world do use them for speech, along with clicking, whistling, and so on). Your speech, then, begins with outgoing breath. You have already experienced moving and sounding from center, so you know the integral connection between your body, activity, emotion, breath, and the voice, which is "vibrating breath." The aim here is to explore and enhance this organic unity of action, emotion, breath, and voice.

There is massive, deep, muscle involvement in breathing. The system of diaphragm, lungs, and bronchial tubes acts as a kind of "bellows." This bellows operates simply: as the diaphragm (see Figure 5.1) pulls downward in the chest cavity, air is drawn into the lungs. As it pushes upward, the air is driven through the bronchial tubes and trachea; through the pharynx; and then into the throat, mouth, and nasal chambers. Feel this process in yourself.

EXERCISE 5.1: BREATH AND VOICE

1. In a standing position, place yourself at rest and in alignment. Place your hands on your waist and breathe slowly, deeply, and fully. Feel the motion of your diaphragm as your whole torso expands and contracts. Then place your hand on your stomach (the center area just above your waist) and feel the movement of the diaphragm. Is it unduly tense, causing its movement to be limited and erratic? Concentrate on eliminating tension here. Check also the areas at the sides of the lower back. Are you breathing and responding 360 degrees around your abdomen? Are you using the entire central section of your body to breathe, or are you a "chest breather," who depends only on the limited capacity of the upper torso?

2. Now produce a continual vocalized tone and explore the variations in that tone that are possible through manipulation of the breath supply alone. Observe how the resonance of the tone is affected by changes in the force of the breath and by controlling the movement of the diaphragm.

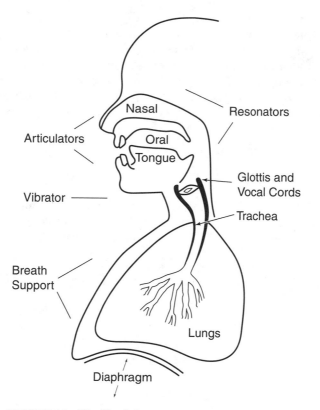

FIGURE 5.1   The Vocal Apparatus

You experienced how the "bellows" formed by the diaphragm and lungs provides the basic support for your breath and, therefore, for your voice. You rarely utilize, in real life, even half of your potential reservoir of air, nor do the demands of everyday speech cause you to develop the muscles that activate this bellows system to any-where near their full potential. The serious stage actor undertakes special study and long-term exercise to develop good breath support, which relates directly to the ability to "project" the voice effortlessly in a large space when needed.

THE CYCLE OF ENERGY

Next we consider the *cycle* of energy that flows from our center outward toward the world *and back again.* Whenever we try to do something, to achieve some objective—in short, whenever we *act*—we send energy flowing out from our center into forms of sound, speech, or gesture in the outer world. We then receive a *reaction* to our action, and this energy flows into us and touches our center, in turn eliciting a further reaction from us, and so on. As this cycle flows out, then in, then out again, we see that there is no truly unilateral action; we do not *do* unless we have been *done to,* and vice versa. In the theater, we like to say that *acting is reacting.*

This sense of a cycle of energy is central to the Asian martial arts, such as t'ai chi ch'uan. Study in these arts can be of great benefit to the actor. Developing this sense of the cycle of energy can also help to open and free the passageway through which the voice naturally flows.

EXERCISE 5.2: THE CYCLE OF ENERGY

Sit up, directly on the bony points you can feel just below the surface of each buttock; spread your legs as wide as is comfortable, with the knees slightly raised (Figure 5.2). Feel lifted from your center out of the top of your head so that your back and neck are long and wide. The head is level, eyes ahead, and the waist is level as well. This is the *sitting alignment.*

1. Breathing out, reach forward and down, keeping your back and neck long and shoulders wide. Imagine that you are bowing to someone sitting at the back of a theater.
2. As you begin to breathe in, draw the breath into the lower part of your body by drawing the small of your back to the rear and scooping "energy" into the funnel formed by your legs with your hands.
3. As the breath begins to fill you, feel its warmth and power flowing up within you. Follow its upward movement with your hands.
4. As the breath rises in your body, it lifts you, straightening and lengthening the upper torso and neck, lifting the head, widening the shoulders and the throat as it flows upward like a wave moving you in a slow undulation. You unfurl like a fern opening.
5. The breath then flows into the outer world; give an "ah" sound to that imaginary person sitting at the back of the theater and accompany it with an unfolding gesture of the arms toward him or her.
6. As the power of the breath begins to diminish, close your mouth so that the "ah" sound becomes an "oh" and then an "m," and you experience a tingling sensation in your mouth and nose areas. The smooth flow of the sound produces a trisyllable word, "ah-oh-m," or *om.*
7. As the breath and sound die away, your body again bows forward and down, your back is still long and wide, and your arms are reaching forward to scoop in a new quantity of breath energy.
8. As the breath and sound are completely used up, your body has sunk low in its bow, and the cycle begins again. Feel the continuity of inward and outward breaths so that the entire exercise becomes one unbroken, flowing experience with no "sharp corners."
9. Repeat this exercise over a period of time. Build up your breath capacity by breathing in for a count of 5, holding for 5, then releasing for a count

FIGURE 5.2   Sitting Alignment

of 10. Gradually lengthen the counts over a period of weeks to 8-8-16, then to 10-10-20.

TONE PRODUCTION

We turn next to the point at which the breath is vibrated and becomes sound. In this, your body works just like any other wind instrument. The outpouring column of air causes vibration as it passes through the vocal cords. This vibration sets the column of air in motion; therefore, the vibration is resonated and amplified. It is then changed in quality (articulated) as it passes through the mouth and nose.

This natural process, unless you resist or distort it in some way, automatically ensures the organic unity of breath, voice, emotion, and activity. Tension in the throat area, however, adversely influences the operation of the vocal cords, unnecessarily restricts the flow of breath, produces a strident and unnatural sound, and quickly causes a sore throat. (It also detracts from a performance because no muscular tension is communicated as rapidly as a tense or sore throat, which quickly produces a wave of "sympathetic" coughing from the audience.)

When we consider how the vocal cords operate, we see that they are capable of four basic types of movement:

1. When the vocal cords are drawn fully apart so that the airstream is permitted to pass through them unhindered, we produce the quality of speech called "voicelessness."

2. When they are closed and tensed, the airstream is forced through them, and they vibrate like reeds in the wind, producing tone. By increasing or decreasing their tension, we increase or decrease pitch.

3. By a quick closing, the vocal cords can interrupt the breath stream suddenly and entirely, resulting in a "glottal stop."

4. There is also a stage somewhere between the first and second that produces a semivoiced tone called a "stage whisper."

Try producing each of these types of sound as you say "hip, hip, hooray." The vocal cords either "voice" the breath stream or allow it to pass freely as a "voiceless" sound. For example, *P* is a voiceless sound, whereas *B* is voiced; otherwise, these two sounds are articulated in the same manner. Try it yourself.

EXERCISE 5.3: VOICED AND VOICELESS SOUNDS

Using the Summary Table of Consonant Sounds (see Table 6.2 on page 48), explore the voiced and voiceless sounds. Do not move your jaw, tongue, or palate while producing each pair of sounds. Make the change only by drawing the vocal cords apart or by allowing them to remain together. Lightly touch your throat and feel it change.

THE VOICE AND INNER DYNAMIC

There is an old story about a highly mannered, flamboyant actress who gestured so indiscriminately that her movements ceased to have any organic relationship to the scene she was performing. Her director tied her hands together with a string. "When your impulse to move is so strong that you must break the string," he said, "then you may move."

The director was forcing her, through the string, to hold her responses in (to suppress them); a psychologist would say he was "raising her threshold of response" so that only the strongest (and, therefore, the most dramatically important) responses would flow over her threshold; the less deeply felt impulses would be filtered out.

I once saw a short film showing the great cinema director Jean Renoir working with an actress in preparation for a highly emotional close-up. He sits her before the camera with the script and instructs her to read the words of her speech without emotion. She goes over the speech several times, and each time her natural response to the highly charged material starts to take over. At the slightest sign of emotion, however, Renoir sternly says, "No, no, just the words!" You can literally see the emotional pressure rising in her as the suppressed responses struggle harder and harder to break free. Finally, when she is about to explode, Renoir calls "action!" and the camera captures a splendid performance. Here is an exercise in which you can experience this for yourself.

EXERCISE 5.4: OVERFLOW

This is an exercise in experiencing the "overflow" of vocal and physical gesture. Repeat Exercise 4.3: read the speech by King Lear aloud but force yourself to speak in a monotone and to remain perfectly still, suppressing all impulses for vocal and physical gesture. Do this several times until you feel the demand for physical and vocal gesture growing so strong that you can no longer "contain yourself" and are finally forced to move and to speak expressively.

As you may have felt in this exercise, the repeated suppression of the impulses tended not only to filter out the weaker, less deeply felt ones, but it also strengthened those that remained by building their "inner pressure," or *inner dynamic*. This is why we often say that "less is more," and why Stanislavski encouraged actors over the course of a rehearsal process to "cut eighty percent" of the activity they began with: with less external activity to release it, internal energy has a chance to build.

In fact, inner dynamic is essential to the sense of drama, because it arouses suspense. A person with a lot of energy "inside" but without much being released "outside" is dramatically interesting; that person commands our attention and makes us wonder "What is he or she going to do?" This inner dynamic produces the quality of excitement or even danger we sense from actors such as Robert De Niro, Dame Judi Dench, or Ed Harris. Here is an exercise that will enable you to experience this inner dynamic and to hear its profound effect on the voice.

EXERCISE 5.5: RUNNING ON THE INSIDE

Stand and run in place, counting every other step aloud from one to fifty, but when you reach thirty, stop running "outside" but continue to run "inside"; hear the effect this has on your voice.

As you noticed here, the voice automatically carries much of your "hidden" energy out into the world, even when you are trying to suppress it! For instance, it is extremely moving to hear newscasters reporting a great tragedy because they are trying to remain "objective," yet, despite their disciplined efforts, the emotion is forcing itself through.

THE VOICE AND ATTITUDE

The words we speak carry the information we wish to impart, but our attitude about that information is usually carried by our tone of voice. If, for example, I feel strongly about what I am saying, I may increase the volume of my voice, elevate my pitch, and enunciate sharply by hitting the hard consonants as a sort of vocal "pounding on the table."

The voice may even communicate attitudes contrary to the meaning of the words. You already recognize such "hidden" meanings as *subtext*. The most obvious example is sarcasm: if, during an argument, I say to you, "Well, you certainly are an expert on the subject," it is my tone of voice that lets you know that I really mean "You don't know what you're talking about!"

In such instances, it is the quality of my voice that communicates my true meaning. It is because these sounds have their source in the common construction of our bodies and in our evolutionary history that they are so powerfully communicative. Remember Charles Darwin's explanation of physical gesture as a vestige of animal behavior in Lesson 4; he also believed that many vocal gestures were symbolic of general bodily functions, as explained here by Robert S. Breen:

> Darwin pointed to the primitive practice of children who expressed their dislike for someone or something by sticking out their tongues and making a sound something like a bleating sheep. Sticking out the tongue was for Darwin a primitive reflex of vomiting or rejecting something distasteful; so, too, was the sound, which got its peculiar vocal quality from the extremely open throat through which it came. The open throat was, of course, a feature of the regurgitation, or vomiting, reflex. It is interesting that the civilized adult will show his contempt or distaste in much the same fashion, though much repressed. We are all familiar with the tone of voice which we recognize as "superior" or "contemptuous" because it has that "open throat" quality.[4]

Think back to the hostess–guest scene in Lesson 4; as the hostess greeted the overdue guest, she *"smiled a closed-toothed smile."* The quality of voice that would go with this gesture has the sound of biting, and although she says, "Oh! We were afraid you weren't coming; but good," her gesture and tone of voice express the subtext, "I'm so furious with you for being late I want to bite you!"

USING YOUR OWN VOICE

From all we have seen so far, we realize that the voice is a tremendously personal thing. As I mentioned at the beginning of this lesson, the word *personality* comes from the Latin root *per sona,* meaning "through sound." Your voice travels from your deepest center on its way toward the outer world, and it carries with it the qualities of your "inner world." The act of speaking literally *turns you inside out.*

This is true when your voice is allowed to function in its normal, undistorted way. But sometimes actors choose to adopt an artificialized voice for the sake of "creating a character," or "playing age," or—especially with Shakespeare—"being poetic." If you do this, your voice is no longer authentically personal.

Your aim is to let your "I" flow into the "me" of the character, and you make that journey first and most actively by doing what the character does, and by *saying* what the character says. If you do not say it with your own voice—if *you are not there*—you are cut off from this primary point of entry into the experience of the character. Although it is true that your voice may undergo some degree of transformation in the course of working on a role, this transformation must be the result of other, deeper changes and cannot be replaced by vocal fakery.

EXERCISE 5.6: USING YOUR OWN VOICE

Select a speech from a play, or use the speech from *King Lear* in Exercise 4.3. Standing before the group, read this speech in your own voice; become aware of any urge to alter your voice in order to "perform." *Allow* yourself to speak the character's words in your own voice, feeling *for yourself* all that the character feels.

Of course, if you intend a professional acting career you must expand the range and responsiveness of your vocal instrument, but no matter how much you may work on your voice you must always do so with an aim to perfecting its own natural qualities. You can do this by becoming aware of good vocal technique and correcting any bad habits you have developed. It is a slow and gentle process best pursued with the guidance of a qualified teacher.

SUMMARY

Vocal gesture is instinctive and universal in appeal and may be the source from which our spoken language evolved. Your voice is an "overlaid function," a sort of double duty performed by organs and muscles that evolved originally for other, more basic activities: the network of muscles that produces the voice begins deep within the body and is central to our emotional life as well.

The arousal of these deep muscles in the act of sounding or speaking builds our *inner dynamic.* Inner dynamic is essential to the sense of drama, because it arouses suspense. A person with a lot of energy "inside" but without much being released "outside" is dramatically interesting.

The word *personality* comes from the root *per sona,* meaning "through sound." The act of speaking literally *turns you inside out.*

SPEECH

Humankind was once described as "the animal who talks." Speech is an amazing capacity: it is based on the ability to *symbolize*. (Nowadays we are examining the possibility that animals such as whales, dolphins, and chimpanzees are also capable of using symbols.)

Philosopher Ernst Cassirer, when theorizing about how the capacity for speech develops in us, observed that at first the sounds we make are part of feelings like hunger, pain, or joy. In this infantile "sensuous" phase, we are not trying to express these feelings to others but are making sounds as part of the feelings themselves:

> When we seek to follow language back to its earliest beginnings, it seems to be not merely a representative sign for ideas, but also an emotional sign for sensuous drives and stimuli. The ancients knew this derivation of language from emotion from the pathos of sensation, pleasure, and pain…it is to this final source which is common to man and beast and hence truly "natural" that we must return, in order to understand the origin of language.[1]

Speech, then, begins with our most fundamental experience of pleasure and pain. We see this in the development of each infant as it learns to talk. In the earliest stage of development, the baby explores the world by grabbing it and literally "taking it in" to its mouth. Later, the baby notices that making a certain sound makes Mommy appear or causes food to be given. The baby notices that *the voice can reach farther than the hand;* it realizes that it can affect the world by producing certain sounds, and at this moment the capacity for symbolic speech is born.

Viewed in this way, speech is *a special kind of doing;* it is the most specific way in which we send our energies into the world in our effort to satisfy our needs. When you deliver a speech on a stage or before a camera, your voice must also be *doing.* Your words should be hitting or caressing or grabbing or whatever the action underlying the speech may be.

This is a particularly useful view of speech for the actor. In a novel or short story, many more words are used to describe feelings, thoughts, and actions. In a drama, these words are eliminated in favor of the dialogue alone and all it can imply and suggest. In creating a drama, the writer has channeled a total human situation full of feelings and actions into the relatively few words of the dialogue.

THE PROCESS OF SPEECH

In our technological world, speech has become primarily a means for the communication of information. But for the actor, speech must retain the feelingful and active qualities I have been describing. Think of speech as *a physical process whereby feelings, needs, and thoughts find their expression in muscular activity that produces articulated sound.* As such, speech is a special type of active gesture intended to produce a real effect on your world.

As you form your thoughts into the physical activity called speech, you make a great many choices that are expressive of your feelings, needs, values, background, and personality. In this way, your process of verbalization expresses the kind of person you are (character) and the way in which you try to cope with your world (action).

It is this living quality of speech *coming to be for the first time* that you must relive to enter fully into your character. If you deliver your lines merely as memorized words, you deprive yourself of the transformational power of participating actively in the character's thought processes that lie behind the words he or she speaks.

This does not require halting speech, long pauses, or the mumbling that too often is used as an easy substitute for an honest participation in the character's thought processes. You don't want to *show* us that you are thinking; you want to be *really thinking.* The words of the dialogue are both your starting point and your final destination: you "take them apart" in rehearsal to discover the thoughts and feelings that drive them; in performance you relive these thoughts and feelings, and the words come out "under their own power."

EXERCISE 6.1: BRINGING A SPEECH TO LIFE

Choose a short speech (perhaps only a few lines) and, after memorizing it thoroughly, go through it so as to experience the thoughts and feelings that drive the words. Begin with the needs and feelings that lie beneath the words and allow the words of the speech to form gradually, like a picture coming into focus. Do this with each phrase or sentence, letting the words come from the need to communicate the idea or feeling behind them.

Does a sense of character begin to emerge as you experience the character's words coming to life? Think of it this way: playwrights, knowing that an actor will eventually speak their words, write not for the eye of a silent reader but for the human voice of an actor; the human voice is deeply involved in the body's muscles; the body's muscles are deeply involved in emotional life and thought.

To sum up: The writer has created your character's speech as the result of a total state of consciousness; by re-creating the needs, thoughts, and feelings that lie behind that speech as you speak it, you begin to enter into the character's life. The more available and responsive your vocal mechanism is, the more powerful your participation in the character's consciousness can be. In the rest of this lesson you will explore the way in which the voice is articulated as it is shaped into words.

In Lesson 5 you experienced the first way in which you articulate, by producing voiced or voiceless sounds. Next, as the breath stream, whether voiced or not, passes beyond the pharynx, it encounters three further forms of articulation. First, the soft palate may raise or lower to direct the breath either into the nose or the mouth; then, if the breath flows into the mouth, it is either impeded or allowed to pass freely; finally, if it is impeded, the location of the point at which it is impeded produces a particular sound. Here is the list of points of articulation of the breath stream:

1. Is the breath voiced or unvoiced?
2. Does the breath pass into the nasal or the oral chamber?
3. If the oral chamber, is the breath impeded?
4. If impeded, at what point is it interrupted?

Let's briefly explore each of these in turn.

NASAL SOUNDS

The first point beyond the vocal cords at which the breath stream is articulated is at the soft palate near the rear of the mouth. As the soft palate lowers or rises, it opens or closes the pathway by which the airstream may pass into the nasal cavity where it is given a special resonance. In English we have only three basic sounds that depend on nasal resonance: *m, n,* and *ng* (as in si*ng*). Nasal resonance plays an important part in causing the subtle variations of tone that produce the individual quality of our speech. Some regional dialects, as well as some speech defects, involve nasal resonance.

EXERCISE 6.2: NASAL SOUNDS

While producing a continual open tone (for example, *a* as in f*a*ther), open and close the soft palate (turning the sound of *a* into *ng*) and feel the vibrations produced in your throat, mouth, and the triangular area of your face surrounding your nose. Try to project the nasal tone into this triangular area (sometimes called *the mask*) with such force that the surface vibrations in this area can be felt with the fingertips.

With the open vowel sound of *a* being formed in the mouth, see how much resonance the nasal cavity contributes even to non-nasal sounds. Check this by snapping the nostrils open and shut between your fingers as you make the vowel sound. Project the tone toward the front of the face, producing strong vibrations in the mask.

ORAL SOUNDS: VOWELS AND DIPHTHONGS

The most complex acts of articulation take place in the mouth. The breath stream, voiced or unvoiced, may be allowed to pass freely or it may be impeded in some way; if it passes freely, it may be "shaped" by the positioning of the mouth's movable parts (mainly the jaw, tongue, and lips). The sounds produced in this "open" fashion are the *vowels*.

The vowel sounds actually used in English far exceed the simple list *a, e, i, o,* and *u* (see Table 6.1). The four categories of vowels include those produced by shaping the mouth at the front (with the lips), the middle (with the tongue), or back (using the rear of the tongue and the jaw). There are also combination sounds called "diphthongs," which are unbroken glides from one vowel sound to another.

EXERCISE 6.3: VOWELS AND DIPHTHONGS

1. Place yourself at rest and in alignment and, using the Summary Table of Vowel Sounds (Table 6.1), make each sound in turn, concentrating on developing the fullest resonance possible and on efficiently using the breath supply. Are you getting maximum volume and resonance for minimum expenditure of air?

2. Exaggerate the "shape" of the mouth in producing each sound. Read the lists in order, concentrating on the movement from front to rear in the mouth and on the increasing "size" as more and more space is created within the mouth.

3. Speak the diphthongs in slow motion for a time to explore the gliding motion from one vowel sound to another. Do you produce a clearly distinguishable sound for each type? A tape recording of your voice is extremely useful in spotting any inefficiencies or peculiarities in your articulation.

ORAL SOUNDS: CONSONANTS

When the breath stream is impeded or interrupted in the mouth, the resulting sounds are the *consonants*. The consonants are necessarily less resonant and more incisive

TABLE 6.1   Summary Table of Vowel Sounds, Arranged from Front to Back in the Mouth as You Read Down and Across

FRONT VOWELS	MIDDLE VOWELS	BACK VOWELS	DIPHTHONGS (GLIDES FROM ONE VOWEL SOUND TO ANOTHER IN A SINGLE SYLLABLE)
we	up	Charles	may
will	further	wants	I
make	further	all	join
them		old	you
mad		books	now
fast		too	Joe

than the vowels. The word *consonant* originally meant "sounding with," indicating that these sounds alone cannot comprise a syllable; they must be combined with a vowel. Although there are subtle exceptions to this rule, the consonants do serve, by virtue of their shorter duration and sharper tonal quality, as punctuation for the beginning or ending of vowel sounds, thus forming syllables.

When we consider the articulation of consonants, there are two principal questions: first, at what *position* in the mouth is the breath stream altered, and second, to what *extent* is it altered? In considering the first of these questions, we see that there are five principal positions within the mouth at which articulation may occur (see Figure 6.1). As the point of articulation moves forward in the mouth, the quality of sound changes.

A.   *Guttural.* The rear of the tongue reaches toward the back of the mouth; guttural sounds appear in some languages (like the *ch* in the Yiddish "*Ch*annukah"), but in English guttural sounds are used only in nonverbal noises.
B.   *Rear Palatal.* The rear of the tongue may rise up to make contact with the soft palate to make sounds like "*g*un."
C.   *Middle Palatal.* A slightly more forward sound may be produced by the middle of the tongue rising up to contact the roof of the mouth as in "*k*ey."
D.   *Dental.* Here the tongue is used in conjunction with either the bony ridge directly behind the upper teeth (as in the sound "*t*ea") or the teeth themselves (as in the sound "*th*ese").

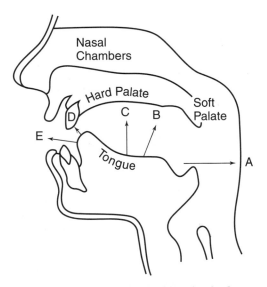

FIGURE 6.1   The Points of Articulation in the Mouth: (A) Guttural, (B) Rear Palatal, (C) Middle Palatal, (D) Dental, (E) Labial

E. *Labial.* The lips may be involved either by contacting the lower lip with the upper teeth (as in *"f*riend") or by having the lips contact each other (as in "*b*oy").

Notice that in each position different sounds are produced by either voicing or not voicing the tone without any other alteration.

At any of these points, the breath stream may be entirely interrupted or only partly impeded. When the breath stream is entirely interrupted, the result is called a *plosive* because the breath stream is cut off and then "explodes" suddenly (*b*oy). When the breath is only partly impeded, the result is a *continuant* because these sounds can be extended (*l*ovely).

Within the general category of continuants, there are several subcategories:

1. *Nasals* (si*ng*) have already been discussed.
2. *Fricatives* are produced by forcing the breath stream through a narrow passageway (*f*riend). Some of these sounds have a hissing quality and are called *sibilants* (*s*orry).
3. *Blends* are combined sounds of plosives that blend immediately into a fricative (*ch*oice, *j*oy).
4. *Glides* are slight momentary constrictions of the breath stream that immediately "glide" into a full vowel sound. Some of these sounds are called *laterals* because the breath flows around the sides of the tongue (love*l*y). Others are called *liquids* because there is only a slight constriction of the breath stream (*r*at).

The summary of consonant sounds in Table 6.2 lists examples of each.

EXERCISE 6.4: CONSONANTS

Using Table 6.2, explore the movement and shape of the mouth required to produce each sound. Exaggerate and read in slow motion. Are you producing a distinctly different sound for each? Are regional peculiarities or bad speech habits affecting any of your sounds? Is the breath supply efficiently used for each? Are you getting maximum resonance from each?

PROJECTION

Many young actors think that being heard in larger theaters is a matter of speaking *loudly;* it is much more a matter of speaking *purposefully* and *clearly.* It has been my experience that actors with even modest voices can be heard in large theaters when they have well-developed speech and are fully focused on what their characters are doing. The actor's study of speech, then, is aimed at developing the voice as *a flexible instrument* that is responsive to the demands of *character* and *style.* To achieve

TABLE 6.2   Summary Table of Consonant Sounds

POSITION IN THE MOUTH	STOPS		NASALS (VOICED)	CONTINUANTS				GLIDES (VOICED)
				FRICATIVES		BLENDS		
	VOICED	UNVOICED		VOICED	UNVOICED	VOICED	UNVOICED	
Labial	_B_OY	_P_ONY	_M_ONEY	_V_ERY	_F_UNNY	—	—	_WOW_
Dental	_D_OG	_T_OY	NO_N_E	_TH_ESE _Z_OO	_TH_INK _S_ORRY	—	—	LOVE_L_Y
				(SIBILANTS)				
Middle Palatal	_G_EEK	_K_EY	CA_NY_ON	PLEA_S_URE	_SH_E	_J_OYCE	_CH_OICE	_R_AT _Y_ES
Rear Palatal	_G_UN	_C_UT	SI_NG_	—	_H_OT	—	—	—

this flexibility, the muscles that control articulation (like any other muscles) need exercise and disciplined development.

Acting for the camera makes its own demands, especially in the area of vocal technique. Increased projection and enhanced articulation, so necessary in larger theaters, seem false in front of the camera, and actors making the transition from stage to screen must often "unlearn" a great deal. When Michael Redgrave, already an acclaimed British stage actor, did his first film scene, he eagerly asked his director how it had gone. The director, who was standing behind the camera, answered, "It was all right, Michael, except that I could hear you." Redgrave's ability to project vocally and physically in a live theater had to be modified for the camera, and the "size" of his performance, in both gestural and vocal ways, had to be greatly reduced.

Unfortunately, the filmic norms of quiet speech and everyday articulation have too often persuaded today's actors that these same norms can be applied on the live stage and that rigorous voice and speech training is no longer necessary. As a result, many of our legitimate theaters now must employ amplification systems in order to make the actors audible. This is a sad state of affairs, and the theater is the poorer for it. Don't let yourself be seduced by the poor speech habits of some of our film stars!

Here is an exercise that will help you discover that good projection and articulation go hand in hand.

EXERCISE 6.5: PROJECTION AND ARTICULATION

Choose any fairly long sentence and stand across the room from your partner. Take turns speaking the sentence to each other.

1. First, experience and emphasize the voiced and voiceless sounds.
2. Next, experience and emphasize the vowel sounds.
3. Finally, experience and emphasize the consonant sounds.

Which types of sounds provided the most clarity and understandability? Did you find that volume was not as important as articulation in making yourself heard and understood?

SPEECH, CONTEXT, AND CHARACTER

You have probably experienced the shock connected with hearing a recording of your voice. We generally have much less trouble orienting ourselves to the way we look than to the way we sound. Besides the fact that we do not hear ourselves accurately "from the inside," our disembodied voices frighten us because there is a tremendously strong sense of personal identity connected with the voice.

For this reason, the vocal aspects of characterization are enormously important, but also very dangerous if misused or approached artificially. Writers take great care in fashioning a character's speech so as to reflect qualities of personality and social, educational, or economic background through word choice, rhythm, tonality, and imagery. We will consider all this in detail in Lesson 17, but for now look at the scene from *Zoot Suit* in Appendix A and see how the speech of the characters reflects their personalities and socioeconomic backgrounds.

Situation and especially our relationship to others also have an enormous impact on articulation. Imagine the same words spoken in a public forum or secretly to an intimate friend or in a dangerous situation. This is why context must always be considered when judging the expressiveness of speech: an evenness of accent and pitch may indicate timidity or quiet authority; a voice extremely active in both range and dynamics may express hysteria or joy; the emphasizing of hard, biting sounds may indicate anger or excitement; the elongation of open vowel sounds may indicate pleasure or pain. Along with the development of your technical control of articulation, you should develop your "ear," your ability to hear the expressive aspects of articulation in real life.

EXERCISE 6.6: ARTICULATION AND CHARACTER IN LIFE

1. Observe around you the articulation habits of all sorts of people. How are laziness, timidity, aggressiveness, pompousness, stupidity, and many other personality traits expressed by articulation?
2. What effect do various emotions have on articulation?
3. What effect does situation have on articulation?
4. Try to re-create the patterns you have observed and examine your feelings when you speak in various ways.

As said earlier, articulation of your character's speech as shaped by the writer is a fundamental step in entering into the life of the character. Good writers, in their shaping of the character's speech, create what might be viewed as a musical score filled with rhythms, sounds, dynamic markings, and implied gestures—much of what you need to create the character.

FURTHER TRAINING OF BODY AND VOICE

These first lessons have briefly explored the most basic expressive skills of the actor. Advanced training in movement, voice, and speech goes far beyond what has been suggested here, and anyone serious about an acting career is advised to seek further specialized study. Opportunities to explore related training in such skills as mime, singing, dancing, clowning, fencing, t'ai chi ch'uan and other Asian martial arts, tumbling, and meditation may also be valuable. Each contributes in its way to useful acting skills and, more important, to the spiritual dimension of acting—for these physical disciplines develop also the mind, emotions, and imagination and, thereby, liberate the actor's creative spirit.

SUMMARY

Speech begins when a baby notices that *the voice can reach farther than the hand.* Viewed in this way, speech is *a special kind of doing;* it is the most specific way in which we send our energies into the world in our effort to satisfy our needs. Think of speech as *a physical process whereby feelings, needs, and thoughts find their expression in muscular activity that produces articulated sound.*

Articulation is a muscular process containing several steps. The breath stream, voiced or unvoiced, passes beyond the pharynx where the soft palate may rise or lower to direct the breath either into the nose or the mouth; then, if the breath flows into the mouth, it is either impeded or allowed to pass freely. Finally, if it is impeded, the location of the point at which it is impeded produces a particular sound. Like every aspect of the voice, articulation is profoundly expressive of personality, feeling, situation, and, especially, relationship, and it must always be understood in context.

Playwrights write not for the eye but for the human voice; the human voice is deeply involved in the body's musculature; the body's musculature is deeply involved in emotional life and thought. This is why the words your character speaks reflect both the psychology and physiology of that character. Your ability to revitalize the process of speech is crucial to your understanding and creation of the character.

WORKING WITH OTHERS

Whatever else a play may mean, all drama is fundamentally about the interaction of people with one another and with their world. It follows that drama can be properly performed only by a team of actors working together to achieve the purposes of the play. Even though most dramatic scenes are based on a conflict between the characters, you and your fellow actors remain teammates working together to realize that conflict.

As playwright August Strindberg commented a century ago:

> No form of art is as dependent as the actor's. He cannot isolate his particular contribution, show it to someone and say, "This is mine." If he does not get the support of his fellow actors, his performance will lack resonance and depth. He will be held in check and lured into wrong inflections and wrong rhythms. He won't make a good impression no matter how hard he tries. Actors must rely on each other. Occasionally one sees an exceptionally egotistic individual who "upstages" a rival, obliterates him, in order that he and he alone can be seen.
>
> That is why rapport among actors is imperative for the success of a play. I don't care whether you rank yourselves higher or lower than each other, or from side to side, or from inside out—as long as you do it together.[1]

Most of the time, your training as an actor will concentrate on your personal skills, and indeed a team depends on the individual strength of every member; but no matter how strong your individual technique becomes, you must also develop the skill of working effectively within the creative ensemble. This lesson explores the sharing of energy that enables a team of actors to work effectively together.

THE BODILY CENTER AND RELATIONSHIP

There is no relationship in which energy is not given or withheld, and there is no way to "fake" a relationship if you fail to involve your deepest bodily energy in it. Have you ever seen student actors trying to do a love scene while both were actually holding their centers back? Or actors on a proscenium stage standing so "cheated out" that each is facing the audience more than they are facing each other? Neither the actors nor the audience can have a truthful sense of the relationship if either partner fails to commit his or her bodily center. Try the following experiment, or at least imagine it in your mind's eye.

EXERCISE 7.1: BODILY CENTER AND RELATIONSHIP

1. With two other actors, stand in a triangle. Stand so that your pelvis is pointed directly at Partner A, then turn your head (without turning your body) so that your face points at Partner B off to your side. Now, whom are you "facing"? That is, with whom do you seem to have the strongest relationship? Can you decide between them, or is the situation ambiguous? Do you see how the ambiguity comes from the fact that your energy is split between them?

2. Take the experiment further. Turn your face back toward Partner A and speak to him or her; Partner B interrupts by asking a question, and you turn your head to B and answer; then you turn back to the original partner and continue. Did you feel that your basic relationship with Partner A was only suspended while you spoke to Partner B, so that the side conversation was only a "parenthesis" within the unbroken relationship with Partner A?

3. Again, speak to Partner A, but this time when Partner B interrupts, turn your pelvis toward B as you answer. Do you feel that you have now established a new relationship with Partner B, and that the original relationship with Partner A has been broken?

You see from this exercise that your bodily energy, emanating from your center, is a fundamental expression of relationship. The active forms of relationship involve energy flowing *toward* someone, or *away* from the person. This is called *approach* and *avoidance*. This is particularly important on stage, where the audience sees your entire body and responds strongly to its total condition.

For example, imagine yourself in the first stages of an argument that threatens to become a fight; you are confronting your opponent with your hands raised, and you appear to be ready for combat. In this situation, imagine rocking your pelvis forward, toward the opponent. Do you feel more truly ready to attack? Now rock your pelvis away from the opponent so that your center of gravity shifts backward. Do you feel on the defensive, only pretending to attack? Exercise 7.2 allows you to experience giving your total weight to another.

EXERCISE 7.2: FALLING

1. Your partner stands in a relaxed alignment, and you stand about three feet behind with one foot thrust back for stability (Figure 7.1). By mutual agreement and talking to each other the whole time, your partner starts to fall backward with his or her body straight but not stiff or tense. You catch the body almost at once and gently raise it back up.

FIGURE 7.1   Falling Exercise

Your partner falls only a short way at first and then gradually farther and farther. If your partner becomes frightened and "breaks" on the way down or remains tense while falling, be encouraging and reassuring. Then reverse roles.

CAUTION: Do not attempt this exercise unless you are confident of being able to catch your partner; otherwise serious injury could result. The person falling controls the situation. The Faller decides when and how far to fall, and how far away the Catcher should stand. The Faller should keep his or her hands at the side, or held together, keeping feet together and legs straight. The Catcher should catch the Faller's shoulder firmly, with his or her strongest leg back for support. Catchers should say when they are ready to catch, and Fallers should say when they begin to fall.

2. After you are comfortable falling and catching in partnerships, try this group version of the exercise. Stand in a circle of Catchers standing fairly close together with the Faller at center. The Faller relinquishes control to the group and is sent gently back and forth, being turned as necessary.

COMMITMENT, SUPPORT, AND COMMUNICATION

The greatness of a play depends on its unity, the way all of its elements have been synthesized into a single meaningful and dramatic experience. Unity must also be a quality of a good production of that play. It can be achieved only when all the many kinds of theater artists—director, actors, designers, managers, and technicians—have aligned their efforts toward the common goal of embodying the action of the play within the performance.

When the actors, the designers, and the director have worked as an ensemble in accord with the text, and the audience has likewise given of itself, there occurs one of those rare moments when true theater lives. All these human energies flow to form one energy that is greater than the sum of its parts; everyone participating in the experience receives more than he or she has given, and we feel truly moved beyond ourselves.

Such rare and wonderful moments can occur in film and television as well as in live theater. They depend entirely on teamwork, and teamwork results from a sense of common purpose and respect. No member of a team needs to sacrifice individuality; rather, each member contributes to the effort of all other members because their work is flowing in the same direction toward the same goal. The ensemble is not a collective in which the individual members have submerged their own identities, but a group of aligned individuals in which each member finds his or her individual power enhanced by membership in the group.

Alignment of effort is achieved within the group when three conditions have been met: first, when each member is genuinely committed to the common purpose; second, when each member supports the others in their particular objectives as members of the group; third, when all agree to maintain the possibility of free and open communication so that any difficulties encountered in the work can be worked out. Let's examine each of these points.

First, *commitment:* it is part of your responsibility as an actor to find a point of personal commitment to your own talent, to each role you play, to each play you perform, to each ensemble of which you are a member, and to the audience you serve through your work. Only when you have committed to your work on all these levels in a deeply personal way can you function at your fullest capacity.

Second, *support for your partners:* we all have different reasons for acting, different reasons for doing particular roles; whatever our reasons, we must support each other's objectives, even if we do not share them.

Finally, *free and open communication:* creating a play or film is rarely accomplished without some tension arising among members of the ensemble. No matter how friendly and supportive we may be, we are all bound to encounter differences of opinion, conflicting needs, or problems that are simply hard to solve. All of these problems can become *opportunities for creativity* as long as we can communicate freely about them.

Commitment, support, and communication: these are the cornerstones of teamwork and are equal in importance to all your other acting skills.

EXERCISE 7.3: LEVITATIONS

1. Form groups of seven or nine: one person lies flat, eyes closed, arms folded across the abdomen. The others kneel beside him or her, three or four on either side, and prepare to lift (Figure 7.2A).

FIGURE 7.2   Levitations

2. You all begin to breathe in unison. When your rhythm is established, *gently and slowly* lift the person, keeping the body perfectly level. The sensation for the person being lifted is one of *floating* or being *levitated.*
3. Float the person up as high as the group can reach and still keep the body level (Figure 7.2B). Then turn in the direction the head is facing so that you can carry the person a short distance, head first, still with the sensation of floating.
4. Slowly come to a halt and begin to float the person down, rocking him or her gently back and forth along the axis of the body, like a leaf settling to earth.
5. Repeat until each member of the group has been levitated.

TRANSACTION AND TEAMWORK

So far your sense of ensemble has been based on a general sense of trust, respect, and commitment. Of equal importance is your ability to use this foundation to enter into the give and take that actually produces a good scene.

As you will explore in greater detail in Part II, it is the exchange of energy, the chain of action, and reaction between the characters, that moves a scene. It is, therefore, crucial that you and your partners be good at receiving and sending the energy of the scene, because each transaction is a link in the chain that moves the play, and a chain—as we all know—is only as strong as its weakest link. This is why Strindberg said that "actors must rely on each other."

This transfer of energy from actor to actor can be described as a continual process of receiving and sending, leading and following, in which all the actors are both senders and receivers, leaders and followers simultaneously. The next three exercises give you the experience of this simultaneous leading and following.

EXERCISE 7.4: LEADING AND FOLLOWING

Blind leading.   You and your partner lightly interlace fingertips up to the first joint. Your partner closes his or her eyes, and you silently lead him or her around the room. As you gain confidence and control, begin to move faster and extend the range of your travels. Soon you can run. If your situation permits, you can even take a trip to some distant destination. Reverse roles and repeat for the trip back.

Leading by sound. Begin as above, but when you are well underway, break physical contact and begin to lead your partner by repeating a single word that he or she follows by sound alone. Again, extend your range and speed.

CAUTION: Be prepared to grab your partner to prevent a collision!

Review the experience of this exercise: as a follower, did you trust your partner enough to truly commit your weight to your movement, or were you only "pretending" to move while still holding your weight cautiously back? As leader, did you receive your partner's energy and respond to the momentum? Let's continue with another exercise to explore simultaneous leading and following.

EXERCISE 7.5: MIRRORS

1. You and a partner decide who is Partner A and who is Partner B. Stand facing each other; A makes slow "underwater" movements that B can mirror completely; try to keep the partnership moving in unison. The movements flow in a continually changing stream; avoid repeated patterns. Notice that bigger, more complete, and more continual movements are easier to follow.

2. At a signal, the roles are instantly reversed without a break in the action. B is now the leader; A is the follower. Continue moving from the deep centers of your bodies; feel yourselves beginning to share a common center through your shared movement; with it comes a common breath. Vocalize the breath and continue to share this common sound, which arises naturally from your movement.

3. The roles are reversed a few more times; each time the leadership role changes, the movement and sound continue without interruption.

4. At last, there is no leader; neither A nor B leads, but both follow, and you continue to move and make sound together. At another signal, both close your eyes for a few moments while continuing to move, then open them again. How well did you stay together?

Watch other partnerships doing this exercise: do you see how intense and connected to each other they seem? Our listening and seeing of each other on stage should always have this kind of literal intensity; you lead and follow each other during a scene just as much as you do in these exercises.

EXERCISE 7.6: COOKIE SEARCH

1. Stand together in a group at the center of your space and close your eyes. Then all spin about a few times until you don't know which way you are facing.

2. Without opening your eyes, move slowly in whatever direction you are facing until you reach a wall or other obstacle. Avoid touching anyone else; feel your way with all of your nonvisual senses.

3. When you all have gone as far as you can (and still have not opened your eyes), begin to search for your partner using only the word *cookie*.

4. When you find each other, open your eyes and wait in silence for all to finish. Feel the drama of the exercise.

In this exercise you were not led but had to find your own way toward your partner's sound. Did you feel lonely while searching for your partner and relieved when you found him or her? Don't be the kind of actor who makes his or her partners feel lonely during a performance.

As you have experienced in these exercises, connectedness depends on how well you see, hear, and feel your partner. As simple as this may seem, such significant seeing and hearing are fairly rare between actors. Some actors are only superficially aware of their teammates; they are aware instead only of what they themselves are doing and react only to their premeditated ideas of the scene. Although such premeditated and false reactions can sometimes fool an audience, the ensemble effort—and, therefore, the play as a whole—inevitably suffers.

Now let's use our collaborative skills to create a group scene.

EXERCISE 7.7: TUG OF WAR

1. Each member of the group "creates" in pantomime a piece of rope about two feet long.
2. Standing in a single long line, each of you "attaches" your rope to those on either side, so the group creates one long rope.
3. Now separate at the center and slide down the rope until two teams are formed.
4. Have a tug of war. At no time can the rope stretch or break. Continue until one team wins.

This exercise is a splendid example of performance reality: the rope ceases to be real if *any* member of the group fails to make the individual part real and connected to the whole; more important, every individual actor must believe in the *whole* rope, and all must create the *same* rope. That is why we say, "There are no small parts, only small actors."

EXERCISE 7.8: TRUST SCENE

Working in groups of three or four, create an outline (a *scenario*) for a simple scene in which each member of the group must demonstrate trust for the other

FIGURE 7.3   Group Levitation

members of the group in some physical way. For example, you might be a group of mountain climbers in danger of falling and so must work together to save yourselves, each of you contributing in a different way.

We'll conclude this sequence on working together with another group exercise.

EXERCISE 7.9: GROUP LEVITATION

1. Stand in one large, perfectly round circle, facing inward. Each of you puts your arms around the waist of the persons on either side (Figure 7.3).
2. Start to breathe in unison, feeling the breath moving the rib cages of the people you are holding. Bend your knees slightly when exhaling, then lift the persons on either side as you breathe in. *Do not lift yourself; lift those you are holding and allow yourself to be lifted by them.*
3. As you breathe out, say the word *higher* and try to lift those you are holding higher and higher. Allow the rhythm of the group to accelerate naturally until you all leave the ground.

Do you see how this exercise symbolizes the way people work together? *When the energy of every member of the group is aligned on the common goal, the result is greater than the sum of its parts: everyone gets more energy back than he or she gives.* And remember that the audience is part of the team.

SUMMARY

All drama involves the interaction of people with one another, so it can be properly performed only by a team of actors with each actor working effectively within the creative ensemble. The foundation of this collaborative skill is the realization that you are, by your very nature, connected to your world and all who inhabit it.

What we do with our energy is the most fundamental expression of our relationships with other persons. There is no relationship in which energy is not given or taken. Our energy moves either toward or away from the other, and the weight of the body is the most obvious expression of this approach or avoidance.

The greatness of a play depends on its unity, and its production must have the same unity. The energies of all the participants must flow together to form one energy. This happens when the ensemble is a group of *aligned* individuals.

Alignment is achieved when three conditions have been met: first, when each member is genuinely committed to the group effort; second, when each member supports the others in their objectives; third, when there is free and open communication.

When the energy of every member of the group is aligned on the common goal, the result is greater than the sum of its parts: everyone gets more energy back than he or she gives. And remember that the audience is part of the team.

ACTION

In Part I you prepared yourself as the "ground" in which the art of acting is to grow. Now, in Part II, you will explore the concept and technique of *action*. It is the "path" that will unlock your power as an actor, give you a sense of purpose, control, focus, and relief from self-consciousness and stage fright.

In this part, many examples will be taken from two great American plays, Arthur Miller's *Death of a Salesman* and Tennessee Williams's *The Glass Menagerie*. I urge you to read both before continuing.

THE FLOW AND SHAPE OF DRAMATIC ACTION

At the outset I must clear up a common confusion about the word *action,* because actors often use it in two different ways. Nowadays we often speak of "my action," meaning what our character does in a scene, and this is the meaning we will explore in detail in the following lessons. However, it is important to first understand the oldest meaning of the term, which comes from the philosopher Aristotle. Writing over two thousand years ago, he used the term *dramatic action* to describe the underlying energy that drives a play.

Aristotle's term in Greek was *praxis,* meaning a force that produces a result, from which we get the word *practical.* So for Aristotle, action is the force that causes the story to unfold and thereby "makes" the drama. For example, Aristotle might have said that the dramatic action driving Tennessee Williams's *The Glass Menagerie* is the struggle between Tom's sense of obligation to his family as the "man of the house" and his need to live his own life. The events of the play are caused by this underlying conflict between opposing forces. This action is "universal" because it involves a conflict all of us experience as we grow up and leave home. It is this Aristotelian sense of dramatic action that we mean when we speak of "the action of the play" or "the action in this scene."

The action of the play is a moving force; the story unfolds from moment to moment as the characters interact with one another, moving constantly toward a resolution of the underlying conflict. It is this flow of dramatic force that makes the play compelling and suspenseful. Everything our characters do, moment by moment, is meant to contribute to this flow, to moving the drama toward its conclusion. This is your main job as an actor; every aspect of your performance—your characterization, your emotion, your movement and speech—must be determined by the contribution your character makes to the flow of the play's action.

Here is an exercise that will give you a chance to experience this flow. Though seemingly simple, this is one of the most important and profound exercises in this book.

EXERCISE 8.1: IMPULSE CIRCLE

With your entire group, sit in a large circle, in chairs or on the floor, about eighteen inches apart. Make the circle perfectly round. Each person puts the left hand out palm up, then rests the right hand lightly atop the left hand of the person to the right.

The leader initiates an impulse in the form of a light, clean slap with the right hand. The slap is passed on from person to person around the circle and is allowed to flow continuously, remaining just big enough to be clearly observable. Once the slap is moving well, try the following experiments:

1. Allow your awareness to go to the slap as it moves around the circle. Begin to experience it *as having a life of its own.* Notice any change in its quality as the group begins to experience it as having its own life.
2. Now allow the slap to move as quickly as it can; see what happens when you "get out of its way." Do not force it to go faster, simply remove any resistance to it so that it flows as instantaneously as possible.
3. Now let it slow down; see how slowly it can go *without dying.* Bring it right to the brink of extinction. Keep the external slap sharp and quick but slow down the impulse as it travels internally. As it moves slowly, see what you need to do to support its life, even while it is not passing directly through you.

Drop your hands and discuss the many ways in which this exercise is like a scene on stage. Consider these questions:

1. What makes it possible for the slap to flow around the group, and how is it like a scene moving forward?
2. As you experienced it as having a life of its own, how did the nature of the flow change? Did your own experience of it change?
3. Did allowing it to be the focus of your awareness reduce your self-consciousness? Did it affect your body?
4. What are some of the ways the scene can "die"?
5. What was different about the experience when it was moving slowly? How did it affect your breathing?
6. Did you begin to feel connected to it at all times, not just when it was "your turn"?

Repeat this exercise on subsequent days; it is a good group "warm- up."

ACTION AND REACTION: THE LIFE OF THE SCENE

As you discussed this exercise, you probably agreed that the movement of the slap, like a scene on stage, depended on *cause and effect* as each of you received and sent the slap in turn. Psychologists call it "stimulus and response," and actors call it *reaction and action.* The flow of the slap depended on the ability of every group member to react and act.

In the exercise, you are slapped by the person on your left; you react to the slap by slapping the person on your right; that person reacts by slapping the next person, and so on. For each of you, *reaction produces an action*. Likewise, in a scene, another character says or does something to which you, as your character, react; your reaction becomes an action directed back at the other character or toward someone else; this evokes another reaction, and so the scene moves through the action–reaction–action–reaction chain of energy passing between the characters.

We might even say that your primary job as an actor at any given moment is to *pass the energy of the scene on in the way most useful to the next actor.* You receive energy, react, and in turn act in a way that moves the scene forward toward its ultimate destination. Each reaction becomes a new action that is a link in the chain of the scene. More simply, we say that *acting is reacting*.

To understand what is required from your action at any given moment, then, you must consider how your individual action fits into the chain of action and reaction that moves the entire scene. This understanding guides you in finding the precise quality of action (and, therefore, of need and objective leading to that action) that best serves the scene.

This understanding of action provides many benefits to you as an actor. During the exercise, when you believed in the impulse as having a life of its own, you became more relaxed and less self-conscious: your awareness opened, your center lowered, your breath became easy, and you stopped judging what you were doing and simply *did* it. Making the slap live became a productive objective, and your focus on that objective took your attention off yourself. You were, in short, *in action*.

When the group related to the slap in this way, you noticed that it began to flow more smoothly and powerfully. When the exercise started, the flow was "chunky," just a sequence of individual actions as each of you waited for your turn, each focused on his or her own part. When everyone focused his or her awareness on the whole, however, all the individual parts merged into one flowing event, which did indeed take on a life of its own.

At that moment, the exercise became "easier." You were no longer *making* it happen; it was making *you* happen. You were receiving more energy from it than you were giving to it, and the whole became greater than the sum of its parts. You also felt that you were part of the whole network through which the impulse flowed all the time, not just when it was "your turn." This is the kind of continuous support and involvement required of everyone in a scene.

These are all ways in which the exercise is like an effective scene on stage. Every actor must be connected to the whole, continuously reacting and acting to contribute to the life of the scene. When this happens, the event begins to take on a life of its own; we say that the scene begins "to play." Your group may wish to repeat the exercise with this awareness.

THE SHAPE OF DRAMA

There are a number of ways in which the previous exercise is *not* like a scene on stage. As much fun as it is, it is not particularly dramatic, though it has the *potential* for drama if certain conditions are met. Let's see what the conditions for drama are by trying another simple exercise.

EXERCISE 8.2: A DRAMATIC BREATH

1. Standing comfortably, try taking a single, complete breath that is as *dramatic* as you can make it. Don't think about it; just do it.
2. Try another; make it even more dramatic.
3. Discuss the things you did to make the breath more dramatic. Did each of these things make it truly more *dramatic* or merely more *theatrical?* If you are in a group, compare notes; was there anything that everyone did?
4. Now discuss situations in life that are naturally dramatic; what qualities do they seem to share? How would your breath be given these same qualities?

When trying this exercise for the first time, most people exaggerate their breath, making it louder and more visible. This, however, serves only to make the breath more "theatrical," not necessarily more dramatic.

Consider for a moment those situations in real life you considered as being naturally dramatic. Let's use a baseball game as an example: what makes for a really dramatic game? The first requirement is that the game must be important to us because the outcome affects the team significantly. The second requirement is that the outcome must be in doubt; the more evenly matched the teams are, and the closer we get to the last pitch with the score tied, the greater the drama.

This, then, is our definition of a dramatic event: *an urgent situation with the outcome in doubt and building toward a climax.*

How would this apply to a breath? At what moment is the outcome of a breath in doubt? The outcome is most in doubt while the breath is being held, and this is why most people who do this exercise hold their breath for a time before exhaling. They naturally feel the holding of the breath as a moment of *suspense* (which literally means "held up," as in "suspenders").

In a play, as in a baseball game, the sequence of events (the *plot*) moves forward as suspense builds; we begin to wonder, "How will this come out?" When the conflict is just on the verge of being resolved, suspense is at its peak. This moment of greatest suspense, as the outcome hangs in the balance, is called a *crisis* (a "turning point"). The function of everything that happens before the crisis is to lead toward it with *rising* energy, while everything after the crisis flows naturally from it with a *falling* sense of resolution (or *denouement,* which is the French word for "unraveling").

This, then, is the fundamental shape of all dramatic events: a rising conflict, a crisis, and a resolution (see Figure 8.1). It is a shape common to all of the performing arts; symphonies and ballets have it. It is the fundamental unit of rhythm, because it is the shape of a muscular contraction and relaxation. It is the fundamental shape of life itself, from birth to death. You can even experience it within a single breath.

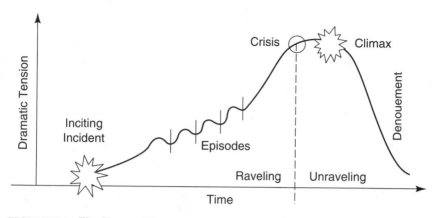

FIGURE 8.1   The Shape of Drama

EXERCISE 8.3: A DRAMATIC BREATH REVISITED

You can experience the shape of a whole play in a single breath. Start as "empty" as you can: feel the rising energy (inhaling); prolong the crisis (holding the breath), feeling the full strength of the held-back energy; then enjoy a full resolution (exhaling). A single breath can be an exciting event.

In this exercise you heightened the "drama" of the breath in two ways: you extended its dynamic range, which we call its *arc,* by stretching the low and high points of the action farther apart; you also *prolonged the crisis* so as to savor the period of maximum suspense. These same principles apply to the shaping of a play, a scene, and the units of action within a scene. We explore the shaping of action within scenes in much greater detail in Lesson 13.

DRAMA AND CONFLICT

In a baseball game, we wonder which team will win, and the greater the rivalry between the teams, the more dramatic the game. In most plays, suspense is built by the collision between two forces, which we call *the central conflict,* and it is useful to identify the central conflict driving the play in the early stages of rehearsal.

In many plays, the central conflict is between two characters, called the hero, or *protagonist,* and the villain, or *antagonist.* In its most simple form, this structure tends toward melodrama and is common in popular entertainment like episodic television. The main question generating suspense here is, "Who will win?"

In more complex plays, this two-person conflict can be used to ignite more profound issues: Shakespeare's Lear and his daughters and Williams's Tom and

Amanda are examples of protagonist–antagonist conflicts, but the issues involved are far more complex than a mere contest between a "good guy" and a "bad guy."

The central conflict may also live inside the protagonist. Such conflicts may not have clear-cut solutions, and many modern characters are trapped in "lose–lose" situations called "double binds." In *The Glass Menagerie,* the central conflict is within Tom: the question is will he stay, sacrificing his own identity, or go, suffering the guilt of having abandoned his family? Either way, he "loses."

A central conflict may also involve a character or characters confronting a difficult situation. There is no antagonist as such in *Death of a Salesman;* instead, the central conflict is within Willy and between him and a world that has made his way of life obsolete.

Whatever its form, then, all plays are organized around a central conflict between opposing forces. Sensing that conflict, we expect that something is about to happen, and this provides the essential ingredient of suspense. In fact, the feeling that something *might* happen, is more important than the event itself. This is how contemporary plays with few "events" in the traditional sense can still be dramatically satisfying, such as Samuel Beckett's *Waiting for Godot,* Harold Pinter's *The Collection,* or Sam Shepard's *The Buried Child,* to name a few.

When creating a role, you must find the connection between your part and the central dramatic conflict of the play and shape your characterization so as to contribute to that central conflict. For example, if you were playing the next-door neighbor, Charlie, in Miller's *Death of a Salesman,* you would have to see that the central conflict of the play is the choice facing Willy between his brother Ben's way of life (which is based on struggle and material success) and Charlie's way of life (which is based on acceptance and spiritual success). Your main purpose in creating Charlie's character would be to embody this alternative way of life, which, if Willy could choose it, would save his life. We call this your character's *dramatic function.* Your understanding of dramatic function is the necessary basis of all your work as an actor. In Part III we explore this essential concept in greater detail.

EXERCISE 8.4: CONFLICTS

1. With a partner, decide on a situation in which there is a *physical* conflict between you; perhaps one of you is trying to leave the room, and the other is trying to prevent it. Improvise within this situation until there is a resolution of the conflict or an impasse is reached.

2. Next invent a situation in which the conflict is *nonphysical* in nature; perhaps each of you is trying to persuade the other of some point of view. Again, improvise until a resolution or an impasse is reached.

3. After each improvisation, discuss with the group the most and least dramatic moments and aspects of it. When did the action seem most believable? Were there gaps in the flow of the action? When was suspense at its height? Was the shape of the experience satisfying? What principles can you deduce from these experiences?

SUMMARY

A scene moves through the action–reaction–action–reaction chain of energy being passed between the characters. Your primary job as an actor at any given moment is to receive energy, react, and in turn act in a way that moves the scene forward toward its ultimate destination. More simply, we like to say that *acting is reacting.*

Every actor must be connected to the whole scene, continuously reacting and acting to contribute to its life. When this happens, the event begins to take on a life of its own; we say that the scene begins "to play."

Our sense of drama springs from an urgent situation of conflict between opposing forces with the outcome in doubt. This central conflict may be between two characters, within the hero, or between the characters and their situation.

The central conflict generates a sequence of events, called the *plot;* the plot moves forward as the conflict intensifies and suspense builds; suspense is at its peak just as the outcome hangs in the balance, and this is the *crisis.* Everything that happens before the crisis leads toward it with *rising* energy; everything after the crisis flows naturally from it with a *falling* sense of resolution.

This, then, is the fundamental shape of all dramatic events: a rising conflict, a crisis, and a resolution. It is the fundamental shape of life itself, from birth to death. You can even experience it within a single breath.

In most plays, suspense is built by the collision between two forces, which is called the *central conflict,* and it is useful to identify it early on. When creating a role, you must find the connection between your part and the central conflict of the play and shape your characterization so as to contribute to that central conflict. This is your character's *dramatic function.* Your understanding of dramatic function is the necessary basis of all your work as an actor.

■ ■ ■ ■ ■

ACTION FOR THE ACTOR

Now that you have begun to understand how the dramatic action of a play or screen-play flows and is shaped to build suspense and provide a sense of crisis and climax, you will begin to explore the special meaning of action for the actor. It is the most important single aspect of the actor's job and unlocks a wealth of riches.

ACTION ACCORDING TO STANISLAVSKI

Early in the twentieth century, the term *action* began to be used in a sense different than Aristotle's when referring to the acting process. The great Russian director Constantin Stanislavski was dissatisfied with the bravura acting style of his time. Too often, he felt, the actor's display of emotion and technique became an end in itself and overshadowed the values of the play. He created a new system of acting aimed at economy, greater psychological truthfulness, and above all respect for the ideas of the play.

He based his system on the idea that everything an actor does as the character has to be justified by the character's internal need. As Stanislavski said:

> There are no physical actions divorced from some desire, some effort in some direction, some objective.... Everything that happens on the stage has a definite purpose.[1]

According to this principle, everything the actor does as the character should grow directly out of the needs of that character; it must be *justified*. The actor can no longer "show off" his or her skills for their own sake; the actor is obligated to per-form in an economical, purposeful way that serves the meaning of the play.

In Stanislavski's terms, the character's needs and desires cause him or her to do something (which he called the *action*) in an effort to achieve a desired goal (which he called the character's *objective*, though some schools of acting use the terms *intention* or *task* to mean the same thing). In other words, *need* causes *action* directed toward an *objective*.

Looked at in this way, your job is to put yourself into the character's circum-stance, experience the character's needs, experience the objectives the character chooses in hope of satisfying those needs, then do the things the character does in an attempt to achieve those objectives. It is this Stanislavskian sense of action as *a purposeful doing directed toward a specific objective* that we use throughout this book.

ACTION IN LIFE

We began in the very first lesson by saying that you are already an actor. You "act" when you do things to get what you want or need. When what you need is important enough, it commands your whole attention and all your energy flows toward your objective.

You have seen people in this condition of total commitment: an athlete executing a difficult play; people arguing a deeply felt issue; a student studying for a big test; lovers wooing. All these people have one thing in common: they have a *personally significant objective,* and as a result they are totally focused on what they are doing. The more important the objective, the more urgent the action and complete the focus, and the more unself-conscious and committed the person becomes. In acting terms, we say that someone who is doing something with this kind of total, unself-conscious commitment is *in action.*

Watching people in action is an invigorating experience; they seem so "alive" that we feel more alive as we watch them, even if their action is extremely simple. For example, a Canadian mime I once saw began his performance in a striking way: the first spectators to arrive found him sitting alone on the stage, applying his whiteface makeup. He worked simply and without the slightest embellishment, but his concentration and involvement were so complete that the spectators quickly became engrossed in watching him. As more spectators arrived, they too fell silent and watched in rapt attention. As the hall filled, the intensity of the experience grew, as if the spectators were adding their energy and attention to his, and indeed they were. When at last he finished, many minutes after the theater was full, there was a tremendous ovation. The bond with the audience that his simple but total action had created was unbreakable for the rest of the evening; because our energy had joined with his, we felt that we had come to *know* him.

Indeed, people reveal a great deal about themselves when they are in action, perhaps more than at any other time. As we say, *actions speak louder than words.* When someone is in action, he or she is so busy *doing* that he or she has no energy or self-awareness left for deception. As a result, we judge someone who is in action as being authentic and believable.

All these are powerful reasons why being in action, *being fully focused on a personally significant objective*, is the best state for you as an actor. Through this focus, you can achieve unself-consciousness, command of your audience's attention, and believability.

The experience of watching someone in action becomes even more exciting when we add conditions that produce suspense, such as an unresolved issue with the outcome in doubt, a deadline, or some other source of urgency. These are the essential elements of drama: *a character pursuing a personally significant objective in an urgent situation with an unknown outcome.* These are the situations that we experience as being the most dramatic in life, as well as on the stage or screen.

You have been in action many times in your life; these experiences can be a foundation for developing the same kind of heightened commitment on stage. Think back: in your life you have had experiences during which you were totally "tuned in" to something you were doing, so engrossed in your activity that you became totally unself-conscious, oblivious of passing time or of outside distractions.

EXERCISE 9.1: ACTION IN LIFE

1. For the next few days, notice which people attract your attention: What are they doing? How do they feel about it? What makes them interesting? Notice especially the people in those situations we think of as highly "dramatic": athletes at crucial moments, people in danger, people in the grip of deeply held beliefs, and the like. Record your observations in your journal.
2. Think about those times when you have been in action. Select one such time and relive it in your imagination. What made it possible for you to achieve this level of complete commitment and focus? Record this in your journal.

INTERNAL AND EXTERNAL ACTION

Action is not just external activity. A jeweler about to split a valuable diamond, hammer raised, is not moving at all; yet we recognize the drama, the sense of "significant doing" in him or her. This is because dramatic action is felt even *before* it has manifested itself in external activity; it lives even in the *potential* for doing. At such moments, the action is literally living *inside* you, so we can speak of both *internal* and *external* action.

Stanislavski called internal action *spiritual* action and external action *physical* action:

> The creation of the physical life is half the work on a role because, like us, a role has two natures, physical and spiritual...a role on the stage, more than action in real life, must bring together the two lives—of external and internal action—in mutual effort to achieve a given purpose.[2]

For Stanislavski it is the *integration* of the internal and external actions—"more than action in real life"—that produces a truthful stage performance, and his acting system is designed to bring about this integration. Best known are his early psychological techniques (such as fantasy and emotional recall), which were designed to work from the internal to the external, from the spiritual to the physical. Later in the development of his method, however, he began to work from the external toward the internal through "the Method of Physical Actions." As he said,

The spirit cannot but respond to the actions of the body, provided of course that these are genuine, have a purpose, and are productive.... (In this way) a part acquires inner content.[3]

During the first half of the twentieth century, the British acting tradition stressed the importance of externals in the acting process, working "from the outside in." Our American tradition, on the other hand, stressed the importance of internals, working "from the inside out." For the past sixty years, however, a real effort has been made in both countries to combine these two approaches. Both are essential, as Stanislavski pointed out:

External action acquires inner meaning and warmth from inner action, while the latter finds its expression only in physical terms.[4]

The most useful approach is to avoid thinking of "inner" and "outer" action as being in any way separable. Imagine instead a single *flow* of action that has an inner phase and an outer phase: something happens to which you respond, and if your response is strong enough, your aroused inner energy flows outward and becomes external action. When this happens naturally, you experience the inner and outer aspects of the flow as a single action.

Unfortunately, actors sometimes disrupt this natural process by being overly self-conscious, by trying to force the inner experience or trying to manipulate the externals in an artificial way. If your performance consists only of external movement and speech unconnected to an inner energy, it will seem hollow and lifeless; if it consists only of inner intensity, without skillful outer expression, it will seem vague and self-indulgent.

EXERCISE 9.2: INTERNAL AND EXTERNAL ACTION

Observe yourself and others to see how action lives in both internal and external forms. What do you notice about the relationship of the two? Which is more suspenseful? Record your observations in your journal.

BELIEVABILITY

Although it is true that we all "act" in everyday life, we do not always act *well:* sometimes our performance is judged to be "insincere" or "unbelievable."

How do we judge the believability of a performance? Social psychologist Erving Goffman points out that our role-playing behavior always sends two kinds of messages: the information we *give* (the impression we are trying to make) and the information we *give off* (the unconscious things we do that reveal how we really feel). In everyday life we intuitively read the information "given off" by watching for traces of unconscious behavior such as "body language" and telltale qualities of the voice; we then unconsciously compare this information with the message being purposely given. When the two are consistent, we judge the performance as believable; when there are inconsistencies, we feel that the person is faking.

For example, if I am trying to convince you that I am extremely interested in what you are saying, but you catch me glancing over your shoulder at the clock, you refuse to believe in my performance. Just so, on the stage, you may see actors glance at the director or audience for approval, or "break" into laughter when the character shouldn't be laughing. Such behaviors that are *inconsistent with the character's reality* make it impossible to believe in the performance.

In life and on stage, the only way to be believable is by being completely committed to your action so that there are no inconsistencies between your conscious and unconscious behavior. Every successful salesperson learns this; it is also the idea behind Stanislavski's system of acting.

INDICATING

Besides inconsistent behavior, we have all learned to recognize another symptom of insincerity, and that is *overeffort*. When someone is trying too hard, being too jolly, too sincere, too lovable, we think that, like Cassius, he or she "doth protest too much." Acting students commonly do too much: in addition to (or instead of) doing what their character is doing, they are also trying to *show* us how the character feels, or what kind of a character they are. Their extra effort is saying something like, "Hey, look at how angry I am" or "Look at what a victim I am."

In real life we sometimes call this "grandstanding"; in performance we call it *indicating*. You are indicating when you are *showing* us something about your character instead of simply *doing* what the character does.

EXERCISE 9.3: A SIMPLE TASK

Select a simple physical activity that requires great concentration, such as building a house of cards or balancing a stick on your nose. Also give yourself a tremendously important reason for doing it: for example, if you can walk all the way across the room balancing the stick on your nose, you will win a million dollars; or if the house of cards falls before you have completed the second level, a loved one will be killed.

As you perform your task, ask your audience to signal by making some sort of noise whenever they feel that you are indicating. Compare their feedback with your own sense of being in action. Did you know when you were indicating? How strong is your impulse to "show" instead of "do," or to "do too much?"

Actors indicate for various reasons: because it is a way of earning the audience's attention; because it is a way of maintaining control over the performance instead of surrendering to the action; or simply because it "feels" like a mistaken notion of acting.

If you recognize indicating and avoid it by committing to a specific action, your action generates and expresses all the emotion and sense of character needed. The essence of good acting is *to do what the character does completely and with the precise qualities required but without adding anything superfluous.*

EXERCISE 9.4: PRETEND AND REAL DOING

1. Take turns acting out a simple "pretend" action, such as looking for a make-believe hidden object.
2. Then substitute a real action; in this example, hide a real object when the performer is out of the room.
3. Discuss the difference between the pretend and the real doing.

Actors sometimes make use of real actions and conditions. In the ancient Greek theater, for example, there was a famous actor who, when performing the part of a grief-stricken father, had the ashes of his actual son brought to him on stage. Nowadays, film actors in particular may use reality to support their performances, since the camera is so demanding in this regard. Robert De Niro, for example, actually gained sixty pounds for his portrayal of a boxer gone to seed in *Raging Bull;* on another occasion, he prepared for a close-up in which he had to exhibit pain by putting a stone in his shoe and running around until it really hurt. Student actors sometimes think of such uses of reality as a kind of cheating. But as Exercise 9.4 probably demonstrated, reality can support and enhance our work.

SUMMARY

Though Aristotle defined *action* as the energy driving a play or scene, we use this term in Stanislavski's sense of *a purposeful doing directed toward an objective.* In life we see people doing things to accomplish important objectives: they are totally committed, unself-conscious, expressive, and believable. We say they are *in action,* and you strive to be in action on stage for the same reasons.

Action exists as a flow of energy both inside you and outside. The internal phase of action gives meaning and believability to the external, whereas the external gives form and expression to the internal. The two are really different aspects of the same energy, and your character can grow both from the inside out and from the outside in.

In life and on stage, the only way to be believable is by being completely committed to your action so that there are no inconsistencies between your conscious and unconscious behavior. This is one reason why you strive always to be "doing" instead of "showing," which is called *indicating.*

ACTION AND THE ACTING PROCESS

The concept of action serves the actor in many ways. In this lesson you will see how it supports your work by enabling you to reduce self-consciousness and to synthesize your actor awareness with your character's awareness. Most important, you will learn how action leads to the transformational process by which character is best created.

PUBLIC SOLITUDE

People who are in action are unself-conscious. For example, an athlete making a play in front of millions of spectators is aware only of the play and may "forget" the spectators entirely. This is a state of mind that Stanislavski called *public solitude.*

He discovered it when one of his acting teachers gave him a simple task: he was to go up onto the stage and count the floorboards while the teacher and the class went on with other business. Stanislavski, like most acting students, suffered from stage fright; he became tense and distracted on stage because he was overly aware of being watched. But while he was busy counting the floorboards, he felt at ease because he became totally engrossed in his task. It was the first time he had ever been on stage without self-consciousness, and the experience was liberating and exhilarating. Stanislavski realized that his total focus on his task had truly allowed him to forget about being watched. He called this state of being "public solitude."

From this experience, Stanislavski developed the concept of the character's objective as a "dramatic task," which, like the task of counting the floorboards, would provide the actor with a point of attention that would reduce self-consciousness and lead to public solitude. The more "in action" you are, the less self-conscious you are, and if this were the only benefit of being in action it would still be of inestimable value.

DUAL CONSCIOUSNESS

It is important that you understand one danger of the concept of public solitude. Many young actors tend to focus so much on the "solitude" that they ignore the "public." Stanislavski would not have approved of you falling into some sort of trance in which you truly forgot that the audience was present: doing so leads to un-craftsmanlike work, which he hated.

The question is: can you be completely engrossed in the action and world of your character while simultaneously being aware of the demands of performance, making artistic choices worthy of your audience's attention?

This question is answered by your capacity for *dual consciousness,* the ability to function on more than one level at a time, maintaining artistic choice while simultaneously becoming the character. As the young actor Kostya in Stanislavski's *Building a Character* put it:

> I divided myself, as it were, into two personalities. One continued as an actor, the other was an observer. Strangely enough this duality not only did not impede, it actually promoted my creative work. It encouraged and lent impetus to it.[1]

Dual consciousness is a feature of all acting, though different performance situations may require more or less emphasis on one level or the other. In TV sketch comedy, for instance, we may allow a bit more of the actor awareness to be present in the performance (this is why stand-up comedians are often successful in TV sitcoms.) In naturalistic stage plays, on the other hand, we strive to reduce our actor awareness to the minimum. For serious dramatic work for the camera, the "actor" must be completely invisible, leaving only the character. In fact, we say that the camera requires "no acting" at all.

Dual consciousness may seem like a difficult thing to attain, but it is really a natural ability. When you were a child, the rain puddle became a vast ocean, but it didn't need to stop being a puddle: you hadn't learned yet that something isn't supposed to be two different things at once, and that we aren't supposed to be in two different realities at the same time. To act, you will have to allow yourself to rediscover this childhood ability.

ACTION AND EMOTION

We've said that the process of acting is basically the pursuit of an objective to satisfy a need. What about the other things we see actors do, especially the emotions and the sense of character they project? As you continue in your study of acting, you will discover that these important things, *emotion* and *character*, develop naturally and automatically from the experience of action as we have defined it. Consider first *emotion.*

Too often, actors think that they must feel something before they do anything. You sometimes hear them say, "I don't feel it yet." Of course you want to find the emotional state of your character so that your actions have the proper quality and tone, but finding the right emotion is a *process* that takes some time. The emotion is the *result* of the process, not its starting point.

You begin work not with the emotion but with the material you get from the script—the things your character says and does (the actions)—and you proceed from the action to discover the emotional life that drives that action. In other words, you don't create an emotion and then do things because of that emotion: rather, you *do* things to fulfill a need, and emotion naturally results from that doing. Remember: *Action produces emotion, not the other way around.*

In real life your emotions spring from your efforts to get what you want. Think of something you want a great deal: if you get it, you're *happy;* if you don't, you're *sad.* If you don't get what you want and it's not your fault, you feel *angry.* When you don't get what you want and you don't know why, you feel *afraid.* When you don't know what you want, you feel *helpless.*

Even if a script gives you an indication of your character's emotional condition in a scene, you do not "play" that emotion; rather, you find it by experiencing the character's action as he or she pursues the objective within the situation. Trying to invent the emotion first is an unreliable and exhausting method that denies the way emotion functions in real life.

EXERCISE 10.1: ACTION TO EMOTION

Take a towel, shirt, or some other piece of cloth and tie a knot in the end of it. Holding the end of the towel so that the knot is away from you, like a kind of soft "club," stand in front of a chair or kneel on both knees. Raise your arms high over your head and breathe deeply from your abdomen. Now strike the chair or the ground with the towel. Repeat this action with growing intensity, each time pausing to breathe deeply before striking. Let your whole body be involved, and let your voice join in. Continue this movement until an emotional attitude begins to grow spontaneously from it. Allow the emotion to develop until it specifies itself. It may even provoke a memory or relate to some specific situation in your life. Allow the emotion to flow and become real for you. Try other gestures, such as clutching your hands over your abdomen and curling into a ball.

This exercise is borrowed from a form of therapy called *bioenergetics.* It is based on the idea that we actually store emotion in our bodily structure and that this stored emotion can be released through physical action. This idea encouraged one well-known American director to advise his actors to "do the act and the feeling will follow." We will explore this idea in greater detail when we discuss the physical aspects of characterization in a later lesson.

ACTION AND CHARACTER

In the same way that emotion arises from action, character emerges from action as well. This is how it happens in real life, too, as mentioned in Lesson 1. Think about how your own personality has developed over the years and how often you "create a character" in real life.

You play a role every time you enter a social situation. In various circumstances, in various relationships, you pursue your needs by behaving in certain ways, doing and saying certain things in certain ways to other people, and reacting to the things they do and say to you. It is this interaction with your world—this give and take of acting and reacting, this adjustment of your behavior to fit your circumstances and those with whom you interact—that shapes and expresses your personality, your character, in everyday life. It is an ongoing process: as your circumstances, needs, and relationships change, they cause changes in you as a person. Mentioned in the first lesson is William James's idea that human personality contains various "me"s that one adopts in various situations but that are all versions of one's central identity, the "I." As you think about how you play various roles in your life, you notice that your sense of "I" tends to flow into whichever "me" you are being at the moment. Some of your "me"s may be more or less comfortable than others, but they are all versions of yourself. If you are in a circumstance that forces you to behave in a certain way, and you allow yourself to remain in that situation for a time, you start to become the kind of person appropriate to that situation.

When you perform as an actor on stage or screen, you still have your "I," but you learn to let it flow into the new "me" of each role you play, even when that "me" is quite different from your everyday self. The qualities of each new "me" have been determined by the writer, who has also created a new set of circumstances, a new world, in which the new "me" lives. One of your most important skills as an actor will be *to allow your "I" to flow fully and freely into the new "me" of the role and its world.* You do this not to "be yourself" but to develop a new version of yourself, perhaps quite different from your everyday self, which is nevertheless "natural" to you, truthful to the writer's character, and appropriate to the artistic purpose for which the role was created.

All this can be summed up by saying that *character grows out of action.* This is the fundamental principle on which all our work is based, and its importance cannot be stressed enough.

EXERCISE 10.2: ACTION TO CHARACTER

Repeat Exercise 10.1, using either the striking action or some other expressive action such as caressing, wringing, or bowing. This time allow the action to engender not only a feeling but also a sense of a character. As you do this thing, who might you be? Follow any associations, real or imagined, and let the personality suggested by the action invade your consciousness. Discuss the results with the group.

PERSONALIZATION AND THE MAGIC IF

You now understand that the dramatic personality evolves according to the same processes of interaction that formed your personality in life. You don't become the character first and then do things "because that's what my character would do"; instead, you allow yourself to do the things your character does, for the reasons he or she does them and in the way that he or she does them, and see whom you turn into.

You must feel your character's needs *as if* they were your own needs, select the objectives that can satisfy those needs *as if* they were your own objectives, and then do what the character does to try to win those objectives *as if* they were your own actions. When you have thus put yourself into the character's place, the natural process of transformation begins, and a new version of yourself, a new "me," evolves. Stanislavski called this process the "Magic If."

This natural process of transformation, however, works *only* if you allow yourself to fully experience *for yourself* what the character experiences with the same urgency and significance as they do. This is called *personalization,* and it is the necessary companion of the Magic If.

There is a potential danger in personalizing the role, however. If you do not truly reach out into the character's experience but instead merely force the character to fit you, you may end up distorting the character and damaging the play. True, every role suggests some experiences and behaviors similar to those you have had in your life, and you certainly want to use these established connections; but every role also offers the possibility of reaching out into *new* modes of experience. Trust that you possess a vast personal potential; if you can engage your own energy in your character's actions within the character's world, you find yourself naturally, effortlessly transformed into a new state of being.

In other words, acting is more self-*expansion* than it is self-*expression.* This expansion, this exploration of new states of being, is the most exciting aspect of the actor's creative process.

EXERCISE 10.3: A DRAMATIC SCENE

Repeat Exercise 9.3, but this time give yourself a character and a dramatic situation. If your task was to build a two-story house of cards, perhaps you are a condemned person about to be executed, waiting for the governor to phone with your pardon. See if you can relax enough to allow yourself to "fall into" action while performing this task. Make it personal; put yourself into the scene as completely as possible.

Were you able to endow your character's need, situation, and action with personal significance? Did doing so begin a transformation into the character? Did emotion begin to emerge? Were you able to avoid indicating and self-consciousness?

THE ACTING PROCESS

In the following lessons we go on to study much more about the acting process, but you now understand its essential elements. We can describe the core of the process as having five steps:

1. You put yourself into the circumstances of your character *as if* they were your own circumstances.

2. You experience the needs of the character *as if* they were your own needs.

3. You allow yourself to form the same objectives the character chooses to satisfy those needs and to care urgently about them *as if* they were your own objectives.

4. You allow yourself to do the things (the actions) the character does to try to achieve those objectives *as if* they were your own actions.

5. If you do all this, simply and completely, you begin to experience a natural process of transformation (the Magic If). A new version of yourself, a new "me," begins to develop according to the same principles by which your personality developed in life.

These five steps lay the foundation of your work as an actor. Beyond them is a sixth step: through your acting skills, you select, guide, heighten, and purify this evolving self. You constantly check this self against the needs of the play, because every character was created to serve a particular purpose within the play. Finally, you arrive at the completed characterization, which is an extension of yourself into a new state of being. It is a marriage between who you are now, the life of the character in the play, and who you become when you begin to live that life.

Your characterization must be the result of this process; there are no shortcuts. As your acting skill develops, you are able to work more efficiently and effectively, but no amount of posturing, false voice, or trumped-up emotion can substitute for this natural process of transformation and artistic development.

By following this process with complete conviction, you not only create living characters of great value in themselves, but you also help to remind your audience of their own potential aliveness. As playwright David Mamet puts it:

> Each time we try to subordinate all we do to the necessity of bringing to life simply and completely the intention of the play, we give the audience an experience which enlightens and frees them: the experience of witnessing their fellow human beings saying, "nothing will sway me, nothing will divert me, nothing will dilute my intention of achieving what I have sworn to achieve": in technical terms, "My Objective"; in general terms, my "goal," my "desire," my "responsibility."
>
> If we are true to our ideals we can help to form an ideal society—a society based on an adhering to ethical first principles—not by preaching about it, but by creating it each night in front of the audience—by showing how it works. In action.[2]

SUMMARY

When you can go completely into action, you achieve *public solitude;* your focus on your task is so strong that your consciousness of being in public recedes into the background. Your ability to be in the character's world while simultaneously attending to your actor concerns is *dual consciousness* and can be recaptured from your childhood playfulness.

In life your personality develops as you interact with your world, and you grow and change as you encounter new circumstances and experiences. The art of acting uses this natural process; your dramatic character evolves in the same way as did the various "me's" that constitute your personality. When you want something in a particular situation and do certain things to get it, your own action changes who you are; character grows naturally out of action.

Your job as an actor, then, is to allow yourself to fully experience the totality of your character's action. You put yourself into the character's circumstances, experience the character's needs, make the choices the character makes, then do what the character does. From this, a natural process of transformation, the Magic If, begins.

Through your artistic skill you guide and heighten this process, working to fulfill the purpose for which the author created your character.

NEEDS, ACTIONS, AND OBJECTIVES

Baseball batters rehearse their stance, grip, swing, and breathing; they study the opposing pitchers; at the plate, they take note of the wind and the position of the fielders. As they begin to swing at a pitch, however, they cease to be consciously aware of all this and focus total awareness on the ball. This single objective channels all of the batter's energy into his action, the swing. Having this single objective allows batters to synthesize all their other concerns, and all their rehearsed and intuitive skills, into a single complete action of mind and body.

For you as an actor, the "ball" is your character's *objective*, what he or she is trying to accomplish at any given moment (also sometimes called his or her *intention* or *task*). Your focus on this single objective at the moment of action provides you with the same kind of integration achieved by the baseball batter. It energizes your action and gives it power, intensity, and control.

In this lesson, you will explore how to define your character's actions and objectives in the most useful way. We begin where the action begins—in the needs of the character.

WANTS AND NEEDS

Your character's behavior, like your own behavior in life, is driven by *wants* and *needs*. There are interesting differences between wants and needs.

First, we may not always want what we need: you may *want* to become a great dancer, but you don't really *want* to spend four hours a day exercising at the barre; you do it because you *need* to. Willy Loman in Miller's *Death of a Salesman* is deeply dissatisfied: he *wants* to be successful, but he doesn't know what he *needs* to do to find success, and his futile search for success drives the entire play.

Second, we may be unconscious of our needs. In *The Glass Menagerie*, Amanda says that she *wants* her children to have independent lives, but unconsciously she *needs* them to remain dependent on her. As in real life, such unconscious needs are usually stronger than conscious wants. The actress playing Amanda is aware of her character's unconscious needs and builds them into the performance, even though they are not in the character's consciousness—another instance when "dual consciousness" is essential to the acting process.

For convenience, we hereafter use the term *need* to refer to both needs and wants. Remember, however, that the differences between them can be important.

ACTION AND OBJECTIVES

A character always feels need as an arousal; the character feels as if he or she has to do something, maybe even without knowing immediately what it is. This arousal can be pleasurable, as in Amanda's expectation of the Gentleman Caller, or painful, as in Willy Loman's dissatisfaction.

As in life, a character may remain aroused for some time without doing anything about it; he or she may simply be in a condition of expectation or dissatisfaction, as in many of Chekhov's characters, and the unresolved need colors the mood and thinking of the character. The longer a need is suppressed, the stronger it becomes, thus building suspense. Hamlet, for example, spends a great deal of time wondering whether to act on his need to avenge his father's murder; his action explodes only in the last scene of the play.

Whether your character acts immediately when aroused or delays action, sooner or later the character must *do* something to try to satisfy the felt need. When your character chooses to act, he or she forms an *objective* that hopefully will satisfy the need and then chooses a course of *action* directed toward achieving that objective. In short, *need leads to objective, which leads to action.*

Notice that the need is *internal* while the objective is *external;* the action is a kind of "energy bridge" that goes from the inner need toward the outer objective. Because the need is inside you, it cannot be made observable in a dramatically satisfying way until it surfaces through action. Until it has produced action, we say that a need is not *playable.* Actors sometimes make the mistake of trying to "play" a need: they try to show us how desperate Willy Loman is or how lonely Blanche Dubois is, and the result is indicating, *showing* instead of *doing.*

Trust instead that the audience will come to understand your character's inner world by observing your action. The writer has constructed your character so that what he or she says and does springs naturally from needs, and those needs can, therefore, be deduced by the audience. It is much more satisfying to allow the audience to make this deduction for themselves, rather than for you to "show" them what the needs are.

EXERCISE 11.1: OBSERVING OBJECTIVES IN LIFE

Watch people interacting in life; see what kinds of objectives produce the most interesting interactions. Notice how people read others and how they deal with failure and success moment by moment. Record your observations and insights in your journal.

DEFINING PRODUCTIVE OBJECTIVES

As mentioned earlier, the purpose of an objective is to *compel your attention,* giving you the kind of focus the batter has on the ball and helping you to be unself-conscious. A useful objective also *energizes* you and leads naturally to stageworthy externals. When an objective does both these things—compels your attention and energizes you—it is what Stanislavski called a *productive objective.*

Experience has proved that objectives become more productive when they are directed toward a *single, immediate,* and *personally important* goal. Let's examine each:

1. An objective needs to be *singular* because you wish to focus your energy on one thing rather than diffuse it by trying to do two things at once. Imagine a batter trying to hit two balls simultaneously.
2. The most useful objective is *in the immediate future,* something that can happen right now. The play must move forward, and your energy must help propel it; never define your character's objective in a way that moves your energy into the past. Although the character's needs may be rooted in the past, the action is directed toward an objective in the immediate future. The best objective is an *aspiration for an immediate change in the way things are.*
3. Finally, an objective must be *personally important* to you. As you have already learned, you must define it in a way that enables you to *personalize* it.

We can remember these three requirements as the acronym "SIP": *S*ingular, *I*mmediate, and *P*ersonal.

While you are learning to act, it may help you to form simple verbal descriptions of your needs, objectives, and actions, step by step through a scene. Remember, however, that these verbal descriptions are valuable only insofar as they contribute to your actual experience of playing the scene. The ability to describe something (which comes from the analytical left side of the brain) is no guarantee of the ability to play it (which comes from the intuitive right side of the brain), and the two sometimes get in each other's way.

Let's examine an objective from a scene to see how these principles are applied. For example, in the second scene of Act Two of Arthur Miller's great play *Death of a Salesman,* Willy Loman wants to be a successful salesman because he has a deeper, lifelong need to be a valuable human being. But he can't be a successful salesman anymore because he's too old to drive all the way to Boston to see his clients; he keeps falling asleep at the wheel. His first boss, who was his friend, has died, and his son, Howard, has taken over the business. Willy goes to see Howard; he must get assigned to a territory in town, and this is his objective in this scene, or *scene objective.*

As Willy enters, he sees Howard playing with a new recorder, and his scene objective gives rise to an *immediate objective,* which is *to get Howard to stop what he is doing and pay attention.* This objective is singular and immediate. It is also supremely important to Willy: if he can't get Howard's attention, he won't be able to get a spot in town, he won't be able to be a successful salesman, and he won't be a valuable human being. His deepest, lifelong need lives in the present moment, giving it all the urgency of a life and death struggle. When objectives are defined in a way that makes them truly SIP, they unlock the entire life of the character in the experience of the actor and best lead to transformation.

For another example of productive objectives at work, consider the second scene in Tennessee Williams's *The Glass Menagerie*. In it, Amanda has returned home after discovering the truth about Laura's failure at Rubicam's Business College. Amanda has no doubt been thinking about what else might be done for Laura instead, and in this scene she hatches the plot that will provide the central motivating device for the entire play: *to get a husband for Laura*. Amanda knows that Laura will need to be coerced into such a plan, so she uses guilt to maneuver Laura into a position in which she cannot refuse to entertain a gentleman caller; this is Amanda's *scene objective*. This scene objective gives rise to several immediate objectives as Amanda moves Laura in the desired direction (we will analyze the scene in detail in Lesson 13). The crisis of the scene occurs when Amanda finally reveals her scene objective by saying, "Of course—some girls *do marry*."

As you see from these examples from *Death of a Salesman* and *The Glass Menagerie*, good playwrights give a character an overall objective within a scene that is worked out, step by step, through a series of immediate objectives. In Lesson 15 you will see how the scene objective itself can be understood as a manifestation of an even larger life objective called the *superobjective*. Having some sense of the superobjective and the scene objective can help you to understand the purpose of each individual immediate objective and how the immediate objectives connect, one to another, so as to move the scene toward its crisis. However, you do not play these larger patterns: your attention in performance is always in the *here and now*, on each immediate objective, making it as SIP as possible.

Here is an exercise to help you explore the power of SIP objectives.

EXERCISE 11.2: A SIP OBJECTIVE

Repeat Exercise 10.3. This time, ask a partner to join you: if you are the condemned person waiting for a pardon, your partner can be a guard or a priest sitting with you in your cell. Form a SIP objective in him or her: perhaps you want your partner to call the governor on your behalf because time is running out. Improvise the scene.

It is always beneficial to enhance the *P* in SIP by finding the most personally important expression of your objective possible, one that truly touches and motivates you as a person while remaining appropriate to the needs of the scene. This is sometimes called *raising the stakes*. Try to "upgrade" your verb to a more active and urgent form: "to question" might become "to interrogate"; "to persuade" might become "to win over." You might even consult *Roget's Thesaurus* for choices of verbs. For example, it lists several possibilities for *persuade: influence, convince, sway, plead with, argue with*. Which arouses you most? Which one best raises the stakes? Which carries the specific quality that is right for the scene?

Your character's energy flows from the character's need toward an objective through action, then your actions join with the actions of the other characters to create the scene. The scene is then shaped by the interactions between the characters so as to serve the needs of the play.

CONNECTING ACTION WITH OTHERS

Because plays are about people interacting with one another, you must understand your objectives in ways that not only energize and focus you by being SIP but also drive your action toward the other characters in the scene.

The best way to achieve this is to think of your objective as being *in* another character, to make it something you need *from that character.* The most productive kind of objective is, therefore, *a desired change in the other character.*

For example, in the Willy Loman scene, your overall objective is to get a spot in town, but as you enter and find Howard busy, your immediate objective will be *to get him to stop what he is doing and pay attention to you.* Defining the objective as being "in him" helps to bring you into meaningful *transaction* with him, producing a livelier, more dramatic scene.

We can take this idea further: in life, when we do something to try to make a change in someone else, we watch that person to see if what we are doing is working or not; if it's not, we try something else. This should be true on stage as well. Ask yourself, "How would I know I am achieving my objective? What changes might I see in the other character that would encourage me that my approach is working?"

Specific, observable change is what you want to bring about in the other character, and it is the best way to define your objective. One director even encouraged his actors to think of this as "a change in the other character's eyes." In the Willy Loman scene, for instance, your first objective might be "to get Howard to look at me with interest." Your full attention is on him, watching to see if your behavior is indeed producing the desired effect, or whether you might have to try a different approach.

EXERCISE 11.3: THE OTHER

Repeat Exercise 11.2, but this time translate your SIP objective into a specific, physical change in the other character, preferably in his or her eyes. For example, if you are a prisoner and your objective is to persuade the prison guard to release you, the change might be "to get him to look at me with compassion." Try the scene with this awareness. Discuss the results with the group.

SPONTANEITY

What you do in performance should feel spontaneous, "as if for the first time," no matter how many times you have done it before. To achieve this spontaneity, you must keep your awareness on your objective rather than on the mechanics of your external action, just as the batter thinks only about the ball and not about the swing. Otherwise you are just "going through the motions," repeating the external aspects of your performance without reexperiencing the internal needs that drive the externals.

In the scene from *The Glass Menagerie*, for example, Amanda has just learned that Laura has not been going to Rubicam's Business College. All her hopes of a career for her disabled daughter have been dashed. On the way home, Amanda has searched for an alternative plan. Either she has decided to try to marry Laura off, or she comes to this decision in the course of the scene (this is for the actress to decide). Either way, the actress playing Amanda must relive everything that has happened before the beginning of the scene, in order to be driven by it, as she turns her attention to her immediate objectives in the scene; as we sometimes say, *every entrance is an exit from somewhere else.* The things that have just happened are Amanda's *motivation*: they drive her, provide force for her objectives, and if fully experienced by the actress will provide a measure of spontaneity to the performance. But she gives her immediate attention to the objectives themselves.

To sum up: You see that motivation is in the past, but it drives you toward your objective, which is in the future. Stanislavski said it this way: *motivation leads to aspiration.* You keep your motivation alive, but you do not "play" it: rather, you allow yourself to be driven by it as you devote your full awareness to your objective. In this way, you will find aliveness and immediacy. It is the *flow* of energy from motivation to aspiration that best provides spontaneity.

Notice that this spontaneity does *not* mean that your performance is erratic or changeable: during the rehearsal process you gradually refine your external action until it becomes dependable, consistent, stageworthy, and *automatic,* just as the baseball batter has rehearsed all the aspects of his swing until he can do it without thinking. As Stanislavski said,

> ...a spontaneous action is one that, through frequent repetition in rehearsal and performance, has become automatic and therefore free.[1]

Because you are able to perform your action without thinking about it, your mind is free to concentrate fully on the objective and to experience what happens "as if for the first time." In other words, because you could "do it in your sleep," you are able to do it fully awake.

SUMMARY

Having an objective, like the batter's focus on the ball, gives your action power, control, and unity. While actually playing a scene, your immediate awareness on the character's objective triggers your well-rehearsed action, just as the batter's focus on the ball synthesizes all his or her rehearsed skills.

Your character's objective is driven by his or her wants or needs, conscious or unconscious. You must rediscover these needs and personalize them, experiencing them *for yourself* as strongly as the character does.

A productive objective energizes you and naturally generates stageworthy external action. It also connects you to the other characters in the scene. The most productive objectives are *a change we want to bring about in another character that is SIP: Singular, Immediate, and Personally important.*

Each of a character's immediate objectives can be understood as a step in his or her larger *scene objective,* which in turn can be seen as driven by a life goal or *superobjective.*

While first learning this technique, it may be useful to form verbal descriptions of your need, objective, and action, though eventually this process becomes largely intuitive. Remember, however, that naming something doesn't guarantee that you can play it, and it sometimes gets in the way.

It can be useful to select the most active, personally important form to describe the objective. It can also help to understand the objective as a change you wish to bring about in the other character.

By reexperiencing the objective every time you perform the action, you keep your performance spontaneous, even though it is so well rehearsed as to be automatic and dependable.

PLAYABLE ACTIONS

In the scene from *Death of a Salesman,* we identified a productive objective. As Willy entered, he saw that the boss was busy; his Single, Immediate, and Personally significant task was to get Howard's attention; this was the *change he needed to bring about in Howard.* Given this objective, the question now is, what does Willy *do* to achieve this objective? What is the *action* that springs from this objective?

This question is, of course, answered by Arthur Miller: Willy is going to *flatter* Howard as a way of winning his attention. Like any good playwright, Miller has envisioned Willy's inner world and has provided an external action that springs naturally from it. It is, therefore, possible for you, as the actor playing Willy, to "work backward" to discover an inner pathway to the given externals provided by the writer.

As the actor creating Willy, you must re-create this process for yourself. You must go on Willy's inner journey and find your own way to the destination provided by Arthur Miller. This is what Stanislavski called *justifying* the external action by finding the inner need that drives it. Only in this way can you have Willy's experience for yourself, and it is that experience that helps turn you into Willy.

Here is an exercise to explore this sense of objectives and actions. It can be done many times until the experience of action becomes familiar to you.

EXERCISE 12.1: SIMPLE ACTION IMPROVISATION

1. Create a need in yourself: loneliness, a need for money, a need to avoid being caught for a crime.
2. Invent an objective growing from this need involving someone in the room: to get that person to go out on a date with you, to borrow money from him, to get her to lie for you. Make it SIP: a single thing, something that person can to do right now that is important to you.
3. Now select an initial strategy that seems likely to succeed with that person, such as "to get Sam to drive me home after class by flattering him."
4. Without revealing any of this to anyone, go for it. Watch to see if your approach is working. If it's not, try a different strategy.

In this exercise you were acting in your own person, inventing your own need, objective, and action. When working on a play, one of your early steps in rehearsal is to discover your character's needs, and each of his or her objectives and playable actions, as provided by the playwright, step-by-step through the scene. By making this analysis early in the rehearsal process, you can begin to experience the logic and momentum of each scene so that it begins to "play." In this lesson you learn how to analyze the action of a scripted scene.

DEFINING PLAYABLE ACTIONS

We have described how to define productive objectives. Now we consider how to define actions springing from those objectives in a way that produces stageworthy externals. These are what actors call *playable* actions.

First, you want the most *active* description possible, so you use *a simple verb phrase* in a *transitive* form, that is, a verb that involves a doing directed toward someone else, such as "to flatter." You avoid forms of the verb "to be," because these are intransitive verbs; they have no external object and their energy turns back upon itself—certainly not a good condition for an actor whose energies must continually flow outward into the scene. You are never interested, for example, in "being angry" or "being a victim" or "being likeable"; these are not playable. Strive instead for *doing,* a transitive condition in which your energy flows toward an object, which, as we have said, is usually a change in another character.

Next, you select a verb that carries a sense of the particular *strategy* employed by the character to achieve the objective. When you choose a course of action in life, you naturally select the one that seems to offer the greatest chance for success in the given circumstances; you ask yourself, "Given what I want, what is the best way to get it in this situation, from this person? What might work?" Characters in plays often do the same.

Let's return to the Willy Loman scene and see how you might describe your action. You have just entered; you desperately need to get a spot in town; you see Howard playing with the recorder. At this moment, you, as Willy, want to get Howard's attention (to get him to look at you), but you want to do it in a way that makes him feel positively toward you. As a salesman, you instinctively appeal to something the "client" is interested in, so you flatter him by praising the recorder and the stupid recording he has made of his family.

Obviously, you have a strong *subtext* here; you seem to be doing one thing, but you are actually doing something else, something that is, for the moment, hidden. But as an actor you *play* the immediate objective (to get him to look at you) through the immediate action (flattery); you trust this immediate action to carry all the hidden pain and hope that lurks beneath it.

From these principles we see that the most complete description of your action as Willy Loman at this moment is *to flatter Howard by praising the recorder* (strategic action) *so he will pay attention to me* (immediate objective), *and I can ask him for a spot in town* (scene objective) *so I can go on being a successful salesman and human being* (superobjective).

Though you may develop such a description of your action as part of your training or study of a scene, you soon discard verbal descriptions in favor of the actual experience of the scene, moment by moment, and have only as much awareness of all this as does the character (except for that little piece of your actor's consciousness that never quite goes away).

So far we have been describing actions that are formed through a process of conscious thought. However, a great many things we do in life and in performance are not necessarily the result of conscious choice. These are sometimes called involuntary responses or conditioned reflexes; Stanislavski called them *automatic* actions.

For example, when riding in a car and presented with sudden danger, you find yourself stepping on the brake, even though you are not driving. Characters on the stage have many responses of a similar kind: when the alarm bell rings, Othello reaches for his sword; when threatened, Laura runs to her menagerie or plays the phonograph. These are habitual actions that serve the needs of these characters on a deep level, and they require little or no conscious thought, but they are, nevertheless, playable *if* the actor has recreated the character's habits as part of the performance. We explore the subject of automatic actions and the demands they make on the actor more in Part III.

UNITS OF ACTION

As we do in life, a dramatic character usually pursues an action until it either succeeds or has been deemed a failure. If it fails, the character shifts to a new action, *even though he or she may not change the objective,* or the character may abandon the first objective, form a new one, and find a new action for it. On the other hand, if the action is successful and he or she achieves the objective, the character moves on to a new objective and forms a new action.

Each change in action, whether there is a change of objective or not, can be felt as a change in the rhythm of the scene; each creates what Stanislavski called a new *unit of action,* regardless of which character has made the change. Actors usually call these units of action *beats,* and the moment in which the change of action occurs is called a *beat change.* (One theory about why we say "beat" is that it was originally the word *bit* said with a Russian accent, although a "beat" as a unit of rhythm is a good description of the way units of action feel as a well-shaped scene flows.)

In the scene from *Death of a Salesman,* Willy Loman tries several ways to get a spot in town from Howard: by flattery, by appealing for sympathy, by appealing to loyalty, by appealing to honor, by generating guilt, by demanding justice, and finally by begging. Each strategic action is abandoned as it fails, and Willy grows more desperate; each shift in action is a "beat change" and moves the scene in a new direction. It is Willy who is "running" the scene at first; he initiates each beat change and Howard only reacts to Willy's shifts in strategy. At the end, however, Howard "counterattacks" and makes the final beat change when he fires Willy.

Notice that the sequence of a character's immediate actions and objectives in a scene has a logical flow aimed at larger objectives. We discuss this flow in later lessons, but for now be aware that this sequence can carry you through the scene, beat by beat, with a sense of momentum. This sense of logical sequence leading from beat to beat is sometimes called the *scenario* of the scene, though Stanislavski called it the *score*.

It is time, at last, for you to begin work on a scene from a play. Choose carefully, as you will work on this scene repeatedly over several of the following lessons.

EXERCISE 12.2: SCRIPTED SCENE: ACTION ANALYSIS

1. With a partner, select a scene (or a logical portion of a scene) no more than five minutes long. Take it from a play you have both read in its entirety, so that you understand how the scene is meant to function within the play as a whole.
2. Analyze the scene by breaking it into units of action. Define your character's need, action, and objective in each unit.
3. Read your scene aloud together in front of the class; simply sit in chairs and make no effort to "stage" it. Your aim here is to begin to experience the give and take that moves the scene forward. Afterward, discuss it with the class. Record your insights and problems in your journal.

THE GIVEN CIRCUMSTANCES

Once you have formed a preliminary sense of the beats of your scene and your character's need, objective, and action in each beat, you have the foundation of a sense of structure, which will prepare you for effective rehearsal. First, however, you should consider also the world of the scene itself.

In everyday life you constantly interact with your environment; its physical, psychological, and social aspects influence your behavior, personality, feelings, and thoughts. Just so, characters in a play or film live in a world created by the author, director, and designers; they and their actions are shaped by that world even more than you are shaped by your world, because they and their world have been created specifically to serve one another. Therefore, you not only work on the inner qualities of your character but also strive to experience the character's world so that your characterization develops in relationship to it.

The specific qualities of the character's world are called the *given circumstances*. These "givens" fall into four categories: who, where, when, and what.

Who refers to the relationship between your character and all the other characters who are important in the scene, whether they are physically present or not. These relationships have two aspects, the *general* relationship (for example, a brother and sister) and a *specific* relationship (Tom and Laura in *The Glass Menagerie* as a unique pair of siblings). The general relationship provides a context; in many ways Tom and Laura are like many other siblings. The specific relationship between them, however, is fraught with blame and guilt over the past and tension regarding the present. The general relationship, then, provides certain basic considerations that make a relationship similar to others of its kind, while the specific relationship reveals what is unique to this particular case.

Where the scene happens also has two main aspects, the *physical* and the *social.* The physical environment has a tremendous influence on the action. For example, many of Tennessee Williams's plays must take place in the hot, humid climate of the South; think what an air conditioner would do to *The Glass Menagerie.* Shakespeare chose to set a play of great passion, *Othello,* in the similar climate of Cyprus, whereas *Hamlet* requires the cold, isolated, and bleak climate of Denmark. Move Hamlet to the tropical climate of Cyprus, and Claudius would be dead by the third act. The bar in which *Cheers* is set is very much a character in the show. It is a home-away-from-home, a place "where everybody knows your name." Here the characters can share their most intimate feelings and problems, as Diane and Carla do in our sample scene (see Appendix A). Social and educational distinctions are unimportant here. In our sample scene, the spunky, street-tough, lower-class Carla is on the same level as her boss, the classy, beautiful but neurotic Diane. Her boyfriend, Ben Ludlow, is an eminent psychotherapist who is attracted to Carla because she's the only one in the bar who doesn't treat him with reverence.

As in the scene from *Cheers,* the social environment established by the writer is as important as the physical environment. The society in which Tom moves in *The Glass Menagerie,* for example, is an active part of his character; we mustn't forget that he works in a shoe factory and his only social life consists of solitary visits to the movies. Think over the plays you have read, and you will see how in each case the influences of the immediate locale and society have been carefully chosen and are indispensable to the specific quality of the action.

When a scene is happening may be equally important, both in terms of the *time of day and year* and the *historical period,* with all its implications of manners, values, and beliefs. *The Glass Menagerie* is set in that period of unrest after the Great Depression and just before World War II, which bears heavily on Tom's personal unrest.

Finally, *what* is happening is the most important element of the scene, and your analysis of its beat structure has begun to provide a sense of it. Consider here also any *antecedent action:* things that we know have happened in the past that affect the present situation, but that the writer has not bothered to actually show us, such as Amanda's visit to the business school where she learns the truth about Laura's lack of attendance.

Here is a summary list of the givens as we have described them:

1. Who
   a. General relationship
   b. Specific relationship
2. Where
   a. Physical environment
   b. Social environment
3. When
   a. Time of day and year
   b. Historical time

4. What
   a. The main event of the scene
   b. Any antecedent action that affects this scene

Each of these given circumstances must be evaluated for its relative importance; don't waste thought and energy on aspects of the character's world that do not contribute to the character's personality or to the action. Remember that you do not play the givens; you simply absorb them and allow them to influence your action and character. Here is an exercise to help you experience the power of the givens.

EXERCISE 12.3: THE GIVENS GAME

1. One member of the group sits quietly. The rest of you watch this person until he or she reminds you of a real person you have known.
2. Remember this person in a particular real circumstance. Recall all aspects of this real scene: who, where, when, what. Keep this information secret.
3. When you have a clear picture of the givens, get up and join the person on stage. Your task is to let the person know who he or she is and what the givens are by simply relating to the person without indicating. You can't, for example, run up and say, "Hey Dad, can I borrow the car?" Don't try to create a whole event; just be there with the person in the circumstances.
4. The sitting person's task is to find out who, where, and when he or she is and what is going on. This is done by simply responding to you in various ways until you are both in the same reality. The rest of the group watches and calls "foul" if they see anyone indicating the givens.
5. When you both feel that you are in the same reality, the game is over. Discuss with each other and with the group what you thought the givens were; compare impressions and notice what produced the strongest and most dramatically satisfying impressions.

Experiencing the givens that most influence the action can be a powerful factor in rehearsing a scene. Consider even working in locations that approximate the conditions of the scene; for example, I have several times held rehearsals for Shakespeare's *A Midsummer Night's Dream* in the woods at night by lantern light, and the "sense memory" of the experience greatly enriched the stage performance.

If the givens of the play are foreign to you, some research is required. The history, architecture, painting, music, and fashion of the time can be very useful. If you are working on *Mother Courage,* you need to know something about the Thirty Years' War; for *The Glass Menagerie,* midwestern city life just before World War II is important.

EXERCISE 12.4: SCRIPTED SCENE: THE GIVENS

1. Working with your partner, analyze the given circumstances of the scene and discuss their influence on your character and on the action.

2. Rehearse the scene in ways that help you to experience the influence of the givens.
3. Read your scene for the class, again without staging it. The audience calls foul if they catch you indicating the givens instead of simply experiencing them.
4. Discuss with them the influence of the givens.

By now, you are well on your way to having your scene memorized; subsequent exercises require that you be comfortably "off book."

SUMMARY

Your character's need generates an objective and an action. Even though the action is provided by the writer, you must re-create the journey from need to objective to action for yourself so that the character's experience can lead you toward transformation.

Your character chooses an action that seems to have a chance for success in the given circumstances; this is the "strategic" aspect of action. You describe an action with a transitive verb phrase that expresses this strategy. You may also include the object of the verb, which is at best a change you want from the other character. You take note of the sequence of actions and objectives that move your character through the scene; this is called the scenario or *score* of the scene.

An action is pursued until it either succeeds or has failed. In either case, a shift is made to a new action. The shift changes the rhythm of the scene and creates a new unit of action called a new "beat." The moment at which the new action is formed is called a "beat change."

You also consider the circumstances of the scene provided by the playwright to understand how the *who, where, when,* and *what* of the scene influence your character and the action.

Armed with your understanding of need, objective, and action; the score of the scene; and the givens, you begin to play the scene. It is here, with the experience of the actual give and take of the living scene, that your true understanding grows and your transformation into the character begins.

BEATS AND SCENES

In Lesson 8 you learned how drama flows and is shaped to provide suspense and a sense of crisis and climax. In this lesson you will experience how the various parts of a play—moments, beats, and scenes—work together to create a unified experience. This may be difficult for the mind to comprehend, but it is easily understood by the muscles, so let's begin with a physical exercise.

EXERCISE 13.1: SHAPING ACTION PHRASES

Perform the following sequence of simple actions, attempting to fully experience the dramatic potential of each. Remember to focus on the *crisis, or turning point,* in each pattern: treat all that goes before as leading up to the crisis, and all that follows as flowing from it.

1. A single step. Where is the crisis of a step? To intensify the experience, involve your breath by inhaling during the rising action, holding the breath during the crisis, and exhaling during the release.
2. Three steps experienced as one phrase, with the crisis in the third step. The first two steps still have mini-crises of their own, but now they lead up to the main crisis in the third step. Let your breath parallel the larger pattern.
3. Three steps with the crisis in the first step, so that the mini-crises of the second and third steps "follow-through" from the first
4. Now try a pattern composed of three units of three steps each, with the crisis of the whole pattern in the second unit of three.
5. Invent patterns of your own; add sound.

In this exercise you experienced how a number of small units of action (like breaths or steps) can be connected into a larger phrase having a shape of its own; likewise, these larger phrases can be connected into still larger patterns, which again have shapes of their own. All these levels have the fundamental shape of rise, crisis, and release, even though the *proportion* or relationship between the parts may be different (see Figure 13.1).

This is how the parts of a play go together to compose the whole play. It begins with the smallest units, the individual transactions between characters, which are

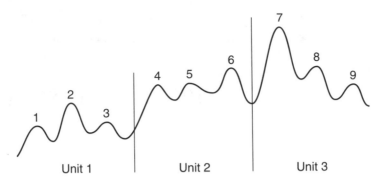

FIGURE 13.1   The Hierarchy of Action. Here, nine steps shaped as three units of action, each with its own crisis, combine to produce one large pattern with the main crisis in step 7.

called *moments*. Moments work together to form larger units called *beats,* and the beats work together to form *scenes;* the scenes flow toward the *main event* of the play as a whole.

This is referred to as the *hierarchy* of action, meaning that action functions simultaneously on several levels that are interrelated. As you rehearse the play, you explore each of these levels, and discoveries you make on one level lead to discoveries on the others. That is, as you experience each moment, you begin to develop some sense of how the beats of the scene flow; as you begin to understand how each scene is structured, you gain guidance to the proper playing of each beat and, therefore, each moment; as you come to understand how the play as a whole is structured, you begin to see what is important about each scene and each beat, and how it fits into the flow of the whole. Thus your performance develops gradually as your experience of small units of action leads to your recognition of the larger patterns they form, and your growing understanding of the larger patterns in turn provides guidance to the proper playing of each smaller element. Be patient; allow this process to develop.

SCENE STRUCTURE

You see now that both beats and scenes are structured like miniature plays: just as a play has an arrangement of scenes (episodes) with a central conflict building to a crisis and climax, so a beat is an arrangement of moments, and a scene is an arrangement of beats. Each has its own central conflict, its own crisis, and its own main event.

Unlike a beat, however, a scene always contains *one major development in the movement of the whole play.* This development may be related to *plot* as a major event, some new piece of information, or a major change in relationship; or it may be a *thematic* development; or both. In any case, every scene contains a "milestone" in the progress of the entire play, and understanding how the scene contributes to the play is crucial to the effectiveness of your rehearsal; it gives your work a sense of priority and direction.

You can identify the scene's function by asking yourself, "What if this scene were cut from the play: what would we lose that would make it impossible for the play to go forward? What would we lose from the meaning of the play?"

Likewise, the main event of a scene is usually obvious; if you have trouble identifying it, ask yourself, "What event in this scene most changes the world of the play? What would have to be provided elsewhere if this scene were cut?" The crisis can then be identified by thinking *backward* from the end of the scene, looking for the moment in which the outcome of the scene most hangs in the balance; this is usually just before the main event. (This same strategy works for the play as a whole.)

Though you may analyze the scene's structure by breaking it down intellectually in this way at first, experienced actors usually approach structure intuitively, developing a shared *rhythmic* experience of the rise and fall of the scene's energy as they explore it in rehearsal. However you develop it, your sense of scene structure must finally live as a sort of underlying "dance" in the flow of the scene, as we feel the energy building toward the crisis, then flowing naturally away from it.

The sense of the underlying structure of the scene is especially important in film and television when a single camera is used. A section of the scene is usually shot from an overall point of view; this is called the "master." Closer individual shots are then made, called "coverage," which are later to be inserted into the master by the editor. Several "takes" of each are usually required, and the whole process can take many hours. Your performance must be consistent from take to take; your close-ups must "match" the master as to timing, position, and expression. This is made even harder by the fact that scenes, and even coverage within scenes, are often shot out of sequence. To make sense of all this and to create continuity, the film actor *must* have a firm sense of the structure of the scene and how every moment fits into it.

In both film and stage work, then, your sense of scene structure is the "map" that traces the energy flow of a scene and permits all the actors to support one another in their journey through it. The map helps you have less fear of becoming lost and makes your work more playful and creative; it also helps you to experience the scene as a single, rhythmic event. One symptom that the scene has started to "play" in this way is that it seems shorter to you when you perform it.

EXERCISE 13.2: SCENE ANALYSIS

Working with your partner, answer these questions about the scene you have chosen for yourselves.

1. What is the major change in the world of the play that occurs in this scene? How does this scene cause the plot to progress? How does it enhance the meaning of the play?
2. What is the central scene conflict? Where is the crisis?

3. Read through the scene aloud on the basis of this analysis. Can you feel the shape of scene action as it flows from beat to beat?
4. Begin to rehearse the scene.

As you rehearse, you explore each *moment* so it fits into its beat and moves toward the *beat crisis;* you develop each beat so that it links with the other beats to create the *scene crisis;* you develop each scene to achieve the shape of the play, leading to the *main crisis* followed by the *main event.*

Rehearsing a scene is much like making a map of an unknown territory. You and your partners, through trial and error, find for yourselves the pathway of action that the author has hidden beneath the surface of the dialogue. Each beat change is a turning point in the journey; the destination is the scene crisis and the scene's main event. It usually takes some time to explore the beat changes by trial and error, but your exploration may be made more efficient if you agree on the destination—the crisis and main event—as you set out. Your initial answers to these questions are necessarily general at first and should be considered temporary. You will discover much more reliable and specific answers later in your rehearsal process, but these early assumptions can help give focus and momentum to your work.

ANALYZING BEATS

The analysis of a scene, beat by beat, is called by some a *breakdown,* by others a *scenario.* As an example of a breakdown, we will consider the scene from *The Glass Menagerie* to which we referred earlier.

The function of this scene within the play as a whole is to establish Amanda's "plans and provisions" to provide a husband for Laura. In the world of the South of Amanda's youth, which she still inhabits in fantasy, the first step in courtship involves visits by suitors called "gentleman callers," and these gentleman callers are expected to vie for the hand of the eligible damsel. In Amanda's fantasy, all that is required is for Tom to go out and recruit a suitable gentleman caller, and Laura's problem will be solved. The visit of the Gentleman Caller becomes the central device moving the play's dramatic action and will eventually precipitate Laura's heartbreak and Tom's leaving.

This scene's main conflict springs from the discovery that Amanda's previous plan for Laura, a career resulting from her attendance at Rubicam's Business College, will not work, and a new plan is needed. In Amanda's mind, marriage is the only alternative, but she knows that Laura will not easily be persuaded to entertain a gentleman caller, and so she must maneuver Laura into a position in which she must accept the plan.

The overall movement of the scene develops as if Amanda were putting Laura on trial. Appropriately, Amanda controls the action and initiates most of the beat changes. As the scene opens, Amanda charges Laura with deception, with being childish, with having destroyed their future; this beat might be called *making the indictment.* Laura soon counterattacks, however, and demands, "Mother, I wish that you would tell me what's happened!" A new, long beat begins as Amanda tells her story of betrayal; this beat might be called *presenting the evidence.* Amanda then demands to know what Laura has actually been doing; we might call this *forcing the confession.* Next Amanda paints a bleak picture of what the future will hold for an unmarried Laura; this is *assessing the damage.* Finally, when Laura's guilt and the enormity of its consequences have been established, Amanda reveals her plan: "Of course—some girls *do marry*"; this is the beginning of *the sentencing* phase of the trial. When Laura admits that there was a boy she liked in high school, Amanda declares the matter closed, and the crisis of the scene is reached and the central conflict is resolved as final sentence is passed: "Sister, that's what you'll do!" Even Laura's protest that she is "crippled" cannot change things.

Each of these beats forms a rhythmic unit within the scene, and the beat changes can be felt as the scene "turns a corner" on its journey toward its ultimate destination.

THE SCORE OF THE ROLE

As you analyze scenes, you will notice that within each beat your character *has a single objective and action.* It is this fact that permits you to translate the architecture of the scene into the thoughts and actions of your character. You follow the sequence of objectives, and it moves you through the scene and arouses and unifies emotion, character, and all other aspects of your performance.

Stanislavski called the sequence of objectives the *score* of the role. There is a logic to the way your character moves from objective to objective as the flow of action and reaction moves you through the scene (more on the score in the next lesson). You discover and learn this score in the same way a jazz musician learns the underlying chord changes of a song, or a dancer learns the choreography. It becomes the foundation of your experience of the scene and can propel your action, giving it pace and momentum.

You *as the actor* understand this structure, and you design the consciousness of the character so as to contribute to it; then, as you play the scene, you can surrender your immediate awareness *to the character's consciousness* while continuing to ensure that your character's thoughts, words, and actions serve the scene. Again, your ability for dual consciousness comes into play (we will explore the score more in Lesson 21).

If all the actors have worked together to develop a shared understanding of the breakdown, the rhythm of the scene is strong and clear. It is as important for actors to agree on the phraseology of their shared action as it is for members of an orchestra to work together to fulfill the phraseology of a piece of music.

EXERCISE 13.3: BEAT ANALYSIS

Working with your partner, answer these questions about the scripted scene you have chosen for yourselves.

1. Do a breakdown of the beats of the scene, as in the example above.
2. Select one important beat.
   a. Define its central conflict.
   b. Specify its moment of crisis.
   c. Decide who makes the choice that changes the beat.
   d. See how this beat grows out of the preceding beat and flows into the following beat.

SUMMARY

The parts of a play go together to compose the whole play: *moments,* the smallest units, the individual transactions between characters, work together to form larger units called *beats,* and the beats work together to form *scenes;* the scenes flow toward the *main event* of the play as a whole.

A scene is an arrangement of beats with its own central conflict, its own crisis, and its own main event. A scene contains *one major development in the movement of the whole play.* This development may be related to *plot* or to *theme,* or to both.

An analysis of the beat structure of the scene is called a *breakdown.* A breakdown greatly simplifies the scene for you. As you rehearse, you begin to feel how each beat fits into the overall structure of the scene.

Within each beat, each character has a single objective and action. It is this fact that permits you to translate the architecture of the scene into the thoughts and actions of your character as the sequence of your character's objectives form the *score* of the role.

Rehearsing a scene is much like making a map of an unknown territory. You and your partners, through trial and error, find for yourselves the pathway of action that the author has hidden beneath the surface of the dialogue. Each beat change is a turning point in the journey; the destination is the scene crisis and main event. This sense of scene structure must finally live as a rhythm as we feel the energy of the scene building toward the crisis and main event, then flowing naturally away from them. If all the actors have worked together to develop a shared understanding of the structure of the scene, the rhythm of the scene in performance is strong and clear.

THROUGH-LINE
AND SUPEROBJECTIVE

As you work on your role, each moment in your performance begins to "fit" with every other in a harmonious way; moments that may have seemed incomprehensible at first begin to fit into the flow of the whole, like steps in a single journey. When finally the whole is in place, each moment of the performance will cumulatively support every other moment, and you will be moved naturally from one to the other by a sense of necessity. This is called the *through-line* of the role. Stanislavski once said that each action fits into the role like vertebrae in a spine, so the through-line is also sometimes called the *spine* of the role.

It is neither easy nor necessary to describe the through-line of a role in words; it is more important to *feel* the sequence and flow of the role, and the "logic" by which one action leads into another, discovering the sequence of objectives which Stanislavski called the *score* of the role. For this reason, the through-line will usually emerge gradually as your individual actions are explored and experienced in rehearsal.

In a production of Brecht's *Mother Courage,* for example, the actress playing the role of Kattrin the mute daughter, needed help with her last scene. In it Kattrin climbs atop a hut and beats a drum to warn the nearby town of an impending attack. The soldiers coax and threaten her, trying to make her stop drumming, but she refuses and is shot. Her choice to sacrifice herself to warn the town is the most important choice of the entire play. It embodies the play's meaning: we have created a world in which love for your fellow human being is suicidal. The dramatic function of Kattrin's character, then, is to provide one glimmer of selflessness against which we can judge the callousness of a world in which love has been sacrificed to economic necessity.

Knowing this intellectually, however, didn't help the actress with the playing of her final action. Rehearsal after rehearsal, she tried different ways of climbing the ladder, different ways of drumming, different ways of thinking through the choice. Nothing seemed to work, and she was in despair.

Her mistake was in thinking that the problem was within this climactic scene; her real problem was that she had not yet found the *through-line* that would bring her to this moment properly. She had to go back to the beginning and examine each moment of her role, each of her previous actions and reactions, to see how each contributed to this final action.

Once she understood this, the actress began to go through rehearsals, moment by moment, asking herself, "What is going on at this moment that will eventually make me climb that ladder and beat that drum?" Each of her moments, beats, and scenes were quickly understood as contributing to this through-line and then climaxing in her final choice to warn the town. At once, her final action became not only easy but unavoidable. This is how the through-line of action brings unity and momentum, what is called *pace,* to every moment of your performance. Once you have fit each moment into its place within the structure of the whole during rehearsal, you are then free in performance to give your full attention to playing each moment, secure that it will also be serving the play as a whole.

We should note that unlike this example, a character's through-line may not be a "straight line." The character may try one thing, then another; he or she may need to discover an effective course of action through trial and error. Think of the through-line as the motivational energy driving your character forward; every time he or she has to choose what to do, the character chooses the thing that *at that moment and in that circumstance* seems best even if it later proves to be wrong.

Here is an exercise to develop your sense of the through-line.

EXERCISE 14.1: THE THROUGH-LINE

Working with your partner, answer these questions about the scene you have chosen for yourselves.

1. Examine the sequence of your character's objectives; do you see its logic as an underlying movement toward your scene objective? In each transaction, try to feel the connection of the immediate objective to the beat objective and the scene objective.
2. Run the scene without stopping and feel the momentum of the sequence of objectives, the *score* of the scene.

THE SUPEROBJECTIVE

You now understand that a play is structured on levels, on a hierarchy, of actions: individual transactions make up beats, beats make up scenes, and the scenes form the overall shape of rising and falling action that give unity to the whole play.

These levels of action relate directly to the inner life of your character because you have an objective (and, therefore, an action) on each level. In each transaction you have an *immediate* objective; the sequence of immediate objectives leads toward your *beat objective;* the objectives of the beats in sequence lead toward your *scene objective;* and your scene objectives can be seen as springing from a deep, overall objective, which is your character's "life goal" or, as it is usually called, your *superobjective.*

For example, consider again the moment from *Death of a Salesman* when Willy finds Howard engrossed in his new recorder. Being a good salesman, Willy tries to get his foot in the door by engaging Howard in conversation and asks, "What's that, Howard?" At this moment, Willy's *immediate objective* is to get Howard's attention by asking about the recorder. Once he accomplishes this, he hopes he can move on toward his *beat objective,* which is to bring up his problem with driving long distances. He would then hope to move toward his *scene objective,* which is to persuade Howard to give him a spot in town. This scene objective is connected directly to his life goal or *superobjective: to prove himself a worthy human being by earning money and respect.* (Notice that the superobjective is described in the same way as all other objectives, by a transitive verb phrase.)

If we were to follow each of Willy's immediate objectives throughout the play, we could see how he is led from objective to objective in pursuit of his superobjective. Again, Stanislavski:

> In a play the whole stream of individual minor objectives, all the imaginative thoughts, feelings and actions of an actor should converge to carry out this superobjective.... Also this impetus toward the superobjective must be continuous throughout the whole play.[1]

Identifying your character's through-line of action as tending toward a super-objective can help you to better understand each of your specific actions, connecting each momentary action to the character's deepest needs and desires. It can also help you to see how the sequence of objectives has a single driving force; thus, you can "play through" each moment and achieve both unity and momentum (called *pace*) in your performance.

Your character's superobjective may be conscious or (more commonly) unconscious. If the character is unconscious of it, you—the actor—can treat it as you treat everything you know that the character doesn't: you take it fully into account as you work, but you do not let your actor's knowledge "contaminate" your character's reality. Remember the idea of dual consciousness: what you know as the actor is not the same thing as what your character knows. The acting teacher Lee Strasberg once said the hardest thing about acting "is not knowing what you know."

Either way, the superobjective functions as an underlying principle that affects all of your actions and establishes your attitude toward life. Willy Loman, for example, is presented with two alternative attitudes toward life. He could, like his brother Ben, strike off on some bold venture and be the "master of his fate"; or he could, like his neighbor Charlie, accept his life as it is and find inner peace. Unfortunately, Willy lacks the courage to follow his brother's example and lacks also Charlie's sense of self-identity. Willy has opted instead to try to earn self-esteem through selling. As a result, Willy has come to confuse success as a salesman with success as a human being. Like many in the U.S. workforce, he "is" what he "does." We would say that his superobjective is "to prove myself worthy as a human being by earning money and respect through selling." What drives the entire play is Willy's constant search for the success that will prove he is a worthy person; his tragedy is that he defines his success by external measures. Each scene, each beat, each moment of the role, and every aspect of Willy's psychology can be understood as reflecting this superobjective.

Because it is so important to the theme of *Death of a Salesman*, Miller was explicit about Willy's superobjective; most plays are not so specific, even in the case of the major character. Most of the time you must *deduce* your character's superobjective from his or her behavior in circumstances. Tom in *The Glass Menagerie*, for example, clearly needs to make a place for himself in the world, but he cannot do so unless he escapes his role as the "provider" for his mother and helpless sister. Tom's superobjective, therefore, translates into the specific need "to leave home without guilt." The through-line of his scene objectives, his beat objectives, and each of his immediate objectives can be seen as being driven by this superobjective. His most important single action—bringing home the Gentleman Caller—is driven by his hope that Jim will replace him as the provider for the family. When he introduces his sister Laura to Jim, the Gentleman Caller, this simple introduction ("Jim, this is Laura; Laura, this is Jim") can be seen as part of his through-line of action moving toward his superobjective:

- *Immediate Objective:* to get Laura and Jim off to a good start
- *Beat Objective:* to lay the seeds of a relationship between them
- *Scene Objective:* to bring another man into the house, hopefully permanently
- *Superobjective:* because if there were another man in the house, I could leave home without guilt since Mother and Laura would be "looked after," and I could get out of here and find my own identity

It is possible for the superobjective of a character to change in the course of the play under the pressure of extraordinary circumstances. King Lear begins his play intent on retiring from the responsibilities of kingship so that he can enjoy his last days "unburdened" and bask in the love of his family and subjects. In the course of his suffering, however, he learns that he has been ignorant of true love, and at the end he surrenders his self-centered superobjective in favor of a desire for universal justice and the simple, personal love he feels for Cordelia.

It may be difficult and perhaps unnecessary to find the superobjective of minor characters, because the playwright has not provided much information; here you can be inventive, so long as your understanding of the character enables you to accurately serve your dramatic function within the play as a whole.

Though you may develop some idea about your character's superobjective before rehearsals start, it is dangerous to become too set in your thinking; these early ideas need to be tested. Ideally, the sense of superobjective emerges gradually from your experience of the specific actions of your character. Let your sense of the superobjective be the result of your rehearsal exploration, not a substitute for it.

Once you have begun to identify the superobjective, you must *personalize* it; you must come to care as deeply about it as your character does. Because the superobjective of most characters is fairly "universal" this is usually not difficult. Like Willy Loman, we all want to be thought of as worthy, and we can all "identify" with

Willy on this basis, however much we can see that Willy's way of pursuing self-esteem is mistaken.

EXERCISE 14.2: THE SUPEROBJECTIVE

Working with your partner, answer these questions about the scene you have chosen for yourselves.

1. Examine your character's actions: can you see a superobjective toward which he or she is tending, whether the character is conscious of it or not?
2. Define the superobjective using a transitive verb phrase.
3. Look through your script: are there any actual lines that sum up your character's superobjective?
4. Now consider ways of personalizing this superobjective so that you feel it with the same intensity as does your character.

Now rehearse your scene again and find how the superobjective is expressed in it.

SUMMARY

One aim of rehearsal is to feel the "logic" by which one action leads into another as steps tending toward scene objectives and through them to the superobjective. As it becomes clear, each moment in your performance begins to "fit" with every other in a harmonious way; this is the *through-line* of your action.

Scene structure translates into the thought of your character because in each transaction you have an *immediate* objective; the sequence of immediate objectives leads toward your *beat objective;* the objectives of the beats in sequence lead toward your *scene objective;* and your scene objectives move toward a deep, overall objective, which is your character's "life goal" or, as it is usually called, your *superobjective.*

Once you have begun to identify this superobjective, you must *personalize* it; you must come to care as deeply about it as your character does.

PART **III**

■ ■ ■ ■ ■

CHARACTERIZATION

In Part I you prepared your body, voice, and mind much in the way a gardener pre-pares the ground before planting a seed. In Part II you developed a way of experienc-ing action, which is the seed from which the created role springs. As you enter into the actions of your character within the given circumstances "as if" they were your own, the transformational process begins to work and a new "me" begins to emerge. In Part III we explore and extend the fruition of this process, the characterization.

THE FUNCTION AND ELEMENTS OF CHARACTER

As a story unfolds, it seems as if the things that happen are "caused" by the characters—their needs, the choices they make, the way they interact with one another—all seem to drive the story forward. This is because first the writer and then the actors have created characters that can believably perform the actions necessary for the advancement of the plot and meaning of the story. So although it seems that the characters cause the story to happen, it is actually the needs of the story that have caused the characters to be the way they are.

This is called the *dramatic function* of character. Your understanding of your character's specific purpose within the story is crucial to the success of your work. Without it, you have no basis for your exploration in rehearsal and no way to judge the results of that exploration. As Stanislavski put it, the actor's most important task is *to understand how every moment of the performance, and every aspect of characterization, contributes to the reason why the story was written.*

This is a powerful idea, equal in importance to the concepts of action and transformation. Your sense of function gives action and transformation a purpose, which makes them capable of serving the story.

DRAMATIC FUNCTION

There are two main ways that your character may serve the story: by advancing the *plot* through actions and by contributing to the *meaning* through the values the character and his or her actions express.

In terms of the plot, your character may commit crucial actions that drive the plot forward; your character may serve as a "foil" to frustrate the intentions of another character, or he or she may simply serve to provide some essential plot information, like the classical messenger. In terms of the meaning of the story, your character may represent certain values or present a contrast to the values of other characters; your character may be the spokesperson for one of several conflicting points of view or an embodiment or extension of the conflict within the main character, like Ben and Charlie who represent the two lifestyles between which Willy Loman must choose in *Death of a Salesman.*

Too often actors approach their characters so personally that they begin to forget the larger purpose for which that character was created. Without a sense of function, they may create a character who is alive and believable but who doesn't fit into the story and doesn't do the job the character was created to do. Even if the audience accepts or is even impressed by such a performance, the story is damaged, and the actor has failed.

EXERCISE 15.1: DRAMATIC FUNCTION

Consider the character you have been developing in the previous exercises: what is that character's dramatic function within the story?

1. If your character were to be cut, what would be missing from the plot? What actions would have to be given to another character for the plot to proceed?
2. How would the meaning of the play suffer if your character were cut? Does your character express some value or point of view that is essential? Would the meaning of the other characters be as clear?

FUNCTIONAL AND LIKENESS TRAITS

In order for your character to serve a purpose within the story believably, the writer has provided him or her with certain traits that make the action required by the story "natural" to the character; for example, because Shakespeare's story requires that Othello strangle Desdemona, he must be capable of overwhelming jealousy.

Aristotle called these *functional traits* because they permit the character to believably fulfill his or her dramatic function. Whatever other traits are suggested by the text, or whatever else you may invent in rehearsal to "round out" the character, you must embody these functional traits first and foremost, and let no other traits obscure or contradict them.

There are other kinds of character traits that do not contribute directly to a character's main dramatic function. These are the traits that help us to recognize the character as a fellow human being, someone we can "know" because he or she is in some way "like" us. Aristotle called these *likeness traits*. Some likeness traits are provided by the writer, but the actor often contributes personal touches to the role.

EXERCISE 15.2: FUNCTIONAL AND LIKENESS TRAITS

Examine again the character you have been developing.

1. What traits must your character have to believably perform his or her function within the story? How has the writer provided or implied these functional traits?
2. What additional likeness traits has the writer provided or implied that help to "round out" your character as a recognizable human being?

CATEGORIES OF CHARACTER TRAITS

Whether they are functional traits or likeness traits, we can classify all characterizational traits into four categories, as outlined here by Oscar Brockett:

> The first level of characterization is physical and is concerned only with such basic facts as sex, age, size, and color. Sometimes a dramatist does not supply all of this information, but it is present whenever the play is produced, since actors necessarily give concrete form to the characters. The physical is the simplest level of characterization, however, since it reveals external traits only, many of which may not affect the dramatic action at all.
>
> The second level is social. It includes a character's economic status, profession or trade, religion, family relationships—all those factors that place him in his environment.
>
> The third level is psychological. It reveals a character's habitual responses, attitudes, desires, motivations, likes and dislikes—the inner workings of the mind, both emotional and intellectual, which precede action. Since habits of feeling, thought and behavior define characters more fully than do physical and social traits, and since drama most often arises from conflicting desires, the psychological is the most essential level of characterization.
>
> The fourth level is moral. Although implied in all plays, it is not always emphasized. It is most apt to be used in serious plays, especially tragedies. Although almost all human action suggests some ethical standard, in many plays the moral implications are ignored, and decisions are made on grounds of expediency. This is typical of comedy, since moral deliberations tend to make any action serious. More nearly than any other kind, moral decisions differentiate characters, since the choices they make when faced with moral crises show whether they are selfish, hypocritical, or persons of integrity. A moral decision usually causes a character to examine his own motives and values, in the process of which his true nature is revealed both to himself and to the audience.[1]

In the following lessons we focus on several of these levels of characterization as they develop through the rehearsal process. First, however, let's look at the information you can get from the play about each of these levels of characterization during your early stages of preparation.

PHYSICAL TRAITS

The first level is *physical.* It is important to you because the external traits of body and voice communicate all the other levels of characterization.

The writer has specified the essential aspects of your character's physical traits. There are four main sources of such information in any text. First, there are the *stage directions* or *prefaces* by the author. Second, there are traits *described by other characters;* of course, we must evaluate such descriptions and determine if they are accurate or perhaps distorted by the other characters' prejudices. Third, many traits can be deduced from the *style of the writing;* someone in a Restoration comedy had better not slouch around like a Sam Shepard cowboy. Fourth, and most important, are traits that are *implied by the action;* if you look at the most important actions that your character commits in the story, you see that there are fundamental physical traits required in performing these actions believably.

EXERCISE 15.3: PHYSICAL TRAITS

Examine the entire story from which your scene comes; find clues to your character's bodily and vocal traits. Check each of the following:

1. Considering the most important actions committed by your character, what physical traits does he or she need for you to believably perform these actions?
2. The stage directions—what does the writer specifically tell you about your character's age, body, and so on?
3. Descriptions by other characters—what can you learn from what others say? Are their descriptions accurate or prejudiced by their points of view?
4. What are the physical implications of the style of the writing?

SOCIAL TRAITS

The second level of characterization is *social* and places the character in relation to the others in his or her world. Just as your personality is greatly influenced by those around you in everyday life, so a dramatic character can be understood only in relationship to the other characters in his or her world.

We always judge character in relationship. If there is a disparity between the way a person wants to be perceived and the way others perceive that person, we always believe the evidence of the relationships. If we are walking down the hall, for example, and I am trying to convince you that I am an important person around here, yet the people we pass are ignoring me, what will you think? Think of the difference between the way Amanda in *The Glass Menagerie* wants to be seen and the actual effect she has on her children.

If you have ever been on stage with someone who failed to relate properly to you, you understand why it is impossible to overcome the false impression another actor can create. For example, if you are supposed to be frightening, but the other actor fails to be frightened by you, there is nothing you can do to correct the audience's impression, because an audience is more influenced by the way others relate to you than by anything you can do on your own. The common idea that the actor creates the character is somewhat erroneous; it would be truer to say that *the actors create each other's characters.* In fact, it is a good idea for you to think less about creating your character and more about *creating the other characters.* If you do that, you will find that you will create your own character in the best possible way.

Sometimes, relationship is the main way a character fulfills his or her dramatic function. In *Death of a Salesman,* Willy has a relationship with each person in the play: father, husband, lover, neighbor, employee, salesman. Each relationship reveals another aspect of Willy's character and adds to the total picture of this complex man, for his "I" is composed of all of those "me's." Each of the other actors creates a part of Willy through these relationships, and so all the actors must cooperate if Willy is to live fully for the audience.

In short, *you create each other more than you create yourselves.*

EXERCISE 15.4: SOCIAL TRAITS

Look for information about your character's social background. If no specific information is given, make the best inferences you can.

1. Childhood environment
2. Educational background
3. Socioeconomic or class background
4. Work experiences

Consider your relationship to every other character in the story. How does each relationship reveal your needs, desires, and values?

Rehearse your scene with your partner: your aim in this rehearsal is *to create each other.*

PSYCHOLOGICAL TRAITS

The *psychological* traits are those which affect the process of thought that produces your character's action. As Oscar Brockett pointed out, "the psychological is the most essential level of characterization" because it *justifies* and *motivates* all the others. Or as Chekhov once said in a letter, "a playwright may invent any reality except one: the psychological." All characters must think before they act.

This is not to say that the psychology of character is always the most important element of the play as a whole. Plays can be organized in one of three ways: by plot, by character, or by idea. Of course, all plays have all three, but one of them will always be the dominant organizational element. In plays in which the external events of the plot are the dominant element, the psychological aspect of character may serve merely to make the action believable. On the other hand, in plays featuring character (like those of Chekhov and O'Neill), the psychology of the characters may be the main interest of the play while the plot is secondary. In plays of ideas, like those of Brecht and Shaw, both the plot and the characters are designed to support the point of the play. You should recognize the priorities of the play in your approach to the role. But since you are always involved with the mind of your character regardless of the purpose it is meant to serve, the psychological level of characterization will always be your main concern.

Your examination of your character's action has already provided you with the basis for understanding his or her psychology, and in the following lesson we extend this understanding in considerable detail. For now, ask these basic questions about the character you have been developing.

EXERCISE 15.5: PSYCHOLOGICAL TRAITS

Consider the mental processes of the character you are developing. Are they:

1. Simple or complex?
2. Fast or slow?
3. Rigid or flexible?
4. Precise or vague?
5. Rational or intuitive?
6. Global or sequential?

Some of these qualities belong to either "right brain" or "left brain" people. Left-brained people tend to be more "rational," whereas right-brained people are more "intuitive." That is, left-brained people tend to reason in a linear way, in verbal and logical terms, but right-brained people tend to think globally, in spatial and emotional terms. If you want to give someone directions to your house, for instance, you should tell a left-brained person to "go three blocks down, turn right, go to the second light, and turn left." A right-brained person, however, has trouble with these verbal, sequential directions and does better if you draw a map on which he or she can see the *shape* of the path to your house. In the sample scene from *Cheers* (in Appendix A), for example, the methodical Diane is clearly a left-brainer, whereas the impulsive Carla is a right-brainer. How would you describe your character: right- or left-brained?

One of the greatest difficulties in writing this book, by the way, was to translate the global and intuitive skill of acting into a linear, verbal sequence; this is why the physical exercises are so important. Many aspects of the acting process must live more in your body than in your mind, and your mind must provide guidance and judgment to your physical work. Acting is a more "whole brain" activity than any other art form, encompassing as it does all the physical skills of the musician and the dancer and all the intellectual skills of the poet and critic.

MORAL TRAITS

The moral level of character refers to your character's values. Most important are the character's:

1. Sense of right and wrong
2. Sense of beauty
3. Religious beliefs
4. Political convictions

The moral aspect of character is rarely complex in the case of minor characters, but major characters usually have highly developed and sometimes complex or conflicted moral traits. When the moral aspect of a character is important, *it will always relate directly to the thematic content of the play.* The moral choice confronting Willy Loman, for example, carries the whole meaning of Arthur Miller's play: our society tends to erode spiritual values and self-esteem by emphasizing material values as a measure of self-worth.

In the previous lesson you defined your character's superobjective. Without knowing it, you were also bringing much of his or her morality into focus; after all, the superobjective and the means used to achieve it are the active expressions of your character's values. Willy feels so inferior that he is driven to lie, even to his family, and finally to sacrifice his life to achieve his misguided sense of "The American Dream." We don't condemn him, but we see him as a pathetic victim of a materialistic society.

EXERCISE 15.6: MORAL TRAITS

Speaking as your character, answer the following questions:

1. My religion is…
2. I believe that when we die, we…
3. The greatest thing one person can do for another is…
4. The person I admire most is…
5. I would define a good person as someone who…
6. The person I detest most in the world is…
7. The most evil thing I can imagine is…
8. The ugliest thing I ever saw was…
9. The most beautiful thing I ever saw was…
10. The proper role of government is…
11. I am superstitious about…
12. I want my epitaph to be…

ECONOMY OF CHARACTERIZATION

We have examined the four levels of characterization. Each works in relation to the others, though one or more may dominate the others. As Oscar Brockett explains:

> A playwright may emphasize one or more of these levels. Some writers pay little attention to the physical appearance of their characters, concentrating instead upon psychological and moral traits; other dramatists may describe appearance and social status in detail. In assessing the completeness of a characterization it is not enough merely to make a list of traits and levels of characterization. It is also necessary to ask how the character functions in the play. For example, the audience needs to know little about the maid who only appears to announce dinner; any detailed characterization would be superfluous and distracting. On the other hand, the principal characters need to be drawn in greater depth. The appropriateness and completeness of each characterization, therefore, may be judged only after analyzing its function in each scene and in the play as a whole.[2]

It is a common impulse of actors to try to play the maid who announces dinner as if she were Lady Macbeth. This is not to say that the maid should not be fully characterized; she should be as fully characterized *as she needs to be to fulfill her dramatic function.* Economy of characterization means giving your character all the traits he or she needs but no more.

Think of a great athlete; "style," grace, and power come from the complete efficiency with which every bit of energy is focused on the job at hand. That athlete doesn't "grandstand"; that is, he or she does nothing that does not directly contribute to the athletic purpose. This is *economy of execution,* and it produces *beauty.* If your purpose is to be a maid answering the door, any energy directed toward creating qualities beyond those necessary for the fulfillment of this task is wasteful and distracting. An overly detailed performance is as disruptive to the story as an incomplete one.

A CHARACTER CHECKLIST

Here is a checklist that reviews the work of this lesson. Use it as you begin rehearsals to be sure you get from the story the information you need to begin work; then check again near the end of rehearsals to be sure that you have considered all the possibilities.

EXERCISE 15.7: A CHARACTER CHECKLIST

What are the physical traits that influence your action?

1. Those specified by the writer
2. Those reported by other characters
3. Those that can be inferred from the action

What are your social traits?

1. Your background and education
2. Your socioeconomic class
3. Your attitudes and behavior toward each of the other characters

What are your psychological traits?

1. Are your mental processes fast or slow?
   a. Rigid or flexible?
   b. Complex or simple?
2. Are you intuitive and global or analytical and verbal? What moral, religious, or political values influence your choices?

SUMMARY

Your character was created by the writer so that your behavior contributes believably to the progress and meaning of the story; you have a specific purpose in relation to the whole. This is your *dramatic function.* No matter how "alive" your character may be, if it does not fulfill your dramatic function, you have failed.

In order that your character may serve his or her purpose within the story believably, the writer has provided your character with certain traits that make the behavior and thought required by the story "natural"; Aristotle called these the character's *functional traits*. Your character also has traits that make him or her recognizable as a fellow human being; Aristotle called these *likeness traits*. In this sense, the needs of the story create the characters more than the characters create the story.

All character traits can be classified on four levels. The first level is *physical,* and it is important to you because the external traits of body and voice communicate all the other levels of characterization.

The second level is *social,* and it places your character in relation to the others in his or her world. As in life, character on stage is perceived mainly in relationship, so remember that you create each other more than you create yourselves.

The third level is the *psychological,* and it is the most important because it *justifies* and *motivates* all the others.

The fourth is the *moral* level, and it refers to your character's values.

A writer may emphasize one or more of these levels. The appropriateness and completeness of your characterization may be judged only after analyzing its function in each scene and in the play as a whole.

THE CHARACTER'S MIND

In the previous lesson I said that your character's dramatic function is to act in certain ways, moment by moment, so as to move the story forward in the proper direction and with the proper qualities of style and meaning. The writer has created your character so that these required external actions are believable and natural. The psychological aspect of characterization results when you have discovered the inner actions that *justify* the external actions required by the plot, meaning, and style of the story. This is what Stanislavski called the actor's most important task: *to understand how every moment of the performance contributes to the reason why the story was written.* You do this primarily by creating the character's mind.

Unlike a novelist, who can take you inside a character's mind to show you the process of thought, a dramatist can only *imply* it through actions. As an actor, you learn to understand the psychology of action so that you can re-create your character's mental processes. This is the greatest creative and personal contribution you make to your performance, for it is the foundation of all the other work you do.

Let's begin to examine the psychological aspects of action by setting up a hypothetical situation: imagine that you see a notice that I am directing a play that is a favorite of yours. This play has a part that you have been dying to play, and you want to approach me about it. Even though you fear my possible rejection, your need is strong enough that you come to see me. You begin by "buttering me up" with your admiration for my work; you express your love for this particular play; finally, you tell me why you are perfect for the part and ask me to consider casting you.

Let's examine what happened here step-by-step. First, you see the notice and it arouses you; this is called your *stimulus.* This stimulus touches your long-standing desire to play the part, and so your arousal has a particular quality that reflects this need; this is called your *attitude.* You are already beginning to form an *objective* (to persuade me to give you the part), and so you begin to *consider alternatives,* various ways of satisfying your aroused need. You might consider asking a mutual friend to approach me on your behalf, or you might consider simply sending a photo and résumé. After surveying your alternatives, you make a *choice* to act in the way you think will work best: to see me in person. This choice unleashes your *action,* which takes the form of *purposeful activity* to gain your *objective.*

This whole sequence is the mental process by which action is formed: *a stimulus arouses a need expressed by an attitude, which generates a strategic choice, which results in action directed toward an objective.* The steps in this process can be summarized as:

- Stimulus
- Attitude
- Deliberation
- Choice
- Action
- Objective

You can see this process represented graphically in Figure 16.1. The large circle represents your skin, the boundary between your "outer" and "inner" worlds. The stimulus sends energy toward you, which enters you through *perception* (seeing, hearing, touching). Once inside you, it arouses a response in you that touches on some *need* or *desire*; it frightens you, or pleases you, or angers you, and this is your *attitude* toward it.

If the nature of the stimulus and situation is such that it provokes an *automatic* action, your reaction is immediate and involuntary, bypassing conscious thought, and results at once in external action (when the alarm bell rings, Othello reaches for his sword).

If, on the other hand, conscious thought is required, you *deliberate* over alternative ways of proceeding until you make a *strategic choice* about how to proceed. This choice is at the center of the process; it is the moment that unleashes the *action* that you hope will win your *objective.*

Remember the impulse circle exercise: like the slap you received, another character in the scene does something, or something happens, and this energy enters you as your stimulus; it passes through you in either an automatic or deliberative way, then leaves you through your action directed toward your objective, just like the slap you passed on. Your action becomes a stimulus for the next person and generates a reaction in him or her, which in turn generates another action, and so the scene moves. Notice also that the energy leaving you as action is not the same in quality or intensity as the energy that entered you as the stimulus; it has been altered by the nature of your needs, attitudes, and personality.

Here is an example of the process of action from the scene in *Death of a Salesman* in which Willy enters and sees Howard playing with his recorder:

1. *Stimulus:* What's that thing Howard's fooling with?
2. *Attitude:* Why doesn't he stop that foolishness and listen to me?
3. *Alternatives:* I should demand the respect I'm entitled to.
4. *Choice:* But that might make him mad. I'd better get my foot in the door first, butter him up a bit.

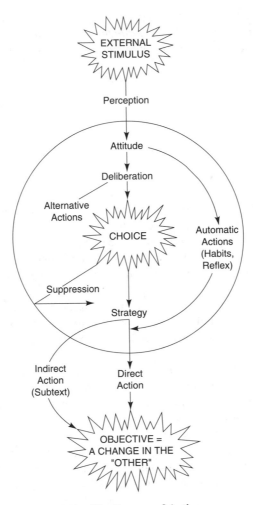

FIGURE 16.1   The Process of Action

5. *Action:* "What's that, Howard?"
6. *Objective:* I want to get his attention in a positive way.

You can see that Willy's needs, values, way of thinking, way of relating to the world—in short, his entire psychology—is involved and expressed in each step of this mental process. Re-creating your character's thought process in this way is the most important single step toward transformation. One way to check the thoroughness of your psychological preparation is to verbalize your character's stream of consciousness. This technique is called the *inner monologue.* Of course, the inner monologue is only an exercise and is meant to be done in private; you must *not* carry it into normal rehearsal, and certainly never into performance.

EXERCISE 16.1: THE INNER MONOLOGUE

Work through your scene with your partner; each of you softly speaks aloud the inner stream of thought that connects the external things you do and say. Go slowly and allow yourself to experience each step in the flow from stimulus to choice to objective. Listen to one another. Note: this is an exercise in *analysis;* make no effort to *perform* the scene in this manner.

THE INSTROKE OF REACTION

In Figure 16.1, you see the energy coming from your external stimulus flowing inward toward your center through perception, attitude, and deliberation. At center, your choice turns the instroke of reaction into the outstroke of action toward an objective: in other words, *choice is the point at which reaction turns into action.* This entire process provides the compelling momentum of a complete action.

Actors sometimes fail to experience the instroke of reaction fully; they *do* something, but they aren't really receiving the stimulus that is *causing* them to do it. They only pretend to perceive what is said or done to them, preferring the safety of working only out of their own heads and refusing to allow the actions of others to influence them directly. When faced with this kind of actor, directors often say things like, "You didn't really hear her say that."

Don't let your fear of losing control of the performance turn you into this kind of hermetically sealed, self-stimulating actor. No matter how strong or how long-standing your character's needs are, the stimulus that triggers those needs is always something "out there" in the scene, something that someone else says or does; learn to look for stimuli that are *immediate* and *external.* Remember: acting is not so much doing things as it is allowing yourself to be made to do them. In short, *acting is reacting.*

For example, there is a scene in Tennessee Williams's *A Streetcar Named Desire* in which Blanche tells Mitch what happened years ago on the night that her young fiancé killed himself. Too often, actresses play this scene as if the pain in Blanche is the main stimulus for the telling of the story. Played in this way, Mitch fades into the background and the story becomes a monologue instead of a scene. The actress must find the stimulus for the story not in her own need but "out there" in Mitch; it is his capacity for understanding that triggers her tremendous need to share, in the hope that he will understand and love her.

Once a stimulus has been received, it is interpreted by your character in relationship to his or her needs. Is this a threat? A good thing? A surprise? The evaluation is expressed as an *attitude* toward the stimulus. Directors often help actors to be specific about attitude by asking, "How do you feel about that?" Learn to ask yourself this question as a regular part of your acting process.

You may notice that your character has a typical way of reacting to most stimuli; this expresses an attitude toward the world in general. Is your character optimistic or pessimistic? Does his or her attitude reveal any personal feeling about him- or herself? Willy Loman, for example, is quick to sense any criticism from others, and it makes him terribly defensive. This almost paranoid sensitivity reveals his fundamental insecurity and low self-esteem.

EXERCISE 16.2: THE INSTROKE OF REACTION

Working with your partner, answer these questions about one of the scenes from Appendix A, or the scene you have chosen for yourselves.

1. In each of your character's actions, identify the external and immediate stimulus.
2. Does your character respond more to some stimuli than to others? How do these sensitivities reflect needs, values, and personality?
3. Consider what each stimulus means to your character; what is his or her attitude toward each? Does it trigger any needs already within the character?
4. What attitudes are typical of your character? What does this reveal about the character's attitude toward the world and about him- or herself?

CHOICE

Because choice is the moment at which reaction turns into action, it is the essence of drama; the most suspenseful moments in plays occur when a character confronts a significant choice. As David Mamet points out, "The only thing we, as audience, care about in the theatre is WHAT HAPPENS NEXT?"[1] From an actor's point of view, this question is really "What is he or she going to do now?"

The suspense is heightened when the choice is difficult, when the character is choosing between equally compelling (or equally unattractive) alternatives. In tragedy, these choices usually take the form of a "double bind" or "lose lose" situation in which there are no good alternatives, as when a character must choose between the sense of truth and life: *Antigone, A Man for All Seasons, Beckett, An Enemy of the People,* and *The Crucible* all center around such a choice. Critic Jan Kott described it like this:

> A classic situation of tragedy is the necessity of making a choice between opposing values.... The tragedy lies in the very principle of choice by which one of the values must be annihilated. The cruelty of the absolute lies in demanding such a choice and in imposing a situation which excludes the possibility of compromise.[2]

In comedy, the choices are not so serious; we might instead wonder something like, "How is he going to get away with it this time?"

Those significant choices that affect the progress of the play demand special attention. In the scene from *Cheers,* for example, Carla's main choice is to not marry

Ben, and Ben's main choice is to accept Carla's rejection with grace. Everything that is said and done in the scene either leads to or flows from these two crucial choices.

Choice is the most revealing point in the process of action. In the making of significant choices, your character is responding to needs; to a way of seeing the world; and to relationships, beliefs, and values. If you can experience all the factors influencing your character's most significant choices, you will be in touch with everything needed to create the psychological aspect of your characterization.

Perhaps more important, your experience of your character's significant choices is the mechanism by which the Magic If produces transformation. When you have entered into your character's circumstances as if they were your own, felt your character's needs as if they were your own, and *made the choices he or she makes given those needs in those circumstances and felt those choices as your own,* then action follows naturally and with it transformation.

Choice cannot be fully experienced without real alternatives. Unless you have alternatives to consider, you can only "act out" your character's choice, not relive it. If a choice is especially significant, the playwright structures the situation so that you know what the alternatives are; but most of the time the writer can only imply your character's view of their alternatives, and you have to supply them for yourself.

For this reason, then, you must consider not only what your character *does* but also what he or she *chooses not to do.* When your character is presented with a significant choice (meaning a choice that affects the progress of the play), you must find for yourself the various alternatives he or she might consider and decide how your character would feel about each. The creation of these alternatives is a powerful way for you to enter into your character's mind, because they represent an inventory of the way the character sees the world.

Following is a list of all the factors that may influence any particular choice. These may be either internal in the character's mind or external in the character's environment.

1. Internal factors influencing choice:
   a. Physiology
   b. Social background
   c. Needs and desires
   d. Psychological processes or "way of thinking"
   e. Ethical values
2. External factors influencing choice (the givens):
   a. Relationships with or attitudes toward other characters
   b. The social environment
   c. The physical environment
   d. Specific immediate circumstances
3. Performance concerns requiring adjustment of choice:
   a. The style or genre of the story
   b. The character's dramatic purpose
   c. The visual and auditory demands of the performance space

Although the last three are clearly "actor" concerns rather than "character" concerns, it is part of your job to justify your performance concerns as organic aspects of your character's inner world. In this way, the two levels of your "dual consciousness" as actor and character work together toward the same goal and eventually come together as a single experience.

EXERCISE 16.3: CHOICE

As in the previous exercise, consider each of your actions in the scene. Focus on the choice from which each action springs.

1. Decide which are the most significant choices (there are probably only one or two in a scene) and examine each in detail: what factors influence each? (Consider the list of factors provided above.)
2. Rehearse your scene with this awareness; take the time to experience each choice fully.

Once the choice to act in a certain way has been made, your outwardly flowing action becomes a *purposeful activity,* either a doing, a saying, or both, directed toward an objective. As you can see in Figure 16.1, this outstroke can take four forms: it can be an *automatic action* that bypasses conscious choice and flows directly from perception to action; it can be a *direct action* that goes at the objective straightforwardly; it can be an *indirect action* that approaches the objective through some other activity; or it can be a *suppression,* a choice *not* to act. Let's examine each.

AUTOMATIC ACTIONS

I mentioned in Lesson 11 that characters often act out of impulse or habit without conscious choice; this is what Stanislavski called "automatic" action. It is extremely useful when approaching a part to identify the automatic aspects of your character's behavior as soon as possible, for it is your task to re-create the character's habits in yourself for the purpose of rehearsing and performing the role.

When you consider how much of a character's behavior falls into the area of automatic actions, you see what an important area of concern this is: the voice, the walk, the wearing of clothes, any special skills (like Othello's swordsmanship) or deformities (like Laura's limp)—these and more must become as natural and habitual to you as they are to your character.

The formation of new habits is accomplished best by regular, spaced repetition over a period of time; you cannot count on rehearsals alone to do the job, nor should you waste the group's time on this sort of personal work. You must develop a program of homework that allows the formation of these habits through short daily exercises. Some psychologists have suggested that it takes three weeks of regular repetition to develop a new habit, so you can't wait very long to start. For instance, if your role involves swords, canes, robes, or skirts, you ask for a rehearsal substitute as soon as you can put down your script.

To sum up, follow this general rule: *whatever your character doesn't need to think about, you shouldn't need to think about; whatever your character does need to think about, you must think about each and every time you perform that action.*

And notice that it is neither necessary nor desirable for these habits to invade your real life. We all have many habits that we "turn on and off" to suit the situation, and the habits you develop to play a role can be restricted to rehearsal and performance of that role. Remember that the aim of this personal work is not to "lose yourself" in your character but to ensure that you don't lose the character in yourself.

EXERCISE 16.4: AUTOMATIC ACTIONS

Again, review your scene with your partner; look for any automatic actions required of your character. Examine them to see what they tell you about your character. What program of homework can you establish to develop these habits in yourself for this role?

DIRECT AND INDIRECT ACTION

We have already discussed how your character selects an action that he or she thinks has the best chance for success in the given circumstances. When possible, your character probably selects a direct action such as persuading, demanding, cajoling, or begging.

However, when there is an obstacle to direct action a character may choose an indirect approach and hide the real objective (*subtext*) beneath some surface activity (*text*). The obstacle that makes the subtext necessary may be *external* in the scene or *internal* in the character's mind.

For example, if I want to tell you that I love you, but I am afraid that you will reject me (internal obstacle), I may choose instead to talk about how lonely I am in this strange town, how dull the people I work with are, how you are the only interesting person I've met here, the only one I feel comfortable with. All this is an indirect way of expressing my love "safely." (This scene is from Chekhov's *The Three Sisters.* Chekhov explored indirect action more than any other playwright.)

Or if I want to tell you that I love you, but your husband is in the room with us (external obstacle), I may choose instead to talk about our pictures in the photo album, how wonderful you looked at the seashore last summer, what a wonderful time I had because you were there—whatever I think can be said without alerting your husband. (This scene is from Ibsen's *Hedda Gabler.*)

Further, the character may be either *conscious* of the subtext or *unconscious.* For instance, in the moment from *Death of a Salesman,* Willy's surface activity is to flatter Howard's recorder, but his subtext is to get Howard's attention; this is a conscious subtext. In *The Glass Menagerie,* on the other hand, Amanda prepares Laura for her gentleman caller, but she also puts on her own party dress and hangs colored lights to make herself look younger; we realize that Jim is also *her* gentleman caller and that she is reliving her youth through Laura. This is an unconscious subtext.

In all these cases, notice that the author has provided a surface activity through which the subtext may be expressed. You must accept this surface activity as your immediate action; *do not attempt to play the subtext.* When actors make the mistake of bringing the subtext to the surface, it destroys the reality of the scene. For one thing, if the audience can see the subtext, they must wonder why the other characters can't.

Trust the text and the audience; they will deduce from the situation what is really going on. Your simple awareness of subtext is enough, and often subtext works even if you are unaware of it. Besides, it is part of the fun for the audience to figure these things out for themselves; if you make it obvious, they don't get to play.

EXERCISE 16.5: SUBTEXT

Work through your scene with your partner; look for any indirectly expressed or hidden objectives.

1. Is the character conscious or unconscious of them?
2. Why can't they be expressed directly?
3. What surface activity has been provided through which they may be expressed?
4. Rehearse your scene with this awareness: avoid playing the subtext.

NOT DOING: SUPPRESSION

There is always at least one alternative available to a character in any situation, and that is the choice *not* to act, to suppress or delay action. Though we often think of "doing nothing" as a passive act, it can actually be a strong form of action because it takes more effort to hold an impulse in than it would to let it out. We call this *suppression*, which literally means "pushing down." Viewed in this way, there are no passive characters on the stage; there are only characters who are aroused but then choose *not* to act, which is itself a positive and playable action.

Suppression is common in drama. Stage characters, like people in life, may often be feeling and wanting much more than their overt actions indicate. The plays of Chekhov are especially rich as studies of suppression and prove that holding an impulse down can be more dramatic than its release. Movement therapist Moshe Feldenkrais says this about the process of delaying or inhibiting impulses:

> The delay between thought process and its translation into action is long enough to make it possible to inhibit it. The possibility of creating the image of an action and then delaying its execution is the basis for imagination and for intellectual judgement....
>
> The possibility of a pause between the creation of a thought pattern for any particular action and the execution of that action is the physical basis for self-awareness....

> The possibility of delaying action, prolonging the period between the intention and its execution enables man to know himself.[3]

The decision not to act heightens dramatic tension and suspense. As you see in Figure 16.1, when a character chooses to *suppress* an impulse, that unresolved energy is reflected back into him or her and builds up to become a source of increasing dynamic tension. There are many characters who spend most of their time suppressing; the most famous example is Hamlet.

One good way to use suppression is to devote some private rehearsal time to releasing the suppressed impulses. By letting the suppressed impulses out, you force yourself to work harder to hold them in when the scene is done in its normal form. It is the effort to suppress the impulse that turns the "not doing" into a "doing" and makes it playable and dramatic.

EXERCISE 16.6: NOT DOING

Work through your scene with your partner. Considering your character in the entire play, do you see a pattern of suppression that reflects the personality or attitude toward life? Rehearse your scene allowing any suppressed material to be released, then immediately repeat the scene and hold in those same impulses.

SUMMARY

Your character is required to act in a certain way, moment by moment, to move the story forward with the proper qualities of style and meaning. The writer has created your character so that these actions and the choices that cause them are believable and natural. The psychological aspect of characterization results when you have discovered the inner process that justifies the external activities and manner of expression required by the plot, meaning, and style of the story.

To re-create your character's mind, you must understand the process by which action is formed: a stimulus arouses you, touching a need expressed by an attitude, which generates a strategic choice, which results in action directed toward an objective. The steps in this process can be summarized as *stimulus, attitude and deliberation, choice, action, objective.*

To keep connected to the scene, learn to look for stimuli that are immediate and external. Remember: acting is not so much *doing* things as it is allowing yourself *to be made to do them.*

Once the stimulus has been received, your character evaluates it in relationship to his or her needs and forms an attitude toward it.

Because choice is the moment at which reaction turns into action, the most suspenseful moments occur when a character confronts a significant choice. Every choice that your character makes that affects the progress of the story (the beat changes) must be well defined and experienced in each rehearsal or performance.

Experiencing choice requires that there be alternatives. Most of the time the writer can only imply your character's alternatives, and you have to supply them for yourself; consider not only what your character *does* but also what he or she *chooses not to do.*

If you can experience all the factors influencing your character's significant choices, you can be in touch with everything needed to create the psychological aspect of your characterization. Only by reliving your character's choices within given circumstances as if they were your own can you enter actively into the world and consciousness of the character. This is what triggers the transformational process, *the Magic If.*

Once the choice to act in a certain way has been made, your outwardly flowing action becomes one of four types: it can be an *automatic action* that bypasses conscious choice and flows directly from perception to action. When approaching a part, identify the automatic aspects of your character's behavior as soon as possible and work to establish those habits in yourself. Whatever your character doesn't need to think about, you shouldn't need to think about.

Your action can also be *direct,* which goes at the objective straightforwardly; or when there is an obstacle to direct action, the character may choose an *indirect* action; we call these hidden intentions *subtext*. The obstacle that makes the subtext necessary may be external or internal, conscious or unconscious. In any case, the author has provided a surface activity through which the subtext may be expressed; it is disastrous to attempt to play the subtext itself. Finally, your action can be a *suppression,* a choice *not* to act, which is itself a positive and playable action that contributes greatly to suspense.

LESSON 17

THE CHARACTER'S LANGUAGE

In the previous lesson you explored the character's mind through action. In this lesson you explore his or her mind through speech, which, as you learned in Part I, is a special kind of action.

Unlike a novelist, a playwright or screenwriter cannot describe the character's thought directly, except in a limited way through stage directions. Though the writer conceives a complete character, the dialogue is all that remains of the fullness of that conception. The words you speak as the character, then, are the *residue* of a complete state of being; it is your job to re-create the fullness of the character by restoring body and consciousness to this residue.

This is made easier by the fact that playwrights and screenwriters, unlike other kinds of writers, know that their language is going to be spoken aloud; they are writing not for a reader but for *you*, the actor. Their first concern is the effect the language has on you as you speak it: not only the ideas and associations it generates in your mind but also what the rhythm of it does to your breathing and your body dynamic, what the sound of it does to your articulatory muscles as you speak it, and the physical sensations its imagery can evoke in you. In a real way, they are reaching deep inside your body and mind through the language of your character.

For example, read aloud this description of death from Shakespeare's *Measure for Measure*. It is spoken by a young man who has just learned that he is going to be executed in a few hours. Feel the physical sensations it evokes, how the rhythm and sound of it can generate his feelings in you.

Ay, but to die, and go we know not where,
To lie in cold obstruction and to rot,
This sensible warm motion to become
A kneaded clod; and the delighted spirit
To bathe in fiery floods, or to reside
In thrilling regions of thick-ribbed ice,
To be imprisoned in the viewless winds
And blown with restless violence round about
The pendant world; or to be worse than worst
Of those that lawless and incertain thought
Imagine howling, 'tis too horrible.

You don't need to be afraid of death to say this speech; the speech itself can terrify you.

You can see how a well-trained actor can find in a good text many specific clues about rhythms, inflections, emphases, and all sorts of characteristics needed to create a role. That is why performing the best writers—like Shakespeare—makes you a better actor. But a play is never like a coloring book; acting is not a matter of simply recognizing the playwright's outline and then "filling it in," or of just "saying the words." The creation of a role is always a collaboration between you and the writer and your director, fellow actors, and eventually your audience. But the words are where you start, and at the beginning they are all you have.

WORD CHOICE: TEXT AND SUBTEXT

You begin by understanding what the words mean and why the writer has chosen to have the characters express themselves in precisely the way they do, not only because you have a responsibility to communicate the meaning of your lines accurately but also because it reveals the way your character thinks and feels.

A character's speech is the result of a process of verbalization; through a lightning-fast sequence of unconscious choices, the preverbal *germ* of the idea is developed into full verbal form. This process automatically reflects the character's mind and personality, education, and social background.

As you relive your character's process of verbalization, you begin to participate actively in his or her mental processes and feelings. You begin by understanding the specifics of the dialogue completely, looking up any unfamiliar words or phrases and considering the effect of historical period on the language. You then ask yourself why your character has chosen to use these particular words instead of some others that might be similar in meaning. What is there about them that is exactly right for the thought and feelings of the character at this moment? This is called the character's word choice or *diction,* in the sense of *diction*ary.

Then you begin to reconstruct the process of thought and feeling from which these particular words spring. Only when you have "worked backward" in this way can you truly speak the character's words as your own; until then, you are merely parroting someone else's words, and you sound mechanical and false.

For example, when Blanche Dubois arrives at her sister's apartment in *A Streetcar Named Desire,* she looks around and says,

> Only Poe, only Mr. Edgar Allan Poe could do it justice. (She gestures toward street) Out there, I suppose, is the ghoul-haunted woodland of Weir.

Under these words is a germinal feeling of revulsion and disappointment: "How awful it is here!" The awfulness of the place reminds Blanche of Poe, the great writer of horror stories, and the visionary painter Weir, whose imagery was fantastic and frightening.

When you take the whole context of Blanche's speech into account, you begin to see the real power of her language. You know that Blanche has arrived here desperate; her life since the grand days on the plantation has become a series of one-night stands in cheap hotels far worse than this place. She must, in her heart, be jealous of Stella who has a home, however poor, and more important, a man, however crude, to take care of her. Blanche has come here as a last resort; it's the end of the streetcar line and the end of her line: the last stop before the asylum.

Understanding this context, you see that Blanche has to denegrate Stella and her home as a way of building herself up; by pretending to be repulsed by Stella's place, she is claiming to be accustomed to much better lodging and, thereby, denying her real past. She exaggerates her revulsion by comparing the place to the creations of two famous lunatics, Poe and Weir.

These artistic allusions are also intended to remind Stella that they share a sophisticated social background; back home in the good old days, she is saying, Stella's present circumstances would have been considered the creation of a demented imagination.

Stella bursts Blanche's bubble with her sardonic dismissal, "No, honey, those are the L and M tracks," which really says, "I know it's not much, but it's good enough for me." On a deeper level, she might also be saying, "Don't play your old games with me."

What we have done here is to *paraphrase* the character's speech, to put it into our own words in a way that expresses our understanding of both its surface meaning and its hidden meanings and attitudes, or *subtext*. This is an excellent technique for personalizing your character's speech; it forces you to return to the germinal meaning and re-create it in your own words, just as if you were translating it from some other language. Of course, in the case of simple naturalistic language, like that in *Death of a Salesman,* your paraphrase may not be very different from the original; still, the exercise is valuable in helping you to understand and internalize your character's speech.

EXERCISE 17.1: PARAPHRASE FOR MEANING AND SUBTEXT

Select a single speech from the scene you have been developing. Write a paraphrase on two levels.

First, write a literal translation of the surface meaning into your own words; be sure you understand the meaning of each word and any references that the speech may make (this inevitably sounds stiff and prosaic). Blanche's speech would look like this:

> *Only that drug-crazed writer of horror stories, only Mr. Edgar Allan Poe could describe this place adequately. (She gestures toward street) The neighborhood looks like one of those terrible, frightening forests full of evil spirits waiting to jump at you, like the ones painted by that insane Mr. Weir.*

Then write a second, more personal paraphrase that expresses the subtext, if any. Again, Blanche's speech:

This is awful! How can you stand it? But then, you were always less sensitive than I am.

Now say all three aloud: the literal paraphrase, the subtextual paraphrase, and finally the original speech. Are you beginning to feel that you "own" the words of the character, that you are speaking real words instead of memorized lines?

RHYTHM

Rhythm is perhaps the single most powerful aspect of language. It functions in three primary ways: to support meaning, to express personality, and to express emotion.

Though rhythm is the most physical and least "intellectual" aspect of language, it is closely tied to and supportive of meaning. It functions not only as tempo (fast or slow) but also in the variations of tempo and force that give emphasis to certain words, sounds, images, or other elements of language.

In addition to supporting meaning through emphasis, rhythm is highly expressive of personality. The blustery, pompous person has a rhythm much different from the thoughtful, introspective person. Even nationality and social background affect rhythm: the Irish, for example, tend to speak each thought on one long exhalation of breath, imparting an unmistakable rhythm to their speech. Good writers build these rhythms into the language that their characters speak, so that a character's speech rhythms are appropriate to his or her personality and social background.

Emotions also have recognizable rhythmic implications. All emotion causes measurable changes in the tension of our muscles, and this has a direct effect on our speech. Take anger as an example: as anger rises in us, the body becomes tense, especially in the deep center where the largest muscles mobilize themselves for action. Tension in the interior muscles is communicated directly to the diaphragm, limiting its movement and forcing us to take shallow breaths. Because we need to oxygenate the muscles for defense purposes, we compensate by taking more short breaths. Tension, spreading to the vocal cords, causes an elevation of pitch, and coupled with the increased pressure of the breath stream, results in a "punching" delivery and increased volume. The vestigial biting and tearing of the jaw related to anger encourage us to emphasize hard consonant sounds so that our speech may become, in rage, similar to the snapping and growling of an angry animal.

A skillful writer shapes rhythm carefully and on several levels at once: syllables, phrases, sentences, and speeches. Let's explore each. The fundamental rhythm of a speech is established by the flow of *accented and unaccented syllables and words.* Look at the following example from Samuel Beckett's *Endgame;* you see that

Beckett has used rhythmic patterns of twos and threes; read it aloud for full rhythmic effect; tap your feet.

> One day you'll be blind, like me. You'll be sitting there, a speck in the void, in the dark, forever, like me. (pause) One day you'll say to yourself, I'm tired. I'll sit down, and you'll go and sit down. Then you'll say, I'm hungry, I'll get up and get something to eat. But you won't get up. You'll say, I shouldn't have sat down, but since I have I'll sit on a little longer, then I'll get up and get something to eat. (pause) But you won't get up and you won't get anything to eat.

The rhythmic flow of these syllables is as highly developed as any formal poetry.

The next level of rhythm involves *breath phrases.* The evolution of our written language was greatly influenced by the way we speak. A simple sentence can be said on a single breath. If a sentence becomes too complex for one breath, we break it up into phrases and create a compound sentence. Each of these phrases becomes a "sub-breath," a kind of "topping off" of the breath supply, within the main breath of the sentence. These sub-breath phrases are usually marked by commas, semicolons, or colons (in music, the comma is still used as a breath mark). The second sentence in the Beckett quote above is a good example.

Good writers use sentence structure to guide you into a pattern of breathing which, as you experienced in Part I, is a powerful factor in the generation of emotion. Try reading the Beckett piece aloud with a small breath at every comma, a full breath at each period, and a large breath at each "(pause)." What emotional experience results?

A still larger pattern of rhythm is developed by the *length of sentences,* each one of which is usually one main breath. Sentence length is usually our best indicator of tempo; shorter sentences usually indicate a faster tempo, and longer sentences a slower tempo, though this is by no means a hard-and-fast rule.

Finally, sentences are grouped into *speeches.* We get a good impression of the rhythm of a scene by looking at the density of the printed script; a mass of long speeches suggests a different rhythm than a back-and-forth exchange of short lines. You can often see changes in a scene reflected in the speech rhythms; for example, one character might have a number of very long speeches, whereas the other has only short replies, until the second "counterattacks" with a long speech, followed by a heated section in which both speak in short lines, often interrupting each other.

By responding sensitively to the rhythms and sounds the writer has built into your character's speech, and by experiencing them fully in your own muscles, you find them a powerful aid in entering into the consciousness of your character. As Stanislavski said:

> There is an indissoluble interdependence, interaction and bond between tempo-rhythm and feeling…. The correctly established tempo-rhythm of a play or a role, can of itself, intuitively (on occasion automatically) take hold of the feelings of an actor and arouse in him a true sense of living his part.[1]

EXERCISE 17.2: RHYTHM

1. Using the same speech as in the previous exercise, mark its rhythmic units on each of the levels we have discussed; invent any system of marking that makes sense to you.
2. Read it aloud to stress each level of rhythm.
   a. The flow of stressed and unstressed syllables
   b. The main breath for each sentence and "sub-breath" for any phrases within compound sentences
3. Now examine the scene as a whole and see how the rhythm created by the give and take of the dialogue relates to the action and relationship. With your partner, read it aloud to experience this fully.

MELODY

In our everyday life we have an intuitive and highly developed sense of the communicative value of sound and rhythm, which together form the *melody* of speech. It is what gives our speech its color and individual flavor, and helps us to catch implications, sarcasm, and other attitudes. Stanislavski again:

> Letters, syllables, words—these are the musical notes of speech, out of which to fashion measures, arias, whole symphonies. There is good reason to describe beautiful speech as musical.[2]

The actor must develop a heightened capacity for the musical aspects of speech. We do this not to produce a beautiful sound but because we must express extraordinary levels of feeling and experience. As Stanislavski put it:

> Musical speech opens up endless possibilities of conveying the inner life of a role.... What can we express with our ordinary register of five or six notes?... We realize how ridiculous we are when we have to express complicated emotions. It is like playing Beethoven on a balalaika.[3]

A good writer selects and arranges words not only for meaning but also for rhythmic and tonal values that support and enhance meaning, character, and emotion. Writers often say that their characters begin to "speak" to them as if they had minds and voices of their own. You can rejuvenate these inherent values of tone and rhythm: if you surrender yourself to experience them fully as muscular actions, you can bring them back to life for yourself and, through your experience, for your audience.

Scholars have formed various theories about the relationship of sound and meaning in language. One of these was the Roback Voco-Sensory Theory. The psychologist A. A. Roback asked experimental subjects to assign meaning to several three-letter nonsense syllables, like *mil* and *mal*. To most people, *mal* seemed to mean something big, and *mil* something little. Roback noticed that saying *mal* requires opening the mouth wide, whereas *mil* makes the mouth small, so he theorized that the meaning came from this physical association.

The theory went on to suggest that much of language was formed by our association of the physical sensation of pronouncing certain sounds with the meaning of the sounds themselves. Words like *rough* feel rough when spoken, and *smooth* feels smooth, just as *rushing* rushes, and *explode* explodes.

The Voco-Sensory Theory can be easily disproved: for example, *small* is made up of "big" sounds, while *big* is made up of "small" sounds. But the general idea is useful to you as an actor: a good writer selects words that have sounds that generate appropriate sensations when you pronounce them. If you can let these sensations resonate in you, the physical act of pronouncing a speech generates and supports the appropriate feeling. As Stanislavski said:

> When an actor adds the vivid ornament of sound to the living content of the words, he causes me to glimpse with an inner vision the images he has fashioned out of his own creative imagination.[4]

On a larger scale, good writers use qualities of sound to help distinguish one character from another, one mood from another, or the changing of emotional states within a role.

You might find in *A Streetcar Named Desire,* for example, that the sounds of Blanche's speeches are more melodious than Stella's, or that Stanley's are animalistic (biting, guttural). You might decide that the dominant sounds in one of these roles suggest a particular pitch range and inflectional pattern. Regional dialect may be important; O'Casey needs to be delivered in an Irish accent as much as Williams needs the Southern accent.

To sum up: The melody and rhythm of your stage language are powerful sources of a sense of character. Remember the work you did on voice in Part I and the profound relationship between sound, breath, energy, and character. But remember: you should *never* adopt an artificial vocal characterization. Always speak in your own voice, however adjusted for the demands of the role. Let the language do the work!

EXERCISE 17.3: MELODY

Using the same speech, read it aloud.

1. What sounds are emphasized?
2. Considering the whole role, is there a pattern of sound or any kind of sound that is dominant?
3. Are there changes in sound that reflect changes in emotion, action, or relationship?
4. Try singing the speech. What kind of music would best accompany your character?

IMAGERY

Drama is one of the most condensed and intensified forms of literature; what a novelist needs thousands of words to do, a playwright or screenwriter must pack into the dialogue alone. Besides the heightened use of diction, rhythm, and melody, the skillful dramatist gets an extra measure of impact and meaning through the potential of language to evoke physical sensation. Stanislavski reminds us that

> To an actor a word is not just a sound, it is the evocation of images.[5]

In its most literal sense, an *image* is "something seen in the mind's eye." The painting of "word pictures" is the most common kind of imagery, but language may appeal to any of our other senses as well: hearing, smelling, touching, tasting, sense of movement, and general body condition. Again read aloud the speech from Shakespeare's *Measure for Measure* at the beginning of this lesson.

Good delivery of imagery like this requires that you re-create the sights, sounds, and other sensations in yourself fully; you then find the character's condition generated in you and through you in the audience. Explore each image, re-create it in physical terms either through fantasy or memory of similar experiences, then allow this experience to remain stored in you as a specially created "sense memory."

EXERCISE 17.4: IMAGERY

Check your speech for any physical sensations it imparts. Dwell on each, re-creating it through fantasy or memory. Then read the speech aloud, taking the time to reexperience each sensation as fully as you can.

In all your work on your character's speech, remember that your aim is to enhance and support the meaning of your character's *actions. Good stage language is itself a form of action!*

SUMMARY

The words you speak as the character are the *residue* of a complete state of consciousness. It is your job to re-create the fullness of the character by restoring body and consciousness to this residue. This is made easier by the fact that the writer's first concern is the effect the language has on you as you speak it: in a real way, the writer is reaching deep inside your body and mind through the language of your character.

A well-trained actor finds many specific clues about rhythms, inflections, emphases, and all sorts of characteristics needed to create a role in the language, but acting is not a matter of simply recognizing the dramatist's outline and then "filling it in."

You begin by understanding what your words mean and why the writer has chosen to have your character express him- or herself in precisely this way (the *diction*), not only because you have a responsibility to the meaning of your lines but also because it reveals the way your character thinks and feels.

You then "work backward" from the words to re-create the thoughts and feelings from which the words spring. As you relive your character's process of verbalization, you begin to participate actively in his or her mental processes and feelings. You must re-create your character's words *as your own,* taking into account the whole context of the character's speech. One good way to do this is to *paraphrase* the character's speech, to put it into your own words in a way that expresses your understanding of both its surface meaning and its subtext if any.

Rhythm is perhaps the single most powerful aspect of dramatic language. It functions in three primary ways: to support meaning, to express personality, and to express emotion. A skillful dramatist shapes rhythm carefully and on several levels at once: syllables, phrases, sentences, and speeches. You can often see changes in a scene reflected in the speech rhythms.

Sound is a powerful component of emotion. Good writers use speech melody, sound, and rhythm to help distinguish one character from another, one mood from another, or the changing of emotional states within a role, and as a reflection of personality.

The skillful writer gets an extra measure of impact and meaning through the potential of language to evoke physical sensation. The painting of "word pictures" is the most common kind of imagery, but language may appeal to any of our other senses as well; your job is to explore each image, re-create it in physical terms either through fantasy or memory of similar experiences, then allow it to remain stored in yourself as a specially created "sense memory."

In all your work on your character's speech, your aim is to enhance and support the meaning of your character's *actions. Good stage language is itself a form of action!*

■ ■ ■ ■ ■

THE CHARACTER'S BODY

In everyday life we can sense the way a person's body reflects his or her personality and immediate emotion. Your work in Part I began to sensitize you to this "body language." The reading of body language has become an important skill in our culture. Lawyers use it to select jurors, salespersons to determine their strategy toward a customer, interviewers to help evaluate applicants, singles to identify likely partners, and politicians to project desirable qualities of personality. In general, we tend to trust body language as a more truthful expression of personality and attitude than spoken language, as we saw in the hostess–guest scene in Part I.

Theater and film make special use of this universal physical language. The image of Willy Loman walking with bent back, shuffling through the opening scene of *Death of a Salesman* communicates a vivid sense of Willy's situation to audiences in Chicago or Peking; so, in their own way, do the formal, precise gestures of the Kabuki actor as he employs the conventions of his theater to express action and emotion.

PERSONALITY IN THE BODY

As you learned in Part I, many aspects of personality come to be carried within the structure of the body. These expressive structural patterns are caused by the cumulative effect of repeated behavioral patterns, especially those in which we suppress or "hold in" certain impulses and reactions. As Alexander Lowen, a psychoanalyst who works in the field he calls "bioenergetics," puts it:

> The muscles can hold back movements as well as execute them.... Consider the case of an individual who is charged with rage and yet must hold back the impulse to strike. His fists are clenched, his arms are tense and his shoulders are drawn and held back to restrain the impulse.[1]

If rage is suppressed in this way often enough, the muscular tension in the hands, arms, and upper back becomes chronic. Because of this long-term tension, the muscles and other tissues in these areas eventually harden, losing their flexibility and sensitivity. The rigidity of these areas eventually affects the person's posture and movement, and a trained observer can diagnose the precise psychological pattern captured in this musculature.

Even without special training most of us can form fairly accurate impressions of people who "harbor a lot of resentment," or are "sitting on a lot of grief," or who "are afraid of their own sexuality," to name a few examples. These expressive bodily configurations are sometimes called the *character armor.*

The suppression of emotion is not the only way this kind of structure is created. The influence of heredity, the infant's mimicry of the parents' bodily motions, and patterns of social response (such as the teenager's slouching) can all become "built in" to the body.

Perhaps in your adolescence you were motivated to play the "tough" by thrusting out your chest, pelvis, or jaw. Years later, even though this social motivation no longer operates, you may find these earlier muscular patterns still operating, literally "built in" to your body by habit; the shoulders still pulled back, the pelvis tilted to one side, the chin thrust forward. These muscular patterns may have become expressive of your personality and continue to influence the way you confront life. People you meet may initially think, "Boy, does *he* have a chip on his shoulder!"

THE CHARACTER'S CENTER

You experienced your own bodily center in Part I. Though it may move in various emotional states (we can be "up" one day and "down" the next), each of us has a location that is our normal center. The location of your energy center and the quality of the energy it contains can be a profound expression of your personality; similarly, in your creation of a dramatic character you work to discover a physiovocal center that is consistent with the character's attitudes and behavior.

We can suggest five primary character centers that by bodily logic and cultural tradition are each associated with a different sort of person: head, chest, stomach, genitals, and anus (Figure 18.1). Let's look briefly at each.

The *head*-centered person may be thought of as cerebral, "other worldly," flighty, scattered, or off-balance. This sort of person always seems "ahead of him- or herself." Energy seems to come out through the eyes or the mouth; if passive, the head-centered person may do a lot of watching; if active, the person may do a lot of talking or being very aware of oral activity of all sorts, which may be a way of sublimating sexual energy. ("Chew, chew, chew," are the first words Amanda speaks in *The Glass Menagerie.*)

The *chest*-centered person might have a lot of "heart" and be quite sentimental, or might be the reverse, tough and "militaristic."

The *stomach* person is usually carrying the badge of self-indulgence; this person may also be good-natured, easygoing, and nurturing, and often makes a good parent.

The *genitally* centered person might be sexy, either in a libidinous way or, contrarily, in a naive way, like the "farmer's daughter."

The *anal* person seems severe, sexually withdrawn, often stingy ("constipated"), dogmatic, and rigid in behavior.

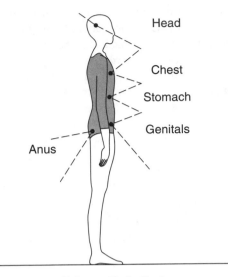

FIGURE 18.1   Primary Body Centers

We have all known people who tend to relate to the world from one of these centers; observe some of your acquaintances from this point of view. Think also of some specific dramatic characters and imagine how this idea of centers would apply to each. What center might Amanda have in *The Glass Menagerie?* Contrast the centers that neighbor Charlie and brother Ben might have in *The Death of a Salesman,* or that Carla or Diane might have in *Cheers.*

When we sense that someone is operating from one or another of these bodily centers, we tend to expect them to behave in the ways associated with that center, so the character's center is a powerful tool of characterization. Moreover, if a character undergoes a radical change in the course of the play, it is possible that center will shift. Think of King Lear; he could be played as a man who is driven out of his mind and into his heart.

The importance of character center is not so much in its influence on an audience; more important by far is its power to affect you as you work on the role, moving you toward transformation. Bringing your own center into conformity with your character's center is perhaps the most fundamental physical characterizational choice.

EXERCISE 18.1: THE CHARACTER CENTER

1. Examine Figure 18.1; try "putting on" some of these character centers. Experience your impulse as initiating in them; move about and enter into improvised relationships. See what attitudes are evoked in you.

    Consider various characters from plays you have read; which center seems right for each? Which center might be right for Willy or Charlie in

Death of a Salesman? For Carla or Diane in *Cheers*? Do any of these characters undergo changes that might result in a shift of their center?

2. Review the section "Your Changing Relationship to Gravity" in Lesson 3 on page 22. Repeat Exercise 3.5 in order to select a specific root and relationship to gravity for the character you are developing.

3. Experiment with the different forms of effort-shape we examined: molding, floating, and flying. Which seems right for your character?

4. Absorb the sense of root and effort-shape you have selected and rehearse your scene with this awareness. Does your experience of the scene change? Are there other aspects of the character that are suggested when you perform it in this way?

THE FLOW OF BODILY ENERGY

As mentioned earlier, the body takes on the qualities we associate with various kinds of characters through the repetition of certain muscular responses to life. We now trace the pathway taken by this muscular energy.

Recall a moment from life or from the scene you have been rehearsing, when you committed some strong physical action. Take a moment to relax and recall the experience as vividly as you can, so that it feels as if you were doing it again right now.

Feel the energy that is in your center; what is your level of arousal? Is it a high charge or a low charge? We call this your *dynamic.*

Next, follow this energy as it flows away from your center; is it moving predominantly *upward* or *downward* or equally in both directions away from your center?

Notice next that the musculature of your body offers two energy pathways running up and down the body. One pathway runs along the *back* of your body, another along the *front.* Because the muscles of the back are large and strong, the rear pathway usually carries your aggressive energies; the muscles and tissues in the front of your body are softer and more vulnerable, so that the front pathway usually carries our "tender" feelings. Which pathway are you using now?

Consider next whether the energy is impeded or even blocked from flowing through certain areas of your body. Some of the most common points of blockage are the jaw, nape of the neck, small of the back, across the chest, or between the shoulder blades. You can perhaps feel such blockages of energy within your own body; are the blocks, if any, habitual to you, or did you intuitively create them as part of the character?

Finally, become aware of how the energy leaves your body: is there an area or part of the body through which it tends to exit?

You now have traced the pathway by which any motion or sound must begin in a deep center and move through the various energy pathways of the musculature until it erupts into the outer world. When it does, it carries with it the tone, color, and shape of the interior world through which it has passed. Through this process, our physical and vocal expressions become a means by which we "turn ourselves inside out" and make a public expression of our private world.

PHYSIQUE AND PERSONALITY

As we said earlier, repeated patterns of behavior may begin to alter the very structure of the body. We come to hold our energy in a way that affects the contours of our body, so that the body soon comes to announce the nature of the energy that inhabits it. This fact is especially important on stage, where the audience sees the whole body more acutely than we do in real life. We consider, then, how the contours of the body may communicate specific impressions of personality.

We must first, however, distinguish between the way the body is held, which is called *alignment,* and the basic structure of the body itself, which is called *physique.* Certain physiques carry particular associations within our culture: the large-abdomened *endomorph,* for example, is thought of as jolly, easygoing, and a good family type; the thin, wiry *ectomorph,* on the other hand, is expected to be nervous and compulsive; and the muscular *mesomorph* is expected to be a lot like Stanley Kowalski.

These body types are of limited importance in the theater. To be sure, it might be unreasonable to cast an endomorphic actor as the mesomorphic Stanley, but within such broad limits it is possible for almost any physique to capture the psychophysical essence of a role on the stage. Though Lee J. Cobb and Dustin Hoffman have very different physiques, they were each successful in creating the role of Willy Loman.

The camera, on the other hand, has no tolerance for fundamental adjustments of physique, which, despite the most skillful makeup and costuming, usually seem false. Insofar as this is true, films and television must be "type cast," at least as far as physique is concerned. Serious film actors sometimes go to extreme lengths in this regard, as did Robert De Niro when he gained weight to capture the degradation of his character in *Raging Bull.*

BODY ALIGNMENT AND CHARACTER

Body alignment, as opposed to physique, can be successfully adjusted both on stage and for the camera, though such adjustments demand enormous skill and practice. They must be fully integrated with the spiritual and psychological life of the character and must never be adopted as mere "externals." The most effective of such adjustments occur automatically and unconsciously as a result of your experience of the character over a prolonged rehearsal period. For now, let's look at the specific qualities that are commonly associated with various body alignments. Examine Figure 18.2 and consider the qualities that each body suggests.

The first body, which features rounded shoulders and back, can have two very different qualities. When it is based on a low energy level, it is called the *oral* body.

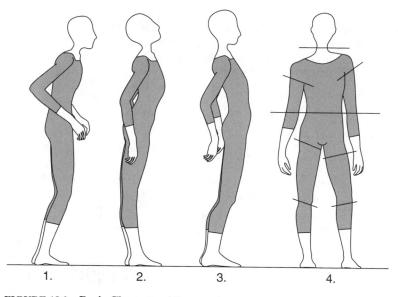

FIGURE 18.2   Basic Character Alignments

The chest is collapsed, and the arms express yearning. The legs are weak, making the body unstable and poorly grounded. Aggressive energies at the rear are blocked, and a great deal of grief is held in the pit of the stomach. This body says, "please hold me."

On the other hand, when this structure is based upon a high energy level, it is called *masochistic*. The shoulders are rounded because of the overdevelopment of the muscles in the upper body, giving a gorilla-like hulking aspect. The bound-in aggressions of this type are turned inward upon the self; notice that the energy pathway along the back begins to approach a circle.

The second body is sometimes called the "militaristic character" because it resembles the stance of a soldier at attention. It is the most hostile of all alignments. The shoulders are thrown back, and an enormous amount of anger is stored in the rigid area between the shoulder blades, the result of a long pattern of inhibited striking. This body is firmly rooted but so rigid in response that it is awkward, even mechanical. Aggressive energies stored in the back dominate, and the tender areas in the front of the body (chest and gut) are made hard—small wonder that we train soldiers to stand this way and to not think for themselves.

The third body is clearly belly-centered. This "heavy" character responds with great equanimity and could be called the "aw shucks" body. We usually think of such characters as unaggressive (the sway back blocks the aggressive energies of the rear body) but jolly and sentimental (as the preponderance of the frontal energies would indicate).

The last body is called *schizoid*. Here the parts of the body are disassociated so that the person is literally "in pieces" and, as we say, "the right hand doesn't know what the left hand is doing." The head is often cocked in a birdlike way. This body is very unstable and poorly grounded; it lacks grace in movement.

EXERCISE 18.2: BODY ALIGNMENT

Try on each of the body alignments described in Figure 18.2. Focus your awareness not on how the body looks from the outside but on *how it feels from the inside.* How does energy flow through it? How does it move? Where is it sensitive, where dead?

Do any of these alignments seem right for the character you have been developing? Try rehearsing your scene in this alignment.

Remember that the theater is a bodily place. All its meanings, philosophical or psychological insights, emotions, and all that may be communicated by a play reach the spectator through the physical sensations that you, the actor, generate. The "instrument" that creates the experience, your organism, is identical with the "instrument" that receives the experience, the spectator's organism, and there is an automatic and unconscious process by which your physical condition is imitated in the deep muscles of your audience; whatever your physical condition is doing to you, it also does to them. It is a real power: use it well.

An exercise follows that reviews all the material we have covered in this lesson. It can help you to apply these principles to the physical life of the character you have been developing. It is important that these physical choices be made *after* you have experienced the character's givens, choices, and actions; you must have this foundation to ensure the rightness of your physical work, or it may become mere posturing.

EXERCISE 18.3: A JOURNEY INTO A CHARACTER STRUCTURE

In this exercise you create the experience of "living inside" the body of the character you have been developing in the previous exercises. You do this by making a series of simple choices as outlined below. Allow at least one hour for this exercise, and do it all in one session. The exercise has three ground rules:

1. Use the full range of everyday movements (walking, sitting, getting up and down) throughout the exercise; do not remain still for too long. Use the voice throughout as well; count, say the alphabet, say your lines, or whatever comes to mind.
2. In each item, make your choices on the basis of what "feels" right; explore the whole range of choice before you settle on what seems to fit your subject. Remember: the basis for the choice is how the energy flow *feels* inside the body, not what "looks" right or what "ought" to be right.

Allow your mind to just settle back and witness; the body is in charge here.

3. The choices are cumulative; stick to the sequence given. After you have made a choice, move on to the next and trust the body to retain the first.

A. Here are the choices in sequence:

1. *Attitude toward gravity:* Experiment with your character's "root." Alternate from "plowing," to "floating," to "flying," and the stages between; select the attitude toward gravity that feels right. Notice the impact of various choices on your walk.

2. *Center:* Review your choice of your character's center from the previous exercise; make it more specific.

3. *Dynamic:* Experience the energy flowing from center as a *low* charge or a *high* charge and the stages between; listen to the changes in the voice.

4. *Energy pathways:* Determine the way energy flows within this body.
   a. Does it flow deep in the *core* or near the *surface*?
   b. Does it flow *upward* or *downward* from center?
   c. Does it flow mostly along the *front* or the *back* of the body?

5. *Blockages:* Are there places in this body where energy is blocked? Try blocking each of these locations and see if it feels right; if it does, allow the block to remain:
   a. Eyes
   b. Jaw
   c. Head/neck
   d. Space between the shoulder blades
   e. Space between the breasts
   f. Pit of the stomach
   g. Small of the back
   h. Genitals (how are they held?)

6. *Body alignment:* Try on each of the five alignments discussed:
   a. Oral
   b. Masochistic
   c. Militaristic
   d. "Aw shucks"
   e. Schizoid

B. Now, allowing the body to hold whatever it retains of these choices, stand in groups of five or six. Each of you speaks a phrase, allowing a new spontaneous ending to erupt for each of you as the phrase goes around the group. If a spontaneous ending does not arise, simply say "pass." When one phrase has made a complete circle, switch to another.

When I wake up in the morning...
Ever since I was a child...
When I look in the mirror...

I can remember...
The child in me...
I need...
I hate...
Strength to me means...
Weakness to me means...
Right now I am aware...
Sometimes I want to cry out to people...
Pain to me is...
I love...
If I could be free to do what I want to do...
My body...
If you could hear the music in me...[2]

Share your experiences of this exercise. What did you learn about your character that you never knew before? What did your body teach you? Learn to treat the body as a source of discovery; there is much about acting that can be found only in physical experience.

SUMMARY

Many aspects of personality come to be carried within the body. These expressive structural patterns are caused by the cumulative effect of repeated behavioral patterns, as well as heredity, the infant's mimicry of the parents, and patterns of social response. Some therapists call such semipermanent alterations in the body's structure the *character armor.*

Bringing your own center into conformity with your character's center is perhaps the most fundamental physical characterizational choice. There are five primary character centers that by bodily logic and cultural tradition are associated with different sorts of people: the *head*-centered person may be thought of as cerebral; the *chest*-centered person might have a lot of "heart" or the reverse and be "militaristic"; the *stomach* person is usually good-natured and easygoing; the *genital* person is either libidinous or naive; the *anal* person seems severe and rigid in behavior.

We must distinguish between the way the body is held, which is called *alignment,* and the basic structure of the body itself, which is called *physique.* Certain physiques carry particular associations within our culture: The large-abdomened *endomorph* is jolly, whereas the wiry *ectomorph* is nervous and compulsive, and the muscular *mesomorph* is a lot like Stanley Kowalski. Within broad limits it is possible for almost any physique to capture the psychophysical essence of a role on the stage. The camera, on the other hand, has little tolerance for fundamental adjustments of physique.

Body alignment, as opposed to physique, can be successfully adjusted both on stage and for the camera, though such adjustments require great skill and practice, and are at best the automatic and unconscious results of your experience of the character throughout the rehearsal period. The oral body has a collapsed chest; the masochistic body has a gorilla-like hulking aspect; the militaristic body resembles the stance of a soldier at attention; the "aw shucks" body is unaggressive but sentimental; the schizoid body has its parts disassociated so that it is literally "in pieces."

Remember that the theater is a bodily place; whatever your physical condition is doing to you, it also does to your audience. Use this power well.

THE CHARACTER'S EMOTION

What is emotion? The root meaning of the word is *an outward movement.* It is any activity that expresses the immediate condition of our organism and is directed toward the outside world, arising automatically out of our efforts to relate to life. Emotion is not primarily for purposes of communication: though there are times when you want to make your feelings known to others, the feelings themselves arise naturally in the course of your interaction with the world and occur even when no one else is present. Emotion serves as a judgment that you pass on your actions: When you try to attain an objective and are successful, you become happy; when you try to attain an objective and fail due to your own actions, you are sad; when you try to attain an objective and are prevented by circumstance or by someone else's actions, you become angry; when you try to attain an objective and fail, and don't know why, you become afraid.

Thus emotion is tied inextricably to action; it arises *automatically* from any significant effort to interact with the world. So it is in performance: *as an actor, you do not create emotion; rather, emotion arises of its own accord out of your action.*

FROM ACTION TO EMOTION:
WORKING FROM THE OUTSIDE IN

Near the turn of the twentieth century, two psychologists, Fritz Lange and William James, developed a theory of emotion of special interest to the actor. (Stanislavski was familiar with it.) This theory holds that emotion is our recognition of a bodily condition that is itself a response to some external situation, or, put another way, that emotion is the physical condition we find ourselves in when we respond to a stimulus.

Let's say you are stepping off a curb when, out of the corner of your eye, you see a car rushing toward you. Immediately you leap back out of danger. You did not jump because you were afraid: you didn't have time to become afraid first; you had to react directly to the sign of danger. In acting terms it was an "automatic action." Your body prepared for "flight or fight," as the psychologists say, and only after you had jumped clear, with your heart pounding, adrenalin flowing, your breath short, did you recognize your own condition and call it "fear." *Your emotion did not cause your action; your action caused your emotion.*

In *Death of a Salesman,* Miller describes Willy's first entrance:

> From the right, Willy Loman, the Salesman, enters, carrying two large sample cases.... He is past sixty years of age, dressed quietly. Even as he crosses the stage to the door-way of the house, his exhaustion is apparent. He unlocks the door, comes into the kitchen, and thankfully lets his burden down, feeling the soreness of his palms. A word-sigh escapes his lips—it might be "Oh, boy, oh, boy."

Try acting this out for yourself just as Miller describes it. This physical pattern by itself is powerful enough to generate an emotional state in you if you perform it with full participation of body and mind. As Plato noted two thousand years ago, the actor mimicking the gestures of an angry person tends to become angry. Or, as some directors say today, "Do the act, and the feeling will follow."

This process aids you in rehearsal. As you try various things—movements, line readings, business—your own emotional response to what you are doing serves to guide you in checking the correctness of your action. This is what the experienced actor means when trying something, but "It didn't feel right"; it is an evaluation of the action itself through its resultant emotion. When you have found the *correct* act, then the *correct* feeling follows, and it coincides with the implied physical condition in the text.

All this is meant to persuade you that you needn't be concerned with emotional behavior as such; if you are able to pursue your character's action with full involvement, the emotion *arises automatically,* and it *is communicated* to your audience. Emotions are states of being, not actions; you are *never* concerned with playing emotion.

A note about stage directions: some acting teachers encourage actors to disregard stage directions because they want the actors to discover the external form of the performance for themselves. This might make sense when you are dealing with an "acting version" of a play in which the stage directions have been inserted by a stage manager to describe what particular actors did in a particular production. But when the stage directions come directly from the playwright, they should be taken into account in the same way that a musician would note the markings for tempo and volume in a musical score. You must consider the internal state that the playwright meant for them to imply.

EXERCISE 19.1: WORKING FROM THE OUTSIDE IN

Examine your scene again, paying special attention to the external actions (words, gestures, movements) and the physical condition suggested for your character. Rehearse it so as to involve yourself in these externals as fully as possible; surrender to the experience that they produce in you.

FROM THOUGHT TO EMOTION: WORKING FROM THE INSIDE OUT

I began by saying that emotion arises out of your attempts to cope with the world and is your way of evaluating these attempts; in this sense, emotion arises from action. But there is another way that emotion is also generated, and that is by your thoughts, expectations, and attitudes. The school of psychotherapy called "cognitive therapy" is based on this fact:

> The first principle of cognitive therapy is that all your moods are created by your cognitions, or thoughts. A cognition refers to the way you look at things—your perceptions, mental attitudes, and beliefs. It includes the way you interpret things—what you say about something or someone to yourself. You feel the way you do right now because of the thoughts you are thinking at this moment....
>
> ...The moment you have a certain thought and believe it, you will experience an immediate emotional response. Your thought actually creates the emotion.[1]

For example, suppose you want to become an actor and are reading this, thinking, "Hey, that sounds good; Benedetti's approach could really help me!" This positive thought makes you feel good. If, on the other hand, you are thinking, "This is too hard, I could never do it," then your feeling is negative and sad.

Psychologists who treat depression have noticed that depressed people are seldom less "successful" in objective terms than many who are not depressed; the difference lies more in the way they subjectively view themselves and their lives. They "send themselves messages" that are negative, and every hint of failure confirms this negative self-attitude.

Some people hold a view of themselves as being unworthy: like Willy Loman, they can't accept praise or success, and they often can't accept the love that others offer them; they feel it must be "earned" because they don't feel worth loving.

Of course, cheerful and optimistic people are also sending themselves messages; they tend to evaluate their transactions with the world in more positive terms, such as "I'm getting better at it," or "What I do makes a difference." If depressed people can identify their negative self-messages and replace them with such realistically positive ones, they can change the way they feel.

In developing the emotional life of a character, it may be useful to examine the character's attitude toward him- or herself. Willy Loman is no less successful in objective terms than is his neighbor Charlie, but he feels like a failure, whereas Charlie feels like a success. Willy is constantly sending himself the message that he has to earn the respect of others and even the love of his own sons; he tries to do this by "selling" himself. He refuses to admit, as Charlie urges him to do, that he is a worthwhile human being. Willy has accepted the materialistic attitude of his society and measures his personal worth in external terms. When the size of his paycheck and the smiles of his clients diminish, he is diminished.

The messages that someone sends him- or herself express a dominant attitude toward life that is clearly reflected in that person's superobjective. Willy's superobjective is "to prove myself worthy by earning money and respect"; the underlying assumption is that he is *un*worthy. He has created an unconscious attitude toward himself, which is his *self-image.*

We tend to become strongly attached to our self-image, even when it is negative. Much of Willy Loman's behavior seems perversely dedicated to proving his own unworthiness, just as Blanche Dubois behaves in ways that prove that she needs "to depend on the kindness of strangers." This kind of repeated pattern of behavior based on the self-image often makes the self-image a self-fulfilling prophecy.

To sum up: Character superobjectives are related to their self-image, which is in turn reflected in the choices they make in "acting out" their lives. Let's apply these ideas to your scene.

EXERCISE 19.2: SELF-IMAGE: WORKING FROM THE INSIDE OUT

What is your character's dominant self-image? What messages does he or she send to him- or herself? Enter into your character's frame of mind and complete these phrases:

1. The most beautiful part of my body is...
2. Happiness to me is...
3. The thing I most want to do before I die is...
4. The most embarrassed I ever was...
5. The ugliest part of my body is...
6. The thing I like best about myself is...
7. Pain to me is...
8. The most secret thing about me is...
9. I can hear my father's voice speaking through my own when I tell myself...
10. Love to me is...
11. The thing I am most proud of is...
12. If you could hear the music in me...
13. I want my epitaph to be...

Immediately enter into the scene and allow these feelings to affect what you do.

As you have seen in the last two exercises, it is possible to work *either* from the inside out *or* from the outside in. Emotion arises automatically out of your involvement in *both* the actions *and* thoughts of your character. Though you may find one approach more powerful for you than the other, *most actors work both ways simultaneously.*

EMOTIONAL RECALL AND SUBSTITUTION

As you begin to participate fully in the actions and thoughts of your character, you begin to have associations or memories of past situations in your own life that were similar. Connecting this personal material with the character's situation can enrich the performance.

Stanislavski experimented with the idea that the actor could develop a wealth of emotional memories as a resource for the acting process, much as a painter learns to mix colors.

> The broader your emotion memory, the richer your material for inner creativeness.... Our creative experiences are vivid and full in direct proportion to the power, keenness and exactness of our memory.... Sometimes memories continue to live in us, grow and become deeper. They even stimulate new processes and either fill out unfinished details or suggest altogether new ones.[2]

Stanislavski worked in the theater at a time when psychology was emerging as a specialized field, and he was deeply interested in it. (The psychologist Pavlov was a friend who contributed to his thinking.) One idea from early Russian psychology that appealed to him was the notion that every cell in the body had a capacity for memory, so the recall of emotional states had the potential to energize the actor in much more than a merely mental way.

We would not entirely disagree with this idea today, though we have other ways of understanding the function of memory. One contemporary school of thought, called "psychocybernetics," describes the operation of memory as serving the needs of survival. Your mind tends to record events that, for various reasons, might be useful as a basis for future action. They remain "on file," ready for recall should a similar situation occur, when we can repeat (or avoid) actions that were in the past successful (or unsuccessful).

For example, you probably suffered some physical injury, discomfort, or severe psychological distress at some time in your childhood, and you have probably "filed" certain prominent details of the event. These details, or things that merely remind you of them, may continue to evoke feelings when they recur, even when the new situation is quite different from the original or when the original has been lost to consciousness. In this way, some events and details continue to evoke strong responses even when there is no longer a direct link to the original situation. (Smells are especially powerful in this regard.)

There are several techniques by which stored memories may be evoked. One of the easiest of these techniques is *visualization*. By relaxing deeply and entering into a visualization of your character's situation, you can invite associations from your store of memories. These associations, or *recalls*, automatically become attached to the character's actions and situation; it is neither necessary nor desirable to "play" them; they are simply allowed to "be there."

Another recall technique that may be useful in certain situations involves making a mental *substitution* of a person, place, or situation from your own life for the one in the scene. If you are supposed to be terribly afraid of another character, it might be useful to recall someone frightening from your own life and substitute this person for that character. Such a substitution is a special kind of emotional recall that often arises naturally as you work. Recalls and substitutions needn't be rooted in real events; *fantasies* sometimes supply more powerful material than real events.

A word of caution: as useful as emotional recall and substitution may sometimes be, there are dangers connected with their use. First, although recalls may be useful for opening an initial connection into the character's experience, you must go beyond this initial connection into the *specific* experience of the character within his or her given circumstances; if you do not, your response may be merely personal without being appropriate to the demands of the character or style of the play.

Second, memories can be very powerful, and those that have not yet been fully mastered can easily overwhelm artistic control. If you fall into your personal memory and emotion too fully, you may lose your necessary dual consciousness. Lee Strasberg claimed that seven years was sufficient time for a memory to have come within the province of artistic control, and he discouraged the use of younger ones. However, as Stanislavski pointed out, some memories grow stronger with age, so there is no guarantee that time alone provides mastery over them.

Third, recalls and substitutions can become obstacles between you and your scene partners. It is awful to be on stage with someone who is looking at you but "seeing" someone else. How much better to find the necessary qualities in the actor who is actually playing the role.

Finally, the emotional power of recalls may distract you from your focus on your objective and action and lure you into playing an emotional state.

For all these reasons, though recalls and substitutions may be useful as training devices, they are of limited use in rehearsal and absolutely *not* intended for use in performance. Stanislavski himself eventually abandoned them entirely. Because memories and associations arise naturally in the course of preparing a role, not much is gained by using them in a premeditated way and much can be lost. Playwright David Mamet said it best:

> The laws of attention which are true off stage are true on stage. The self-concerned person is a bore and the self-concerned actor is a bore. And whether the actor is saying, "I must play this scene in order to be well thought of," or, "I must remember and recreate the time my puppy died in order to recreate this scene well," makes no difference. In both cases his attention is self-centered, and in both cases his performance will tell us nothing we couldn't have learned more enjoyably in a library.
>
> Acting, as any art, must be generous; the attention of the artist must be focused outward—not on what he is feeling, but on what he is trying to accomplish.[3]

EXERCISE 19.3: EMOTIONAL RECALLS AND SUBSTITUTIONS

Place yourself comfortably at rest and do the Phasic Relaxation exercise.

Now go through your scene mentally; picture the entire circumstance and live through your character's actions as if you were actually doing them in those circumstances. Let your body respond freely.

As you live through the scene, notice the emotional associations that arise. Do you remember events from your past? Do the other characters remind you of people you have known? Avoid internal censorship; release into these memories fully.

Now examine the most significant of these recalls. Ask yourself the following questions about this memory:

1. Where in my body is it located?
2. What is it like? How big is it, what color is it, how much does it weigh, and is it hot or cold?
3. How does it make me feel about myself? About the other people in this memory?
4. Are there ideas, attitudes, or beliefs connected with this memory?
5. Do I recall making any choices at this time, even unconsciously, that have affected me since?
6. Are there images from even earlier times contained in this memory? If so, experience these: continue to allow such images to flood up and take you back further and further in time.

Review this exercise and evaluate any connections that were made; are they useful to the scene? Do they need to be specified or altered to meet the exact demands of the scene?

Rehearse your scene and simply allow these associations to "be there."

THE ROLE OF EMOTION IN PERFORMANCE

Finally, we must say something about the way in which you will experience your character's emotion in performance. Young actors sometimes think that they must re-create the character's emotion to generate each performance "truthfully," but this is an exhausting and unreliable way of working.

We may sometimes be tempted to admire the emotionality of the actor who loses control and is overwhelmed on stage, but the display of emotion for its own sake is never our true purpose. The great actor aspires to use emotional technique to realize the truth of the character according to the demands of the play; the ultimate test of a performance is not only its emotional power but also the completeness with which it contributes to the whole play as a work of art; emotion is a means to this end, never an end in itself.

Because emotion arises from action and thought, you need only *do* what your character does and *think* the thoughts that produce the action; the performance itself then gives you the emotion. This was the position to which Stanislavski had come by the time of his last book, *Building a Character,* in which he said:

> Our art...requires that an actor experience the agony of his role, and weep his heart out at home or in rehearsals, that he then calm himself, get rid of every sentiment alien or obstructive to his part. He then comes out on the stage to convey to the audience in clear, pregnant, deeply felt, intelligible and eloquent terms what he has been through.

At this point the spectators will be more affected than the actor, and he will conserve all his forces in order to direct them where he needs them most of all: in reproducing the inner life of the character he is portraying.[4]

The important idea here is that in performance, *the spectators will be more affected than the actor.* This is necessary for several reasons. First, strong emotion interferes with your craftsmanship; as Stanislavski put it, "a person in the midst of experiencing a poignant emotional drama is incapable of speaking of it coherently."[5] Second, it is unreliable to depend on emotion to generate a performance that must be done repeatedly and on schedule. Stanislavski used the example of the opera singer who, at the moment the music requires a certain note with a certain feeling, cannot say to the conductor, "I'm not feeling it yet, give me four more measures." Finally, and most important, your aim is the creation of a *transparent* performance, one through which we get a clear view of the events, characters, and ideas of the play. If your performance calls undue attention to itself, you have failed. As an audience member I am not here to watch *you* weep; I am here to weep *myself.* (Acting for film requires a different and more direct use of emotion.)

SUMMARY

An emotion is any activity that expresses our immediate condition and is directed toward the outside world. In everyday life emotion serves as a *judgment* that we pass on our actions. In this way, emotion arises automatically from any significant effort to interact with the world. It should be so on stage as well: *you do not create emotion; rather, emotion arises of its own accord out of your action.*

The James–Lange theory holds that what we call emotion is our recognition of a bodily condition that is itself a response to some external situation. As some say, "Do the act, and the feeling will follow." When you have found the correct act, the correct feeling follows, and it coincides with the implied physical conditions in the text.

It follows that you needn't be concerned with emotional behavior as such; if you are able to pursue your character's action with full involvement, the emotion *arises automatically* and *is communicated* to your audience. You are *never* concerned with playing emotion.

Although it is true that emotion arises from action, it can also be generated by your thoughts, especially the messages you send yourself about yourself. This is the first principle of cognitive therapy. In developing the emotional life of a character, it may be useful to examine the character's attitude about him- or herself. A character's superobjective is related to self-image, which is in turn reflected in the choices the character makes in "acting out" his or her life.

You see that it is possible to work either from the inside out or from the outside in. Emotion arises automatically out of your involvement in *both* the actions *and* thoughts of your character. Though you may find one approach more powerful for you than the other, most actors work both ways simultaneously.

As emotion arises in rehearsal, it often brings with it associations or memories of past situations in your own life. Stanislavski experimented with the idea that the actor could develop a wealth of emotional memories as a resource for the acting process. There are several techniques by which stored memories may be evoked; one of the easiest is *visualization*. Another involves making a mental *substitution* of someone from your own life for one of the other characters in the scene. Recalls and substitutions needn't be rooted in real events; *fantasies* sometimes supply more powerful material.

As useful as emotional recall and substitution may sometimes be, there are dangers connected with their use. Because memories and associations arise naturally in the course of preparing a role, not much is gained by using this process in a premeditated way, and much can be lost.

Young actors sometimes think that they must re-create the character's emotion in each performance to be "truthful," but because emotion arises from action and thought, you need only *do* what your character does and *think* the thoughts involved in his or her action; the performance itself gives you the emotion.

Emotion in performance must be held at a reduced level for three reasons: first, strong emotion interferes with your craftsmanship; second, it is unreliable; finally, and most important, your aim is the creation of a *transparent* performance. Acting for film, however, requires a different and more direct use of emotion.

PART IV

THE WORKING PROCESS

Having now explored the development of character through the pursuit of action and its refinement, we turn at last to the actual work process of the actor in rehearsal. This part will focus on the preparation of a play for performance in a live theater. The rehearsal process for film and television is very different, and while it is touched on here, it is discussed in detail in my book *Action! Acting for Film and Television*.

FINDING THE CONTENT

Though there are various ways in which stage directors may choose to structure the rehearsal process, the work of the actor always has this typical sequence with ten steps:

1. Auditions and casting
2. Preparation and homework
3. Early readings
4. Exploring the action
5. Establishing the score
6. Getting up and off book: blocking
7. Pacing the performance
8. Polishing the performance
9. Technical and dress rehearsals
10. Growth after opening

The first five are the early period of exploration when the *content* of the performance is being developed; we discuss them in this lesson. The last five are devoted to establishing the *form* of the performance; these are discussed in Lessons 21 and 22.

GENERAL AUDITIONS

Though not usually thought of as part of the rehearsal process, auditions are in fact a time when you may form an initial approach to a role that can greatly influence your later work.

Auditions are a nerve-wracking but necessary part of the actor's life. If it is any consolation to you, directors are under even more pressure during auditions than are actors. The casting of a play, film, or television show is the most important single decision directors make, yet they often have to make it with only minimal knowledge of the actors.

In general we can divide theater auditions into two types, "general" and "specific." Most general auditions, sometimes called "cattle calls," are used for preliminary screening for a role or for membership in a company. In this type of audition you are usually asked to present two monologues of different types, such as modern and classical. If you are involved in this kind of auditioning, you should develop a repertoire of at least three or four carefully chosen and prepared monologues, including comedy and tragedy, poetic and modern styles. About two minutes is a good length for each, though some might be as short as one minute, others as long as three. Beware of going on too long; it is much better to make a strong initial impression and leave the auditioners hungry for more.

Your repertoire of speeches should be chosen to demonstrate your abilities to the best advantage, but most important, they should be material that you love; it is a tremendous advantage to you if your positive feelings for your material outweigh your negative feelings about auditioning.

Introduce yourself and your selections clearly and in a businesslike way. Dress neatly and appropriately to the material you are going to perform but not in a "costume." Take time to prepare yourself and the space but work efficiently. Your focus should be on the work itself; let your appetite for acting motivate you.

Shape each speech to have a smooth, logical progression; this requires some judicious editing, and internal cutting is allowable. In monologues in which another character is assumed to be present, be careful to "create" the other person by the way you relate to that character; place him or her (in your mind) somewhere just off center (not off to one side) a bit closer to you than the auditioners. Do not look directly at the auditioners unless the speech is intended by the author as direct address. Make sure each piece has a satisfying ending, even if that is not how it would be performed in context. This shows the auditioners that you have a desire to satisfy an audience.

Provide a well-organized and attractive résumé, and an eight-by-ten black-and-white photo. This "head shot" assists the auditioners in remembering you; it should be current and "neutral"; that is, it should look like you and not limit the impression it provides of you to one quality such as "sexy," "likable," or "dangerous."

SPECIFIC AUDITIONS

When auditions are for specific roles, various techniques are used. Most directors have developed their own auditioning style, some of which can be rather disarming, but usually you are asked to read a scene from the play, film, or television show. In the live theater, you are usually able to read the entire play in advance and prepare a selection from the role. In film and television, you are often given only a few pages from the script and only a short time for preparation (though it is a union rule that an entire script must be made available if you ask to see it). Don't hesitate to ask questions about the character's given circumstances, about the contribution the character is expected to make to the show, or about the approach the director intends to take.

If you have limited time to prepare for an audition, your immediate job is to find a productive objective and playable action in the material and to make that objective important to you through some kind of personalization. Use the principles you learned in Part II.

Some actors can give good cold readings with only a few moments' work, but directors are sometimes suspicious of this; many times these slick cold-readers fail to develop much beyond their initial reading. In television, however, quick results are required; here, casting is often done by producers who are result-oriented; they want to see exactly what you will do on the set.

Perhaps the greatest challenge in an audition is to allow yourself to really be in the here and now. Usually, you come away from an audition with only a vague sense of what happened or who was there. Take a moment at the beginning to breathe, to see where you are and who is there; treat it like a social situation in which you are glad to be present.

Then, as you perform, go for it. Make the event live. Don't be tied to your script (but don't ignore it completely). It is better to be a bit rough on the lines but alive than to be technically correct but mechanical. Most important, make contact with the person you are reading with, whether that is an imaginary character, a stage manager, or a casting director. As in any other acting situation, the scene can live only *between* you. Put your objective into him or her, try to affect him or her.

In film and television auditions, don't try to create a character or some special emotional state: just let yourself say and do what the character does with your own voice and your own body. They don't want a character; they want to see *you*. Film and television actors are cast so that they bring some interesting quality to the role in their very presence before the camera.

Auditions are much more enjoyable if you approach them without a sense of competitiveness. Think of them not as a contest with other actors but as an opportunity to communicate your potential to a director or producer. Take the long view and remember that the opinion formed of you at an audition may be important at some future time; it is therefore important that you honestly present your best abilities and avoid falsifying yourself for the sake of the particular instance. The question young actors most often ask about an audition is, "What do they want?" A much better question would be, "How can I best show them what kind of actor I am?"

Above all, do not take auditions personally. It usually requires many auditions before you land a part. (In film and TV about twenty seems to be an average, in live theater it varies tremendously.) You can't take every rejection as a reflection on your talent. Auditions do not test your artistry so much as they test your usefulness for the specific role at hand. True, you have to deliver the goods, but first you have to be in the right place at the right time.

EXERCISE 20.1: AUDITIONS

Set up a general audition situation in your class. Each of you is to present two monologues, one modern and one classical. They should be no more than a total of four minutes: a timekeeper will stop you when your time is up. After each audition, the class critiques the work. Also simulate auditions for a film. Use specific scenes.

PREPARATION AND HOMEWORK

Now that you have been cast in your role, you must do some important preparation before rehearsals begin. Analysis, private experimentation, beginning to learn the lines, and private rehearsal of special skills must be accomplished outside the rehearsal hall. Never should you waste the time of your fellow actors and director by failing to do your homework, even if it must be done overnight, as it usually is in television.

Remember that homework is a *preparation* for rehearsal, not a *substitute* for it. Your prerehearsal work identifies the possibilities that are then explored in rehearsal with your fellow actors; it does *not* determine the form of the finished product. Unfortunately, some actors are so insecure that they prepare for rehearsal as if it were performance, creating a rigidly premeditated form; the director then must be a "referee," mediating between the various actors' ideas of how to play their roles. Remember that rehearsal is a time for *mutual* exploration through trial and error.

Depending on the demands of the material, your preparation may take various forms. Certainly you study the play as a whole and develop a preliminary sense of your character's dramatic function. You also examine each of your scenes and do a preliminary breakdown of your action, looking for your beat and scene objectives, and beginning to form a sense of your superobjective.

There may be technical demands on your voice or body related to the specific character; Sir Laurence Olivier devoted a full year to his vocal preparation for *Othello;* Robert De Niro did extensive physical preparation for his role as a prizefighter in *Raging Bull.* As mentioned in Lesson 18, many of the physical and vocal aspects of character and the character's habits have to be practiced almost daily throughout the rehearsal period, and it is never too early to start.

Besides technical preparations of vocal and physical skills related to the external behavior of the character, you also want to prepare yourself to enter the character's mind as well. For this purpose you may need to do research into the intellectual world from which the character comes. You are most interested in those things that established the character's psychological and moral qualities, such as the religious and philosophical beliefs of the time, the educational experiences of the character, the quality of home life, the work environment, the system of government and justice, and so on.

You might also need to develop certain technical skills related to the style of the production, such as fencing, dancing, tumbling, the use of canes, fans, large skirts, or robes. For period plays especially, you may want to do some research into the fashions of the time, the ideas of grace and beauty, and social behavior. Experiencing the music, painting, and architecture of the time is valuable; documents such as diaries, letters, and newspapers can also be helpful. Review your list of the given circumstances; be sure you have considered all the possibilities.

The social backgrounds of plays as recent as *The Glass Menagerie* or *Death of a Salesman* are different enough from our own to require you to learn about life in the Great Depression and World War II and about the popularity of "The American Dream" through such self-help methods as the Dale Carnegie books. Our credit-card culture, for example, cannot fully appreciate the importance to Willy Loman of "weathering a twenty-year mortgage" or the humiliation for Amanda Wingfield of having to ask Garfinkle's Delicatessen for credit.

Two good ways to focus your research into the character's inner and outer worlds are by writing an autobiography and a diary entry for them.

EXERCISE 20.2: AUTOBIOGRAPHY AND DIARY

Imagine that as your character, you have been asked to write a short autobiographical sketch of yourself. Limit yourself to two pages, and include only those things that were most influential in your life; title your essay, "The Things That Made Me Who I Am."

Imagine also that you keep a diary. Select an important day within the time frame of the play and write the diary entry for that day. Check your list of given circumstances and be sure you have covered all the operative elements.

As valuable as it is to do this sort of personal preparation, your characterization should also develop in a way that emphasizes the differences between your character and other characters in the story. In the scene from *Cheers,* for example, we can assume that Diane is college-educated and perhaps from a rich family, whereas Carla barely finished high school and comes from a tough, working-class background. The differences between them enrich their relationship and give them obstacles to overcome in dealing with one another, all of which make for a more satisfying dramatic experience.

Remember too that your character is a creature of the theater; it will be useful for you to understand the theatrical world in which the character was created. Reading other plays by your author and his or her contemporaries can help; so can study of the physical and social environment of the theater of the time. For instance, the open-air, thrust quality of the Elizabethan playhouse with its pit in which the "groundlings" stood throughout the performance is important to an understanding of Shakespeare's plays. Just so, it is revealing to learn that the Moscow Art Theatre in which Chekhov's plays were first presented sat 1,200 persons, so that the scale of the performances must have been somewhat larger than we usually think.

Likewise, coming to understand the literary conventions that influenced the playwright may help you to understand your character. It is revealing to learn of Chekhov's passion for the writing of the French Naturalists and their "scientific" approach to personality and behavior; this is even more illuminating when we consider his training as a doctor and the fact that he wrote his four great plays after learning that he was dying of tuberculosis.

In the same way, understanding the playwright's psychological and moral values can be revealing. It is helpful to know that Bertolt Brecht was an ambulance driver in World War I and was permanently affected by the carnage and misery he experienced then.

EARLY READ-THROUGHS

Now rehearsals begin, and you are meeting for the first time with your fellow cast members. Your director may greet you in a variety of ways: some outline their interpretation and approach to the play; some lead a discussion about it; some may do exercises to "break the ice" and to establish a working rapport in the ensemble; many dispense with any such preliminaries and begin at once to read the play.

These early "table readings" are your first forays into the heart of the material. Begin to work at once on the play as a whole; listen to it in the living voices of your fellow actors and begin to discover how it lives within this particular group of people.

Above all, read *in relationship,* with a spirit of give and take, reaction and action; get your awareness and your eyes out of your book as much as you can and contact the other characters in your scenes. Begin to search for the action that lives only in the specific transactions between the characters. Read also with deep muscle involvement, so that you involve your whole self even though you are probably sitting at a table; you will find that a wealth of associations and ideas well up.

These early rehearsals are exploration, but never indiscriminate exploration. Any meaningful exploration has a sense of goal that prevents it from degenerating into blind groping. There is usually in the vision of a play as communicated by the director some sense of the direction in which your exploration must go.

Not all of your rehearsal discoveries result from purposeful experimentation, of course; the accidental is an important part of all creative processes. You must have the courage to be playful, to invite the *happy accident* to happen, and to benefit from it. Such spontaneous discovery grows best from the receptiveness and responsiveness of each cast member to each other and to the moment. In these early stages of rehearsal, as rapport is being established within the company, it is especially important that each actor makes an act of faith to work together toward the defining of goals with respect, trust, good humor, and a generous heart.

EXPLORING THE ACTION

The main business of these early rehearsals is for you and your partners to begin to shape and specify the transactions of action–reaction that form, link by link, the chain that binds the scenes and the play together. Your preliminary breakdown of the role is being tested and refined, moment by moment, beat by beat, and scene by scene. The rightness of each of your actions is being determined by the way it fits into the cause–effect chain of interactions between characters, which in turn moves the play. As you *feel* the connectedness of every moment with every other moment, your through-line begins to emerge. (In film and television, rehearsal is extremely limited and this process must occur very quickly; the fact that film scenes are usually shot out of sequence makes it necessary for you to establish the through-line *before* you begin shooting any individual scene.)

As the correct sequence of actions begins to form, your scenes begin to play, to flow "under their own power." You no longer have to *make* things happen, you can *let* them happen; and your scenes begin to feel simpler and shorter.

The many choices you must make during rehearsal cannot be prejudged or set-tled by endless discussion; you must actually do a thing to know whether it is right. One of the most common expressions you should hear during rehearsal is "Let's try it." Each choice you make reveals more about the whole play, and in turn each of these revelations of the larger pattern helps you to find the rightness of each detail.

EXERCISE 20.3: MAKING CONNECTIONS

Work through your scene with your partner; either of you may stop the rehearsal at any point when you do not feel connected to the flow of the action, when you are not being "made" to do what you must do next. At each point of difficulty, examine the moments that lead up to it; what can your part-ner supply to correct the problem? What do you need to be getting from your partner to be *made* to do what you do next? Work it out between you until every moment of the scene grows organically out of the flow of action and reaction.

Note: You do *not* tell your partner what to do; you only say what you need from him or her; you might say something like "I need to be more threatened by that," but you leave it entirely to your partner to determine how best to ac-complish this.

This exercise can help you to realize that a difficulty at one point in a scene is often caused by problems earlier in the scene, or even earlier in the play. Don't always try to fix a problem by making an immediate adjustment; trace backward and see if the answer lies in some earlier action, value, or relationship.

ESTABLISHING THE SCORE

You come to understand the score partly through analysis but mostly through trial and error in rehearsal. As the score emerges from the actual experience of action and reaction, stimulus and response, between you and your partners, you begin naturally to assimilate it until it becomes part of you, an "inner model" that guides you through the scene.

The score eventually becomes habitual; you absorb it so totally that you can begin to experience the scene fully, moment by moment. This is the point at which your actor's awareness begins to give way more and more to the character's consciousness; when the score is completely automatic, then you can give yourself fully to each moment with complete attention to "the here and now," confident in the knowledge that the scene can move toward its proper conclusion. In a way, you must be able to do the scene "in your sleep" to be able to do it fully awake.

In *Creating a Role,* Stanislavski describes the operation of the score like this:

> With time and frequent repetition, in rehearsal and performance, this score becomes habitual. An actor becomes so accustomed to all his objectives and their sequence that he cannot conceive of approaching his role otherwise than along the line of the steps fixed in the score. Habit plays a great part in creativeness: it establishes in a firm way the accomplishments of creativeness. In the familiar words of Volkonski it makes what is difficult habitual, what is habitual easy, and what is easy beautiful. Habit creates second nature, which is second reality. The score automatically stirs the actor to physical action.[1]

Elsewhere he says:

> The law of theatrical art decrees: discover the correct conception in the scenic action, in your role, and in the beats of the play; and then make the correct habitual and the habitual beautiful.[2]

At what point do you commit to a choice and allow a particular element of the score to become habitual? Some actors wait a long time before making their final choices and approach their roles warily in early rehearsals, gradually filling in the full performance. Others work at performance levels right off, though they maintain enough flexibility to make changes later as necessary.

You have to determine your own best approach in relation to the disposition of the director, your fellow actors, the nature of the play, and the length of the rehearsal period. To lie back and play the waiting game is usually unfair to your coworkers because they depend on you for their reactions, but neither should you make final choices too soon, committing yourself to insufficiently tested actions.

As the score emerges, your through-line of action and the full experience of your superobjective emerge with it and provide unity and momentum to the performance.

SUMMARY

As nerve-wracking as they are, auditions are a time when you can form an initial approach to a role. For general auditions you should develop a repertoire of three or four prepared audition pieces chosen to demonstrate your abilities to the best advantage, preferably material that you love.

When auditioning for specific roles, your immediate job is to find a productive objective and playable action in the material and to make the objective important to you. In the audition itself, allow yourself to be in the here and now; make the event live. Make contact with the person you are performing with (even if imaginary) and try to affect that character.

Take the long view and remember that the opinion formed of you at an audition may be important at some future time. Think "How can I best show them what kind of actor I am?"

Once cast, you begin your preparation: analysis, beginning to learn the lines, and private rehearsal of special skills must be accomplished outside the rehearsal hall. Remember that homework is a *preparation* for rehearsal, not a *substitute* for it.

At the first reading begin at once to search for the action that lives in the transactions between the characters; read *in relationship,* with a spirit of give and take. As soon as possible, put your book aside so that you can explore the action on your feet. Keep the action going while you call for lines in character without apology. This is the time to start using your rehearsal clothing and props regularly.

The breakdown of the scene now begins to emerge. The rightness of each action is determined by the way it fits into the action–reaction chain between characters; this binds you to the other actors and them to you. Each of you has the right to receive, and the obligation to give, what best serves the common purpose.

The sequence of actions that Stanislavski called the *score* of the role is now starting to develop. The score eventually becomes habitual; you must be able to do the scene "in your sleep," to be able to do it fully awake. This is also the time that your *superobjective* starts to come into focus.

At what point do you commit to a choice? You have to determine your own best approach; to play the waiting game is unfair to your coworkers because they depend on you for their reactions, but neither should you make final choices too soon.

DEVELOPING THE FORM: SCALE AND BLOCKING

During much of the rehearsal to this point, you and your fellow actors have been exploring the individual connections that form the chain of action and reaction that move the play "under its own power" and have begun to set this sequence of actions and their objectives, which Stanislavski called the *score* of the role. This is the "map" of your performance, which you will follow each time you take the journey. (We will focus exclusively on live theater from this point on; in film and television the external form of the performance, since it needs to be repeated only for several "takes," is not established as firmly as in live theater, where it must be repeated for days, weeks, or months.) Now, having found much of the content of your stage performance during your early rehearsals, you begin to develop a form that is expressive and reliable.

GETTING UP AND OFF BOOK

As soon as possible, begin to put your book aside so that you can explore the action on your feet. This, of course, requires learning the lines (in film and television, you are expected to report for the shooting of a scene with lines fully memorized). You have to find your own best method for line memorization. Some actors like to have a friend read the other parts (*cue* them); some make a tape recording of their lines to listen to at night; some even write out their lines. Many find it useful to begin working in paraphrase, finding the ideas behind the lines in their own words first.

However you work, be sure to learn the *action* as well as the lines; that is, learn the words in the context of the give and take of the scene, paying considerable attention to what the other character is saying. This is not only an easier way of learning lines, but it also makes learning them a useful step in your exploration of the action.

The transitional rehearsal period during which you are putting the book down can be a frustrating one. During this period you must not waste rehearsals by stopping the flow of the emerging action; it is expected that you will have to call for lines, so don't waste time apologizing, and above all *keep the action going while you call for lines in character.*

This is the time to get your rehearsal clothing and props and start using them regularly. Pay special attention to the effect of the character's clothing on your body, and be sure to wear the correct type of shoes to rehearsal so as to establish the correct relationship to gravity.

THE STAGE

We must next consider the demands of the space in which you will work. A stage is *any* space in which actors create for their audience the patterned experience called drama, including the film or television "sound stage." Stages come in many sizes, shapes, and types: a circle scratched in the dirt, a rug spread in a marketplace, the back of a truck in a field, or an elaborate building filled with high-tech machinery. Never before has such a wide variety of stage types confronted the actor.

A stage is defined by its relationship to the audience, and in the theater there are four basic configurations: *proscenium, thrust, arena,* and *environmental* (Figure 21.1). Let's consider what each of the basic types means to the actor.

Proscenium

The traditional proscenium stage features an arch through which the audience sees the action. This "picture frame" evolved as a way of establishing a point of reference for settings painted in perspective (hence the word *pro-scenium,* which means "in front of the scene"). To enhance the illusion of perspective, the stage floor was originally sloped upward away from the audience; for this reason, moving away from the audience is called going "upstage," and staying there during a scene so that the other actors are forced to turn their backs on the audience to speak to you is called "upstaging." Moving toward the audience, on the other hand, is called going "downstage."

The actor on the proscenium stage must realize that the audience is limited to one side of the playing area and adjust his or her use of the space accordingly, but it is certainly not necessary to always "cheat out" (to turn your body partly out toward the audience). Doing so makes your character appear to be more interested in speaking to the audience than to the other characters in the scene. And don't underestimate how much acting you can do with your back.

Thrust

In the 1950s the thrust stage (so called because it "thrusts" into the midst of the audience) became very popular. It features the same stage–audience relationship as the classical Greek and Elizabethan theaters. It places the actor into close proximity with

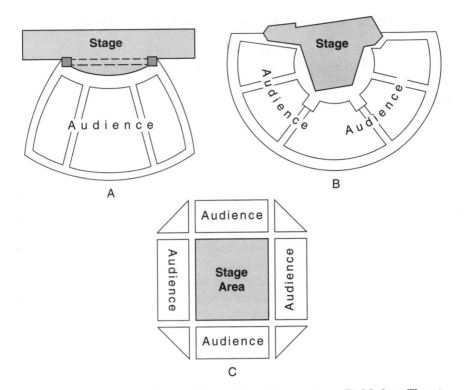

FIGURE 21.1   **Types of Stages: (A) Traditional Proscenium; (B) Modern Thrust; (C) Arena**

the audience but limits the use of scenery; for this reason, it is very much an "actor's" theater. There is some added responsibility here to keep *open* to audience view, or at least to distribute your presence equally to all sections of the house, but the increased sense of audience contact inherent in the thrust stage makes such accommodation easy and natural. Blocking and movement most often are oriented to the two strong diagonals that form an "X" on the stage floor.

Arena

The arena and other types of full-round stages stand at the opposite extreme from proscenium stages. Here the audience completely surrounds the stage and the actor enters through the audience area, either down the aisles or from openings in the auditorium called "vomitoria" (see Figure 21.2). Here you don't worry too much about keeping "open" because your back is always to someone; rather, you play with full three-dimensional reality, except that in both thrust and arena, it is important not to stand too close to other actors because you will block each other from audience view.

FIGURE 21.2   A Full-Round Production: *Six Characters Looking for a Writer,* **as staged by the author for the Quantum Theatre, Pittsburgh, 2002.**

The full-round offers a sense of intimacy unlike any other type of stage, and such theaters are usually quite small. For this reason, audiences tend to expect a more detailed and subtle performance, something closer to what is required for the camera.

Environmental

Although most stages are of the three basic types already described, we sometimes create special environments for specific productions, some of which may abandon entirely the separation of stage and audience. Here, of course, the proximity of the audience demands total commitment and attention to detail, just as the camera does in film acting. For example, my production of Kafka's *The Trial,* at the California Institute of the Arts, was mounted as an enormous fun house; small audience groups moved from room to room, each accompanied by an actor performing the role of the hero, and in each room a scene from the novel was played out. As in this example, most environmental productions happen in very small spaces, so a fully naturalistic style of performance on a scale appropriate to film is usually called for.

To sum up: regardless which of these stages you work in, remember that it is the total theatrical space that is your true working area, not the stage alone. Your adaptation to the position of the audience and to the vocal demands of the shape and size of the entire auditorium is essential.

DIRECTIONS ON STAGE

You need to be able to find your way around on stage according to the traditional terms used by directors and scripts. Though there are many different kinds of stages today, we generally use the nomenclature developed for the proscenium stage, even in film and television.

Vertical Directions

As mentioned earlier, the proscenium stage floor was originally sloped upward away from the audience, so we speak of "*up*stage" as being away from the audience, and "*down*stage" as being toward the audience. To stand "level" with another actor is for both of you to stand perpendicular (in profile) to the audience. In TV sitcoms you notice that actors often play "level" in relation to the cameras. Here are the most common forms of stage movement directions:

> **Lateral Directions** are determined by the actors' view as they face the audience or the camera. Thus *stage right* is the same as audience or camera left; *downstage right* means toward the audience and to the actor's right (Figure 21.3).
>
> **Turns** are described as being either *in* (toward the center of the stage, whichever side of the stage you are on) or *out* (again, away from center).

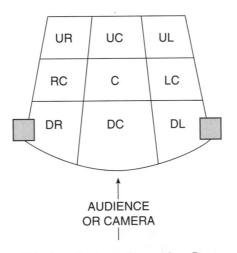

FIGURE 21.3   Locations on a Proscenium Stage

Crossing (that is, moving from one point to another) may be in a straight line or in a slight arc so that you end facing more in profile to the audience. A cross with an exaggerated arc is called a "circle cross" (or sometimes a "banana").

Positions as you pivot relative to the audience or camera are called "one-quarter," "half," and "three-quarters" depending on how far you turn from one side to the other. Thus a director may tell you to "cheat out one-quarter," which means to pivot 45 degrees away from center. This system of directions soon becomes second nature.

EXERCISE 21.1: DIRECTIONS ON STAGE

Have your partner stand in the center of the stage and stand beside him or her on the stage right side; your partner will "play director" by giving you the following directions; then reverse positions.

> *Go down right. / Turn out and go up right. / Turn and cheat down one-half. / Take a long cross down left, going upstage of me. / Turn in and do a banana cross up, passing on the downstage side of me and ending level with me on the right. / Cheat out one-quarter. / Now turn in one-quarter. / Go straight down and hold center. / Circle up to the right around me and exit left center.*

THE SCALE OF PERFORMANCE

The type and size of the performance space require a fundamental adaptation in the size or scale of the performance. Adjusting the scale of performance is a matter of increasing or decreasing its size without distorting the content, just as you might raise or lower the contrast or color level on a television set without changing the content of the picture.

For example, an intimate scene can be played in a large theater by making an overall increase in its size and volume, as long as the behavior and attitudes of the characters continue to conform to the demands of intimacy in all other respects. Your audience accepts the necessity of the adjustment and by convention reinterprets the scene in their own minds to compensate for it.

In the live theater, the problem of scale is usually a matter of this sort of enlargement. For certain intimate spaces, however, such as small full-round stages or environmental productions, you may need to *reduce* scale so as to focus on the minute details of physical and vocal behavior.

The most extreme instance of small-scale work is acting for the camera. Because of its closeness, the camera lens tends literally *to record your thought*; it is usually "too much" for the camera if you do anything more than *think* your way through a scene and allow the rest of your behavior to remain as it would be in life; some actors actually have to reduce the scale of their real-life behavior for the camera.

Many of the actors who act both on stage and for the camera report the importance of learning to "do nothing" for the camera.

Because small details of behavior are usually beyond the bounds of conscious control, the completeness of your inner work and the intensity of your concentration are at a premium before the camera or in intimate theatrical situations. In general, we can say that *as the external scale of a scene decreases, the level of inner dynamic and detail must increase.*

Scale is determined not only by the size and distance of the audience but also by the style of the material being performed. Broad comedy and especially farce, for instance, depend on a size, energy, and tempo of performance that is heightened beyond the limits of everyday behavior; on the other hand, the naturalism of Chekhov places behavior "under the microscope" of a nearly scientific scrutiny, and great meaning is attached to even the tiniest details. A more filmic approach is needed here.

When performing in large spaces or in broad comedy, it is important that you do not judge the scale of your performance according to your everyday kinetic sense. I have sometimes videotaped performances requiring large scale (such as an outdoor Shakespeare festival), and when the actors see themselves they invariably say, "I thought I was moving more than that!" Although they had increased the scale of their movement beyond that of everyday life so it felt like quite a stretch, a much greater extension was actually needed.

In all, your ability to adjust the scale of your performance to fit the needs of your stage and the style of the play is similar to the way you adapt the size of your behavior to fit different contexts in real life, except that the extremes of largeness or smallness are often greater when acting than in everyday life.

Here is an exercise to explore the effect of scale on your performance.

EXERCISE 21.2: THE SCALE OF PERFORMANCE

Go through your scene several times, each time performing in a smaller scale:

1. As if in a huge proscenium theater
2. As if in a medium-size thrust
3. As if in a tiny full-round theater
4. As if for a camera close-up shot

What effect does each have on your experience of the scene? Can you keep the essential action alive in each? Is one more appropriate to the needs of the scene than the others?

THE GROUND PLAN AND SETTING

The shaping of the stage space and the placement of entrances is a decision made with particular care by the director and scenic designer; we call this the creation of the *ground plan.* When directors and designers discuss ground plan and setting, for instance, they often pay special attention to "territoriality": To whom does the space belong? Whose taste does it reflect? Are there areas within it that belong to certain persons? Do the entrances and exits reflect status or relationship (for example, strangers use the front door, whereas family and friends always come in through the kitchen)?

When the ground plan has been correctly established, you find that your character moves within it naturally as the action unfolds; the room itself provides the reason for moving here or there as different needs are felt. For this reason, some directors say that "the ground plan really blocks the show."

Usually, the scenic design has been completed before rehearsals begin, and a picture or model of the set is shown to you early on. As soon as you put the show "up on its feet," the ground plan is usually taped out on the floor of the rehearsal hall and you must visualize the space as it will eventually look in the completed set. You can then rehearse within the ground plan so you are ready to move onto the real set with a minimum of disruption.

Work with your stage manager to select rehearsal props and costumes with care as accurate substitutes for the real things. Take full advantage of costume fittings to get the feel of your clothes, making all the movements your part may require (and to alert the costumer to any problems of motion). Once the set is in place, make it part of your homework to spend some time in it, walking your part or simply getting the feel of the environment.

Although all aspects of the physical set, costumes, and props—the period, decor, color, and so on—are usually determined by the director and the various designers, only *you,* the actor, can endow the space with life by justifying every aspect of it. No amount of scenery, costuming, and lighting can compensate for your failure to "live" in the character's world. Remember: an elaborate production can feel like a dead museum tableau, but a skillful actor can create a whole world on an empty stage.

BLOCKING

The patterned use of space in a stage performance is called *blocking.* Good stage blocking is much more than the creation of pleasing spatial arrangements; it must also reflect the nature and relationships of the characters and most of all the underlying action of the scene. Who is dominant at this moment in the scene? What space do they control? Who is on their side? Who is on the attack? Who is retreating? When do they counterattack? These are the things that determine good blocking.

Although the sense of spatial relationship is artistically heightened on the stage, it is based on our sense of blocking in everyday life. Remember the hostess–guest scene in Lesson 4: do you see how the prolonged encounter at the door, the guest's unwillingness to cross the threshold and enter the hostess's territory, expressed the situation? Once inside, the guest refused to surrender his coat as a symbol that he was only a temporary visitor, that he "didn't belong." How would you imagine him moving in that room? How would he sit in a chair? Where would he sit? How would he eat?

EXERCISE 21.3: BLOCKING IN LIFE

Spend a few days watching the "blocking" of everyday life. Notice how attitude, relationship, and action are expressed in the way people place themselves in a room and in relationship to each other. Record your observations in your journal.

Blocking evolves in the course of rehearsal in a variety of ways, depending on the approach of the director. Some directors plan the blocking in detail and lay it out for the actors at an early stage of rehearsal (this may be especially necessary in shows with large casts or with highly stylized material). Most directors, however, prefer that the actors provide the basic movement impulses that generate the blocking, with the director then editing the pattern as needed. Some directors do no blocking at all, waiting for the actors to find the spatial patterns that best express the action of the scene as it unfolds during the rehearsal process.

No matter how the director works, it is your ability to experience the way in which your movements are organic to the action of the scene that makes blocking truly alive and expressive. Even without a director's help, you should be able to utilize your stage environment to create spatially logical patterns that express the action of your scene and your relationship to other characters.

Blocking for film and television is an even more critical matter. Here your movements are expressed not in feet but in inches. Once a shot has been established by the director and director of photography, strips of colored tape are placed on the floor to mark the exact position of each actor's feet; if there are movements within the shot, each interim destination is marked in the same way. As you do the scene, you must "hit your marks" exactly, without looking down. It can even matter which foot your weight is on, because the composition of the shot and the focus of the camera may require your head to be in a precise location at a precise time.

The nature of film also requires that your eye movements be "blocked"; that is, you must look in precisely the right place at the right time because the apparent location of the other character must be exactly the right distance away from the lens. If the "eye line" isn't consistent in the various shots of a scene, it can't be edited together.

Eye movements are also one of the major factors that determine when an edit is made, so you may have to provide "a look" to a precise point at a precise moment in a scene to motivate a cut to another character. When the camera is seeing only one character in a scene, the other actors usually stand off camera to provide the correct eye lines.

As difficult as all this sounds, even this kind of critical positioning becomes second nature after a time. As you develop your performance, be it for the camera or for the stage, the blocking emerges and is incorporated as a natural part of your total action. By concentrating on what your character is doing, you naturally make the correct movements to the correct locations without thinking.

JUSTIFYING THE BLOCKING

Blocking is "dead" movement until it is endowed with meaning by the way you motivate it as an expression of your character's action. For example, if the director suggests that you move upstage of the sofa while you say, "I don't want to hear this," that movement may be desirable for spatial or pictorial considerations: the director may, for instance, want you to move there so that focus is thrown to a doorway through which someone is about to enter (this is called "setting up" an entrance).

At first, this movement may feel awkward and unnatural to you and probably would appear that way to an audience as well. There is a marked difference between the way we move when we are responding to the external commands of another person and when we are responding to an internal need of our own. The audience unconsciously senses that difference when you move to the sofa; in acting terminology, you have not yet *justified* the cross.

Your task now is to justify the movement as a believable action performed by your character at this particular moment in the scene out of a real need. You might, in this example, find that your character needs to protect him- or herself from what the other person is saying at this moment and so goes to "hide" behind the sofa.

By justifying your movement and your spatial relationship to the setting and the other actors in this way, your blocking comes to life as believable movement. You also find that justified blocking is easy to remember; because it has become a natural expression of your character's action at a particular moment, you need only concentrate on what your character is doing and the blocking "happens on its own."

You also find that the *timing* of lines and crosses makes a critical difference in the process of justifying a line or a cross. Deciding whether you should say "I don't want to hear this" before, during, or after the move can change the psychological meaning of the line; it can feel right one way and quite wrong another.

All these decisions are usually made by trial and error, and that is one of the main functions of rehearsal. As you gain experience, your ability to justify movement or dialogue or to determine the timing of a move or line eventually becomes almost intuitive and almost instantaneous.

EXERCISE 21.4: BLOCKING YOUR SCENE

Together with your partner, decide on what type of stage (full-round, thrust, proscenium) you would like to perform the scene you have been preparing. Design a ground plan for the scene and set up your own rehearsal hall, arranging furniture as needed. Rehearse the scene and allow the blocking to emerge; get the help of a director if possible. Work to justify the blocking. Perform the scene in class and discuss.

SUMMARY

As an actor, you have a special relationship to the environment in which you work; the stage and your fellow actors are your partners in creation. A stage is defined by its relationship to the audience. The four basic types of theater configurations are proscenium, thrust, arena, and environmental.

When describing movement on the stage, we generally use the nomenclature developed for the proscenium: We speak of "downstage" as being toward the audience and "upstage" as being away; lateral directions are determined by the actor's right and left as he or she faces the audience. Turns are described as being either "in" (toward the center of the stage) or "out." Positions as you pivot are called *one-quarter, half,* and *three-quarters* depending on how far you turn.

The type and size of the performance space require an adaptation in the scale of the performance, increasing or decreasing its size without distorting the content. Your audience accepts the necessity of the adjustment and by convention reinterprets the scene in their own minds.

The most extreme instance of small-scale work is acting for the camera. Because of its closeness, the camera lens tends literally to record your thought, and many actors report the importance of learning to "do nothing" for the camera.

In general, as the external scale of a scene decreases, the level of inner dynamic must increase. Scale is determined not only by the size and distance of the audience but also by the style of the material being performed. In large spaces or broad comedy, do not judge the scale of your performance according to your everyday kinetic sense; much larger movement may be needed.

The shape of the environment in which the play occurs is the *ground plan.* When the ground plan has been correctly established, the room itself provides the reason for moving here or there; some directors say that "the ground plan really blocks the show."

The patterned use of space in a stage performance is called *blocking.* Good stage blocking must reflect the nature of the characters, the character relationships, and most of all the underlying action of the scene. Most directors prefer the actors to provide the basic movement impulses that generate the blocking, with the director then editing the pattern as needed. Blocking for film and television is a critical matter; once a shot has been established, strips of colored tape are placed on the floor to mark the exact position of each actor's feet; you must "hit your marks" exactly, without looking down. The camera may even require that your eye movements be blocked.

But no matter the situation, it is your ability to experience the way in which your movements are organic to the action of the scene that makes blocking truly alive and expressive. Blocking is "dead" movement until you *justify* it as a believable action performed by your character out of a real need. Justified blocking (and dialogue) is easy to remember because it has become a natural expression of your character's action.

PREPARING TO OPEN

With your score and the blocking having been more or less established, you move into the final phase of rehearsal in which the stage performance is given its final form before opening. One of the major developments in this final phase is the perfecting of the show's rhythm, which lives in its shape and pace.

SHAPING AND PACING THE PERFORMANCE

When you and your fellow actors established the score, you began to experience how each of your individual actions and objectives contributed to the flow of the show, each beat change leading to each scene crisis, and each scene moving toward the crisis of the entire play. This *shape* is now to be perfected as you set the tempo-rhythms of the performance. Each beat change, each scene crisis, and the momentum toward the major crisis of the play are brought into sharp focus, and the flow of action that connects these milestones is established and smoothed to provide momentum, a sense of drive, urgency, significance, and rising dramatic tension, which we call good *pace;* by contrast, a performance lacking in pace feels "flat" and fails to compel our attention. Note that "pace" refers to the momentum of the action, regardless of its "tempo," which refers to its speed.

When a performance lacks pace, there is a temptation to speed up or artificially "hype" the action; this is always a mistake. Good pace results only from the natural flow of the action when each transaction of reaction and action between the characters is real and complete. Rushing or forcing the scene only blurs these connections and harms the pace. Paradoxically, poor pace is usually best corrected by taking the time to reestablish the connections within the scene.

The best source of pace is the underlying conflict of the play itself as it lives in each scene. Whatever form the conflict has been given, it provides momentum by driving the conflicting forces against one another as the need for a resolution grows. If you can experience the conflict in this way, scene by scene, it can provide momentum as part of the intrinsic reality of the play, thus avoiding an artificial heightening of energy by rushing or forcing your action.

The given circumstances may also supply a sense of urgency: there may be an *external deadline* that requires that an objective be achieved as quickly as possible, such as someone about to enter or the fear of discovery. More commonly there is an *internal deadline,* such as the need to do something before you lose your nerve, to say something before breaking into tears, and so on.

In some cases, because no writer is perfect, it may be necessary for the actors and director to invent some external or internal source of momentum for a scene. This might involve redefining the given circumstances to provide urgency. Another strategy is to invent some surface activity, such as sewing, smoking, drinking, eating, or playing cards, that might help you to channel your energy outward and thereby move the scene forward.

On the other hand, it may be that at moments of great tension or emotion, *containment* and *stillness* produce better pace than activity. Remember that activity "spends" energy and that you must invest your stage energy with great discrimination; it is often true that "less is more," *if* it is the right "less."

One important element of good pace is *cueing,* the way in which one character begins to speak after another has finished. In real life, if you and I are discussing something, I listen to you to understand the idea you are trying to express. When I have grasped that idea, I form my response and am usually ready to begin answering *before* you have actually finished your sentence. Listen to real-life conversations; do you hear how we actually overlap one another's speeches slightly, or at least are *ready* to respond before the other person has stopped talking? This is good "cueing."

Sometimes pace is harmed by the actors doing "too much," engaging in extraneous business, unnecessary pauses for thought, or emotional displays. Any action, any piece of business, any emotion, or any character trait that impedes the pace of the scene should be discarded. As Stanislavski was fond of saying, "Cut 80 percent!"

EXERCISE 22.1: SHAPING AND PACING THE SCENE

Examine your scene with your partner; is each beat change and the scene crisis fully realized? Can you feel these as changes in the scene's rhythmic shape?

Look together for those aspects of the situation that provide urgency or a sense of deadline and thereby contribute to the scene's momentum:

1. The physical environment: time, place, and so forth
2. The social environment: customs, the presence of others
3. The situation: internal or external factors that create urgency or tension
4. The conflict between the characters

Practice your listening and responding skills to produce good cueing. After rehearsing your scene to achieve good shape and pace, perform it for your class. Ask them to signal whenever they feel the shape of the action becoming vague or the pace dropping.

MAKING FINAL ADJUSTMENTS

Having laid the foundation of your score and characterization, having set the basic form of the blocking, and having established good shape and pace, your production is ready to add the final technical elements in the last days of the rehearsal process. During this period you have to make many *final adjustments.*

Of course, you have been making adjustments throughout your rehearsal process, and your ability to make complete adjustments quickly is one of your most fundamental and useful acting skills. An adjustment is any alteration in the form of your performance made to meet some external need, such as a blocking problem, a lighting or scenic concern, the need of a fellow actor for support in a particular moment, and the like. The adjustments you make in this final stage of rehearsal, however, are more demanding because the form being adjusted is more fully set, and the anxiety you feel as opening approaches makes you less flexible.

Although the adjustment is in the external form of your performance, it must still be *justified* by being the result of some change in the inner phase of your action. If you alter only the external form of your activity without adjusting the process of thought from which it springs, the results seem forced, unnatural, and incomplete. For instance, if the director yells, "Louder!" you do not merely say the line more loudly: you intuitively review the process of inner action from which the line springs and adjust something in the perception, attitude, or choice so that the line *must* be said more loudly.

Although almost all adjustments can be made in your inner phase of action, you can also make adjustments by redefining the given circumstances. Because your stimulus is almost always the action of another character, you can even make adjustments by asking your fellow actor to provide you with a stimulus that can better elicit the desired response.

TECHNICAL AND DRESS REHEARSALS

The final phase of the rehearsal period is devoted to incorporating the physical production elements: makeup, props, costumes, set, lights, and sound. Ideally, this is a time of completion and crystallization of your performance; many actors do not feel that their work comes fully to life until all the physical production elements are in place. Stanislavski spoke of completing a characterization only when, in full makeup and costume, he would rehearse before a mirror to be sure that his external appearance was correct and that his inner life was in harmony with his external appearance.

In most U.S. theaters, only the final week of rehearsal is devoted to the assimilation of all the completed technical elements. This can be a period of tremendous frustration and distraction for you if you have not prepared yourself for it in the earlier stages of rehearsal.

Above all, avoid the temptation to "freeze" your work during this final phase of rehearsal. Many fine performances wither on the vine before opening because the outer form becomes the focus of the actor's attention and the inner phase of action ceases to live and grow. Use the addition of the technical elements as an opportunity to extend and specify the score of your role and to explore further the life of the character within a more complete environment.

There are two main ways in which you can be prepared for this final phase: first, have a solid score, the "sequence of objectives," which helps you to keep your focus on the action without being distracted by all the new technical elements; second, use good rehearsal substitutes for props, costumes, and ground plan.

During this period, you probably have less rehearsal time available to you as the energies of the production are taken up with technical matters. It is important that you continue to work on your own to prepare yourself for the coming of the audience. One way to do this is to *visualize* the performance as it will be under audience conditions. Visualization is an excellent form of private rehearsal; it is most effective when used during periods of relaxation when your deep muscles actually participate. Here is an exercise in the technique called Visuo-Motor Behavior Rehearsal, which was first developed for the 1980 Winter Olympics and used by athletes such as Jean-Claude Killy with great effectiveness.

EXERCISE 22.2: VISUO-MOTOR BEHAVIOR REHEARSAL

Using the Phasic Relaxation, put yourself into deep muscle relaxation and mental restful alertness.

Now visualize the following: you are about to open in the play from which your scene comes; the theater is ready, you hear the buzz of the audience in the house, and you are standing in your costume with your fellow actors ready to take your places.

In your mind, go into the set and take your opening positions: feel the stage lights shining on you; smell the makeup; feel your clothing; see your fellow actors and the set.

The scene begins; live through it totally; let your deep muscles respond to the experience; feel the props and all the business.

Tests have shown that this form of rehearsal can be just as effective as ordinary rehearsal and sometimes more so.

GROWTH AFTER OPENING

In the live theater, the opening of the show is never the completion of your work but only the start of a new phase of the growth process. The audience contributes in many ways, perhaps most by providing the responses that complete the rhythmic shaping of the work. These responses take many forms, from the overt (such as laughter or sobs) to the covert (such as rapt stillness or restlessness, or just the "feeling" inside the auditorium). Whatever their form, the audience's responses are an important element in the rhythm of the scene. So far, you have been guessing what those responses may be, and your director has been substituting for them as "an ideal audience of one," but now you have the real thing, and you can fine-tune the shape and flow of your action accordingly. This is the business of "preview" performances, or invited audiences at dress rehearsals, if you are lucky enough to have them.

The audience's presence also causes change in the way you experience your own work. Some things you thought would work well may turn out to be too personal or obscure, whereas other things that you hadn't really noticed turn out to be powerful or worth developing further. At last you have a sure basis for judgment.

This sure basis for judgment naturally causes you to begin economizing. You find after a time that you expended more energy during rehearsals than you do in performance and that you generally expend less and less energy as the run continues. This is not because you begin doing your part mechanically, without thought or feeling, but because you penetrate deeper and deeper to its essence; as this happens, unessential detail begins to fall away. Your performance is made more effective by distilling it to its essentials in this way; you are doing more with less.

SUMMARY

The *shape* of each beat, scene, and the show as a whole is now to be perfected as you set the temporhythms of the performance. The flow of action that connects these milestones is established and smoothed to provide momentum, a sense of drive, urgency, significance, and rising dramatic tension, which we call good *pace.*

One important element of good pace is *cueing,* the way in which one character begins to speak after another has finished.

By now your production is ready to add the final technical elements in the last days of the rehearsal process. During this period you have to make many final adjustments in form to meet external needs. These adjustments must be *justified* by being the result of some change in your inner phase of the action. Technical and dress rehearsals can be a period of tremendous distraction for you if you have not prepared yourself properly with a strong score and effective use of the rehearsal ground plan, props, and costume pieces.

The opening of the show is never the completion of your work but only the start of a new phase of the growth process. At last you have a sure basis for judgment, and you can penetrate deeper and deeper to its essence; as this happens, unessential detail begins to fall away. Your performance is made more effective by distilling it to its essentials; you are doing more with less.

THE ACTOR AT WORK

Underlying all the techniques and principles you have studied so far are your attitudes and values as an actor. These are reflections of the motivations that brought you to acting, your personal beliefs, your relationship to your world, and your hopes for your future as an actor. These values and hopes profoundly affect the way you work, though their influence is often unconscious. If you can develop productive attitudes as the foundation of your working process, you will be a more effective actor, and you will be better able to take charge of your own growth.

An effective work process depends on three things: good communication skills, a creative attitude, and a clear sense of purpose. We end our study by exploring these fundamental attitudes.

SUPPORTING EACH OTHER

The interactive nature of drama means that your individual creation cannot be separated from the work of all the other actors and the director. Your attitude toward your fellow workers is as important as your attitude toward your own work. Remember this observation by playwright August Strindberg quoted in Part I:

> No form of art is as dependent as the actor's. He cannot isolate his particular contribution, show it to someone and say, "This is mine." If he does not get the support of his fellow actors, his performance will lack resonance and depth.... He won't make a good impression no matter how hard he tries. Actors must rely on each other.... That is why rapport among actors is imperative for the success of a play. I don't care whether you rank yourselves higher or lower than each other, or from side to side, or from inside out—as long as you do it together.[1]

Your working relationships are most effective when they are based on three principles: first, mutual *commitment* to the working relationship and to the work itself; second, mutual *support* for one another's individual objectives and methods; third, free and open *communication* so that problems can be thrashed out and thereby become opportunities for creative interaction. Let's examine each.

First, you are *committed* to the working relationship because it enables you to do better work as an individual. Friendship results from most of your working relationships; there is a wonderfully warm sense of kinship among actors. Often you meet another actor for the first time and because of your mutual friends you know at once that you are family. But commitment to the working relationship is not necessarily the same thing as being "friends," and it is possible to work effectively with people you don't particularly like.

Although group membership requires generosity, good humor, and a spirit of reasonable compromise, it should *not* involve either the sacrifice of self-esteem or the surrender of personal standards; the need to be "nice" should never cause you to falsify your values or discipline. Remember: the group doesn't make good work because it is a good group; it becomes a good group because it creates good work.

Second, your *support* for one another's objectives and methods is the basis of respect. You might not share other actors' reasons for doing what they do, nor work the same way, but you respect their motives and their right to work in their own way, just as you expect respect for your own motives and methods. If your different ways of working cause a problem (as they sometimes do), negotiate compromises on both sides, which, as much as possible, meet everyone's needs equally.

Finally, the possibility of free and open *communication* is critical. Problems arise in any creative process, and they must be worked through and negotiated; only good communication makes that possible.

FREE AND OPEN COMMUNICATION

Free and open communication does not mean that we say everything that's on our minds in the name of "honesty"; some things are best left unsaid—as Falstaff says, "discretion is the better part of valor"—but the *possibility* of discussing problems needs to be felt by everyone. Otherwise an atmosphere of repression develops and tensions mount, perhaps to a boiling point.

In addition to the group's need for good communication, you have an individual need for it. We have already discussed how actors depend on feedback more than most other artists; the notes you get from your teachers, directors, and fellow actors are tremendously important in guiding your growth. Actors, therefore, have a solemn responsibility to provide accurate and useful feedback to one another. The most effective feedback we can give each other is based on a few basic principles.

Most important, say *what you see* and *how it makes you feel.* Don't say, "Why are you hiding from us," say, "I noticed that you rarely looked at your partner during this scene, and that made me feel as if you were hiding. What was going on?" Do you see the difference between these two statements?

In the first statement, you *interpreted* the reason for what you saw, then reported your interpretation as if it were true. If the other person doesn't feel that he or she was "hiding," that actor will reject your input. In the second statement you reported your specific observation, then reported the feeling it engendered in you. This way of speaking is preferable because it does not involve interpretation: you saw what you saw, and it made you feel a certain way. Now you can go on to discuss the situation profitably.

Once you have an effective message to send, consider some effective ways of sending it:

1. Be *clear* about your message before you deliver it.
2. Be *specific, simple,* and *direct;* use examples.
3. Pick an *appropriate time* to communicate.
4. *Check* to see if your message was received accurately.

Here is an exercise to practice these communication skills.

EXERCISE 23.1: ATTRACTIONS AND RESERVATIONS, AGONIES AND ECSTASIES

Join with one of your fellow workers to share impressions of your own and each other's work. Take turns completing the following statements; be specific and direct; supply examples.

1. My greatest agony about my own work just now is...
2. The greatest reservation I have about your work is...
3. The thing I feel best about in my own work is...
4. The thing that attracts me most about your work is...

Compare your feelings about praise and criticism. Which do you take more seriously? Did you learn equally from each? Are you benefiting from the feedback of others enough? Or are you *too* dependent on them?

Unfortunately, despite the nature of their work, most actors have no better communication skills than anyone else. Here is a list of the most common pitfalls in good communication. Think back over your working experiences: have you suffered from or been guilty of any of the following communication disorders?

1. *Fogging:* Using generalities without referring to specifics. Example: "You need to work on your voice."
2. *Mind-raping:* Assuming you know what someone is thinking without bothering to check. Example: "Why are you hiding from us in this scene?"
3. *Defusing:* Excessive self-criticism that makes it impossible for anyone else to criticize you. Example: "I know the scene was terrible, but I just couldn't concentrate at all today."
4. *Dumping:* Using criticism as an emotional release or as a weapon
5. *Gunnysacking:* Saving up grievances until an explosion becomes likely
6. *No trespassing:* When unstated rules exist within a group that certain people or certain issues may not be criticized

7. *Holier-than-thou:* Criticism of others for the purpose of avoiding criticism of self

8. *Doomsaying:* Feedback that emphasizes only the negative without acknowledging the positive

YOU AND YOUR DIRECTOR

The relationship between actor and director deserves special attention. Because the director is the focus of the group's working process, your ability to work effectively with your director is critical. It helps if you have a clear sense of what each of your functions, rights, and responsibilities is.

The director has three main functions: (1) to guide the development of an overall interpretation for the production, (2) to align the efforts of all the different artists contributing to the production, and (3) to provide feedback during rehearsals by being an ideal audience of one. The interpretive function makes the director a "central intelligence" for the production, establishing its point of view. The director either provides this focus at the outset or guides the cast in discovering it during rehearsals.

Your performance, like every other element of the production, must be aligned toward this central interpretation. Even if your personal preference might be for a different interpretation or emphasis, once you have accepted the role it is your job to work effectively within the director's production concept.

Perhaps the most destructive attitude is that of actors who become apologists for their characters, arguing from the characters' points of view as if every scene "belonged to them." Group interpretation can be ruined by actors who insist on adopting their characters' points of view at the expense of the play as an artistic whole.

On the other hand, we do a great disservice to our director, our fellow actors, and ourselves if, out of our desire to avoid conflict, we fail to express ourselves honestly. An actor who is too pliable is as destructive as one who is too rigid. Your ideas are appreciated if they are presented in a reasoned, timely, and respectful fashion. Although a show has only one director, everyone connected with it must feel responsible for the whole production and provide any ideas that may be of value.

There are many ways in which the responsibilities of director and actor overlap and where compromise is necessary. The actor, intimately involved with the life of the character, possesses insights into the life of that character that are denied to the director. At the same time, the director has an objective overview unavailable to the actor. In an effective working relationship, both respect and value the insights of the other and seek to join their points of view to the best possible advantage.

Even in the best situations there are times when insoluble disagreements occur; when this happens, ties go to the director. The director has assumed public responsibility for the interpretation of the production, whereas you have assumed public responsibility only for the portrayal of your character within the context established by that interpretation. Once the director's interpretation has been clarified, it is your responsibility to find the best possible means of implementing it; if this proves to be impossible, the relationship must be severed for the sake of the play. Unless you have become a major star, this means that you get fired.

Besides interpretation, another important function of the director is to establish a common approach in the conduct of rehearsals. Each director has a characteristic way of working, and it is easier for the actors to adapt to the director's method than for the director to adopt an individual approach to each of the actors. It is, therefore, part of your job to adapt, as much as is reasonable, to the director's approach, and to help the director develop the most effective channel of communication with you.

To sum up: You and your director are coworkers, not master and slave. Though you share many responsibilities, you have essentially different functions that are interdependent and equal. The director's first responsibility is to the overall patterning of the play as a theatrical experience; your responsibility is to bring your role to life so as to best contribute to that pattern.

THE FEAR OF FAILURE

The fundamental drive for most actors, like most people, is the desire for success and its flip side, the fear of failure. Everyone has both, of course, though one may be said to be dominant over the other in many individuals. Each is a powerful source of energy, but the differences between them are important.

At the 1984 Olympics in Los Angeles, the champion athletes were tested to see which were driven primarily by a desire for success and which were motivated primarily by the fear of failure; it was found that over 70 percent were driven by the desire for success, whereas less than 30 percent were motivated by the fear of failure. I would suspect that those motivated by fear of failure tended to be technically precise but cautious, whereas the larger group would include more "inspired" athletes who were greater risk-takers. The fear of failure encourages safe and conservative choices, but the desire for success can generate energetic though sometimes risky choices.

No one has ever tested a group of actors in this way, but I suspect that a larger proportion of actors would be found to be driven by the fear of failure. There are many unsuccessful or marginal actors who hang on in the business for year after undistinguished year, whose work is competent but uninspired, who deliver reliable but cautious performances, and who simply don't "go for it." Their motto seems to be "nothing ventured, nothing lost."

The fear of failure encourages the attitude that "I must do it exactly right," producing, at best, technical skill, precision, and consistency. These are qualities that are rewarded for their own sake, but technical skill never entirely compensates for a lack of creativity. For the actor, technical skill is only the means toward the expression of an artistic vision.

An excessive fear of failure can cause you to censor creative impulses, fearing that "I'll look foolish." When you censor an impulse, you must literally "hold it in," and this causes muscular tension. It is no accident that we tell overly cautious people to "loosen up."

Finally, and most important, the fear of failure may cause you to continually judge your own performance to see if you are "doing it right," and this encourages self-consciousness. As George C. Scott once observed in an interview:

> I think you have to be schizoid three different ways to be an actor. You've got to be three different people: you have to be a human being, then you have to be the character you're playing, and on top of that, you've got to be the guy sitting out there in row 10, watching yourself and judging yourself. That's why most of us are crazy to start with or go nuts once we get into it. I mean, don't you think it's a pretty spooky way to earn a living?[2]

EXERCISE 23.2: THE FEAR OF FAILURE

Think back to your most recent work in an audition, rehearsal, or performance: do you remember censoring yourself? Were you sending yourself messages like, "This isn't going to work" or "This might make me look stupid." What physical tensions resulted from "holding in" your impulses?

Next time you work, notice these moments of self-censorship as they occur: simply release the tension, take a breath, and get back to work.

THE DESIRE FOR SUCCESS

A working actor needs the drive, courage, and long-term tenacity that a strong desire for success can provide. Each of us must define success for ourself: what constitutes true success for you?

There are really two ways of measuring success: in purely internal terms, such as pride, sense of accomplishment, and feelings of growth, and by external measurements, such as reviews, grades, and the response of the audience. Obviously, all actors are, and should be, concerned with both. What we need is perspective and balance between the two.

Most actors err on the side of emphasizing external measures of success over internal. Even if they have a sense of their own worth, they usually don't trust it, and they feel so dependent on the opinions of others that a negative response from anyone damages their self-esteem.

Of course, it hurts any actor when his or her work is not well received. But the serious actor strives to balance the understandable desire for immediate success with the equally important long-range demands of artistic development. You should approach each new role, each rehearsal, and each performance with a desire not only to please others but also a desire to *learn and grow* for yourself. When evaluating the experience, you must not only ask "Did I do the job well?" but also "Am I now a better actor for having done it?"

Winning parts, applause, and good reviews, as important as these things are, are not enough. I know some actors, especially in film and television, who are wildly successful in commercial terms but who derive little personal satisfaction from their careers. The "business" demands that they use the same skills, play the same sort of character in the same type of material, role after role; no matter how highly developed these skills may become, they can bring only limited artistic satisfaction.

Serious actors insist on continuing to develop and extend their abilities with disciplined regularity throughout their lifetimes. There is no real substitute for meeting the day-to-day demands of rehearsal and performance; this is why the actor in a repertory company, preparing a continual variety of roles, may develop much faster than the actor who works in long runs or repeatedly plays the same kinds of roles.

Most difficult is the situation of film–TV actors who, unless they are among the 6 percent who work regularly, work only a few weeks out of every year. Classes, workshops, and occasional theater roles are the only chances such actors have to maintain and extend their skills. In the waiting room at a TV audition, I heard one actor tell the others this joke:

> Three actors were complaining about being out of work. "Heck," said the first actor, "I haven't had a part for four months." "That's nothing," said the second actor, "I haven't even had a decent *audition* for a year!" "I've got you both beat," the third actor said, "I haven't acted for six years. It's gotten so bad, I'm thinking of leaving the business."

EXERCISE 23.3: MEASURING SUCCESS

Think back to your most recent performance. Did you have your own independent evaluation of it? Did you trust that evaluation? How did the comments of others affect you? Did you distinguish between the short-term measurement of your success in the role and the long-term benefits of the work to you as a developing artist?

YOUR SENSE OF PURPOSE

We use the word *professional* to imply a high level of skill, reliability, and commitment in many fields, but it means something special among actors. When actors want to pay someone a real compliment, they say, "You're a real pro." But what is it that defines a professional?

In athletics, we distinguish between professional and amateur on the basis of money: the professional is paid, whereas the amateur (from the root *amat,* "to love") participates only for the love of the sport itself. But in acting, *professional* seems to mean much more than the fact that someone receives money; the term carries an implication of integrity, reliability, high standards, and most of all *commitment.*

The root of the word comes from an old French verb, *profes,* which meant "to make a solemn vow," as in joining a religious order. In our culture, professionals have special knowledge or skills that give them power over other people: doctors, lawyers, clergy, and others of the "professional class" are responsible for the well-being of their clients. Society has placed a special trust in them, and in return they are expected to use their special powers only for the benefit of those they serve. Thus a professional is *someone who has taken a solemn vow to maintain an ethical standard.* He or she has accepted personal responsibility for work that affects the lives of others.

As an actor, you have special power over others. We don't usually take acting as seriously as that, but it is true. With this power comes a public responsibility for the well-being of those whose lives you affect, and this demands an enormous commitment.

This commitment operates on three levels simultaneously: First, you must be committed to *your own development as an artist.* Without this commitment to yourself, you cannot offer to others all of which you are capable.

Second, you must be committed to *your work.* If you are merely using your work to advance yourself, you obscure its value to others.

Third, you must be committed *to the world you serve through your work.* Acceptance of this social responsibility gives you a sense of purpose to something greater than yourself, and this can lead you to extraordinary accomplishments.

Theater is the most human of all the arts, and we can preserve and expand our humanity through our art in ways denied us by everyday life. As David Mamet says:

> What can be preserved? What can be communicated from one generation to the next? Philosophy. Morality. Aesthetics.
>
> These can be expressed in technique, in those skills which enable the artist to respond truthfully, fully, lovingly to whatever he or she wishes to express.
>
> This is what can and must be passed from one generation to the next. Technique—a knowledge of how to translate inchoate desire into clean action—into action capable of communicating itself to the audience.
>
> This technique, this care, this love of precision, of cleanliness, this love of the theatre, is the best way, for it is love of the *audience*—of that which *unites* the actor and the house; a desire to share something which they know to be true.[3]

The desire of which Mamet speaks, this *need to express the truth within the techniques of art,* is not merely personal. It involves a sense of service to something greater than ourselves, and as such it is the deepest and most lasting motivation of the actor. As he says:

> Our workers in the theatre—actors, writers, directors, teachers—are drawn to it not out of intellectual predilection, but from *necessity.* We are driven into the theatre by our need to express—our need to answer the question of our lives—the questions of the time in which we live. Of this moment.[4]

This need "to answer the question of our lives" demands both the highest artistry and the deepest humanity. Again, Mamet:

> Who is going to speak up? Who is going to speak for the American spirit? For the human spirit?

Who is capable of being heard? Of being accepted? Of being believed? Only that person who speaks without ulterior motives, without hope of gain, without even the desire to *change,* with only the desire to *create:* The artist. The actor. The strong, trained actor dedicated to the idea that the theatre is the place we go to hear the truth, and equipped with the technical capacity to speak simply and clearly.[5]

This sentiment, expressed recently by one of our leading writers, hearkens back to the original impulses of the founders of our modern school of acting when, more than ninety years ago, Stanislavski and Nemirovich-Danchenko debated the requirements for actors to be taken into the company of the Moscow Art Theatre:

"Take actor A," we would test each other. "Do you consider him talented?"

"To a high degree."

"Will you take him into the troupe?"

"No."

"Why?"

"Because he has adapted himself to his career, his talents to the demands of the public, his character to the caprices of the manager, and all of himself to theatrical cheapness. A man who is so poisoned cannot be cured."

"And what do you say about Actress B?"

"She is a good actress, but not for us."

"Why?"

"She does not love art, but herself in art."

"And actress C?"

"She won't do. She is incurably given to hokum."

"What about actor D?"

"We should bear him in mind."

"Why?"

"He has ideals for which he is fighting. He is not at peace with present conditions. He is a man of ideas."

"I am of the same opinion. With your permission I shall enter his name in the list of candidates."[6]

It is important, then, for you to consider how you may serve through acting. Traditionally, artists have announced their specific commitment through the publication of a *manifesto;* this was their way of taking the same kind of public vow that lawyers and doctors take when they are licensed. A manifesto is a brief, passionate, and personal statement of belief and purpose. It requires considerable thought and should be as simple and direct as possible.

EXERCISE 23.4: YOUR MANIFESTO

Write your own manifesto for the art of acting. Make yours just two paragraphs long:

1. What do you want to do for the world through your acting? How do you want to make a difference?

2. What techniques and process are necessary to achieve your purpose? What skills and capabilities must *you* develop to empower yourself to achieve your purpose?

When you are satisfied with it, publish it in some public forum, read it in class, or put it up on the wall.

TRANSFORMATION

Your sense of purpose grows from your respect for your own talent, your love for the specific material you are performing, and your desire to use both to serve your audience. It is this drive to be *at service* through your art that finally overcomes the self-consciousness of your ego and carries you beyond yourself, giving you a transcendent purpose from which come dignity, fulfillment, and ongoing artistic vitality.

Stanislavski called this ongoing artistic vitality "theatrical youthfulness." Near the end of his life, he addressed a group of young actors who were entering the Moscow Art Theatre with these words:

> The first essential to retain a youthful performance is to keep the idea of the play alive. That is why the dramatist wrote it and that is why you decided to produce it. One should not be on the stage, one should not put on a play for the sake of acting or producing only. Yes, you must be excited about your profession. You must love it devotedly and passionately, but not for itself, not for its laurels, not for the pleasure and delight it brings to you as artists. You must love your chosen profession because it gives you the opportunity to communicate ideas that are important and necessary to your audience. Because it gives you the opportunity, through the ideas that you dramatize on the stage and through your characterizations, to educate your audience and to make them better, finer, wiser, and more useful members of society....
>
> You must keep the idea alive and be inspired by it at each performance. This is the only way to retain youthfulness in performance and your own youthfulness as actors. The true recreation of the play's idea—I emphasize the word true—demands from the artist wide and varied knowledge, constant self-discipline, the subordination of his personal tastes and habits to the demands of the idea, and sometimes even definite sacrifices.[1]

The art of acting has always had a very special service to render, one that has become increasingly important today: it is rooted in the actor's ability to transform, to become "someone else." At a time when mass culture, big business, and bigger government make us, as individuals, feel more and more insignificant and impotent, the actor's ability to be "in charge" of personal reality can be a source of hope and inspiration to others.

The actor's ability to undergo transformation is itself a kind of potency, a kind of power over the future. Although a play may teach us something about who we are, it is the actor's ability to be transformed that teaches us something about who we may *become*. The actor's ability to redefine personal reality before our very eyes reminds us of our own spiritual capacity for self-definition, and thus the theater becomes a celebration of our vitality and of the ongoing flow of life.

The actor who works in this spirit finds his or her horizons being continually broadened by a renewed sense of ethical and spiritual purpose. It can be a wonderful time to be an actor if you make it so.

SAMPLE SCENES

FROM *CHEERS*
BY TOM REEDER[1]

Note: Carla works as a waitress in the Cheers bar, where her boss is Diane. In this scene, Carla has just received an offer of marriage from Ben Ludlow, an eminent psychologist she has been dating. She has reacted strangely to the proposal and has gone into the back room to think. Diane follows her to see what's wrong.

[*Int. Pool Room Carla is standing lost in thought.
Diane enters.*]

DIANE:

Carla, I couldn't help noticing that you're not exactly leaping for joy. Bennett Ludlow is a wonderful catch.

CARLA:

[*With difficulty*] There are things he doesn't know about me.

DIANE:

A little mystery is good for a marriage. What haven't you told him?

CARLA:

Well, I haven't been completely honest about my kids.

DIANE:

What haven't you told him about them?

CARLA:

That they live.

DIANE:

He doesn't know you have children?

CARLA:

Shhhhh.

DIANE:

Carla, you have to tell him. He's going to wonder who those little people are running around the house.

CARLA:

I'm hoping he'll be too polite to ask.

[*Off Diane's look.*]

CARLA (*cont'd*):

I didn't want to scare him off.

DIANE:

Seriously, Carla, it's only fair that you tell him immediately that you have five children.

CARLA:

Six.

DIANE:

Okay, six. But if you wait, if you put this off—I thought it was five.

CARLA:

It was. But I just came from the doctor.

[*Diane groans with recognition.*]

DIANE:

Carla, when you took hygiene in high school, did you cut the "how-not-to" lecture?

CARLA:

I had to. I was pregnant. I tell you I'm the most fertile woman who ever lived. For me there's only one method of birth control that's absolutely foolproof, but it makes me sick to my stomach.

DIANE:

What's that?

CARLA:

Saying no.

[*Ludlow enters.*]

LUDLOW:

Carla, are you all right?

DIANE:

Well, I'm going to go celebrate with the others. We're like a big family here at Cheers. You know what they say about a big family—more to love. I always say—

CARLA:

Beat it.

DIANE:

Bye.

[*Diane exits.*]

LUDLOW:

Carla, my proposal wasn't received with the enthusiasm I expected it to be. In fact, it occurred to me that I never actually heard you say "yes."

CARLA:

I know. Benny, I have to tell you some things about myself.

LUDLOW:

This sounds serious.

CARLA:

It is. Benny, have you ever seen "The Brady Bunch"?

LUDLOW:

Yes, I think so.

CARLA:

Picture them with knives.

LUDLOW:

I don't understand.

CARLA:

I have five children.

LUDLOW:

Five?

CARLA:

Well…five and counting. You're going to be a daddy.

[*Ludlow sits down.*]

LUDLOW:

This is quite a day.

CARLA:

You now have my permission to withdraw the proposal.

LUDLOW:

Do you want me to withdraw the proposal, Carla?

CARLA:

I want you to do what you want to do.

LUDLOW:

I want to marry you.

CARLA:

You're kidding. Wow. What class.

LUDLOW:

I still haven't heard you say yes.

CARLA:

I know. [*Genuinely puzzled*] Why do you think that is?

LUDLOW:

I think if you examine your feelings, you'll know.

CARLA:

Yeah, I guess I know. I love somebody else.

LUDLOW:

Who?

CARLA:

I don't know his name. I haven't met him yet, but I've had this real clear picture of him in my mind for what seems like forever. He's going to walk into this bar some night.

Actually, not walk. More like swagger. You know, confident but not cocky.

He's okay-looking, but he's no pretty boy. He's a swell dresser. He's wearing this burgundy leather jacket. His nose is broken in all the right places. He's got this scar on his chin he won't talk about. He cracks his knuckles all the time. Drives me up the wall, but, what can you do? Doesn't talk much. Doesn't have to. He falls for me hard. I hurt him a few times. He gets over it. We get married.

[*She turns to Ludlow.*]

CARLA (*cont'd*):

So you see, it would be kind of messy if I was already married when he gets here.

LUDLOW:

You know something, Carla? I sort of have a dream girl myself.

CARLA:

What's she like?

LUDLOW:

She's a spunky, hearty, little curly-haired spitfire, who doesn't know what's good for her.

CARLA:

I hope you find her some day.

LUDLOW:

Me too. And I want you to know I intend to take care of this child financially.

CARLA:

You bet your buns you will, Benny Baby.

[*He exits. Carla stands there considering her fate.*]

FROM *ZOOT SUIT*
BY LUIS VALDEZ[2]

Note: *This 1978 play chronicles a real event, the 1943 trial of a Mexican American gang for murder. Fueled by war hysteria and racist fear of the "Pachucos" with their long hair and zoot suits, the trial was a travesty, resulting in life sentences for the boys (later overturned on appeal). The play uses narration, direct address to the audience, and other techniques that make special demands on the actor. In this scene, the hero's girlfriend testifies in court about the night of the murder. The end of the scene has been modified to eliminate several other characters who enter and act out the murder scene.*

DELLA: After the dance that Saturday night, Henry and I drove out to the Sleepy Lagoon about eleven-thirty. There was a full moon that night, and as we drove up to the Lagoon we noticed right away the place was empty…(*A pair of headlights silently pulls in from the black background upstage center.*) Henry parked the car on the bank of the reservoir and we relaxed. (*Headlights go off.*) It was such a warm, beautiful night, and the sky was so full of stars, we couldn't just sit in the car. So we got out, and Henry took my hand…(*Henry stands and takes Della's hand.*) We went for a walk around the Lagoon. Neither of us said anything at first, so the only sounds we could hear were the crickets and the frogs…(*Sounds of crickets and frogs, then music faintly in the background.*) When we got to the other side of the reservoir, we began to hear music, so I asked Henry, what's that?

HENRY: Sounds like they're having a party.

DELLA: Where?

HENRY: Over at the Williams' Ranch. See the house lights.

DELLA: Who lives there?

HENRY: A couple of families. Mexicanos. I think they work on the ranch. You know, their name used to be Gonzales, but they changed it to Williams.

DELLA: Why?

HENRY: I don't know. Maybe they think it gives 'em more class. (*We hear Mexican music.*) Ay, jijo. They're probably celebrating a wedding or something.

DELLA: As soon as he said wedding, he stopped talking and we both knew why. He had something on his mind, something he was trying to tell me without sounding like a square.

HENRY: Della ... what are you going to do if I don't come back from the war?

DELLA: That wasn't the question I was expecting, so I answered something dumb, like I don't know, what's going to keep you from coming back?

HENRY: Maybe wanting too much out of life, see? Ever since I was a kid, I've had this feeling like there's a big party going on someplace, and I'm invited, but I don't know how to get there. And I want to get there so bad, I'll even risk my life to make it. Sounds crazy, huh? (*Della and Henry kiss. They embrace and then Henry speaks haltingly.*) If I get back from the war ... will you marry me?

DELLA: Yes! (*She embraces him and almost causes them to topple over*).

HENRY: ¡Orale! You'll knock us into the Lagoon. Listen, what about your old man? He ain't going to like you marrying me.

DELLA: I know. But I don't care. I'll go to hell with you *if* you want me to.

HENRY: ¿Sabes qué? I'm going to give you the biggest Pachuco wedding L.A. has ever seen. (*Another pair of headlights comes in from the left. Della goes back to her narration.*)

DELLA: Just then another car pulled up to the Lagoon. It was Rafas and some drunk guys in a gang from Downey. They got out and started to bust the windows on Henry's car. Henry yelled at them, and they started cussing at us. I told Henry not to say anything, but he cussed them back!

HENRY: You stay here, Della.

DELLA: Henry, no! Don't go down there! Please don't go down there!

HENRY: Can't you hear what they're doing to my car?

DELLA: There's too many of them. They'll kill you!

HENRY: ¡Chale! (*Henry turns and runs upstage, where he stops in a freeze.*)

DELLA: Henry! Henry ran down the back of the Lagoon and attacked the gang by himself. Rafas had about ten guys with him and they jumped on Henry like a pack of dogs. He fought them off as long as he could, then they threw him on the ground hard and kicked him until he passed out.... (*Headlights pull off.*) After they left, I ran down to Henry and held him in my arms until he came to. And I could tell he was hurt, but the first thing he said was...

HENRY: Let's go into town and get the guys. (*Music: Glen Miller's "In the Mood."*)

DELLA: It took us about an hour to go into town and come back. We got to the Lagoon with about eight cars, but the Downey gang wasn't there. That's when we heard music coming from the Williams' Ranch again. We didn't know Rafas and his gang had been there too, causing trouble. We all went there yelling and laughing. At the Williams' Ranch they saw us coming and thought we were the Downey Gang coming back again … They attacked us. An old man ran out of the house with a kitchen knife and Henry had to hit him. Then a girl grabbed me by the hair and in a second everybody was fighting! People were grabbing sticks from the fence, bottles, anything! It all happened so fast, we didn't know what hit us, but Henry said let's go!

HENRY: ¡Vámonos! Let's get out of here.

DELLA: And we started to back off… Before we got to the cars, I saw something out of the corner of my eye … It was a guy. He was hitting a man on the ground with a big stick. Henry called to him, but he wouldn't stop. He wouldn't stop … He wouldn't stop … He wouldn't stop … (*Della in tears, holds Henry in her arms.*) Driving back in the car, everybody was quiet, like nothing had happened. We didn't know José Williams had died at the party that night and that the guys would be arrested the next day for murder. (*Henry separates from her and goes back to stand in his place. Della resumes the witness stand.*)

USEFUL PLAYS

The following plays are good sources of scenes with the qualities most useful for this book. Most of them are available in inexpensive paperback "acting editions" if the publisher is indicated. There are also a number of anthologies of scenes for student actors on the market. One useful reference book that indexes scenes in a variety of ways (male–male, female–male, female–female, and by genre and ethnicity) is *The Ultimate Scene and Monologue Source Book* by Ed Hooks (New York: Backstage Books, 1994).

Absence of War by David Hare
After the Fall by Arthur Miller (Dramatists Play Service)
Ah, Wilderness! by Eugene O'Neill (Samuel French)
Albertine, in Five Times by Michel Tremblay
All My Sons by Arthur Miller (Dramatists Play Service)
The Amen Corner by James Baldwin (Samuel French)
American Buffalo by David Mamet (Samuel French)
The Andersonville Trial by Saul Levitt (Dramatists Play Service)
And Miss Reardon Drinks a Little by Paul Zindel (Dramatists Play Service)
Angels in America by Tony Kushner (Theatre Communications Group)
Anna Christie by Eugene O'Neill (Vintage Books)
Arcadia by Tom Stoppard
Balm in Gilead by Lanford Wilson
Bedrooms: Five Comedies by Renée Taylor and Joseph Bologna (Samuel French)
Bent by Martin Sherman (Samuel French)
Birdbath by Leonard Melfi (Samuel French)
Born Yesterday by Garson Kanin (Dramatists Play Service)
Brighton Beach Memoirs by Neil Simon
Career Girls by Mike Leigh
The Caretaker by Harold Pinter
Cat on a Hot Tin Roof by Tennessee Williams (Dramatists Play Service)
Cell Mates by Simon Gray
Ceremonies in Dark Old Men by Lonne Elder III
Chapter Two by Neil Simon (Samuel French)
The Chase by Horton Foote (Dramatists Play Service)
The Children's Hour by Lillian Hellman (Dramatists Play Service)
Cloud Nine by Caryl Churchill
The Colored Museum by George C. Wolfe (Broadway Play Publishing)
Come Back, Little Sheba by William Inge (Samuel French)

Come Back to the 5 & Dime, Jimmy Dean, Jimmy Dean by Ed Graczyk (Samuel French)
Comedians by Trevor Griffiths
A Coupla White Chicks Sitting Around Talking by John Ford Noonan (Samuel French)
Crimes of the Heart by Beth Henley (Dramatists Play Service)
Crossing Delancey by Susan Sandler (Samuel French)
The Crucible by Arthur Miller (Dramatists Play Service)
The Dark at the Top of the Stairs by William Inge (Dramatists Play Service)
A Day in the Death of Joe Egg by Peter Nichols (Samuel French)
Death and the Maiden by Ariel Dorfman
Death of a Salesman by Arthur Miller (Dramatists Play Service)
The Death of Bessie Smith by Edward Albee (Plume)
Dejavu by John Osborne
A Delicate Balance by Edward Albee (Samuel French)
Division Street by Steve Tesich (Samuel French)
Duet for One by Tom Kempinski (Samuel French)
The Eccentricities of a Nightingale by Tennessee Williams (Dramatists Play Service)
Ecstasy of Rita Joe by George Ryga
Effect of Gamma Rays on Man-in-the-Moon Marigolds by Paul Zindel (Bantam)
Enter Laughing by Joseph Stein (Samuel French)
Extremities by William Mastrosimone (Samuel French)
Fences by August Wilson (Samuel French)
Fool for Love by Sam Shepard (Dramatists Play Service)
Frankie and Johnny in the Clair de Lune by Terrence McNally (Dramatists Play Service)
The Gingerbread Lady by Neil Simon (Samuel French)
The Glass Menagerie by Tennessee Williams (Dramatists Play Service)
Glengarry Glen Ross by David Mamet (Samuel French)
Golden Boy by Clifford Odets (Dramatists Play Service)
A Hatful of Rain by Michael Vincente Gazzo (Samuel French)
The Heidi Chronicles by Wendy Wasserstein (Dramatists Play Service)
The House of Blue Leaves by John Guare (Samuel French)
The Immigrant by Mark Harelik (Broadway Play Publishing)
I Never Sang for My Father by Robert Anderson (Dramatists Play Service)
I Ought to Be in Pictures by Neil Simon (Samuel French)
It Had to Be You by Renée Taylor and Joseph Bologna (Samuel French)
Joe Turner's Come and Gone by August Wilson
Jumpers by Tom Stoppard
Kiss of the Spider Woman by Manuel Puig
Last of the Red Hot Lovers by Neil Simon
Last Summer at Bluefish Cove by Jane Chambers (JH Press)
Laundry and Bourbon by James McLure (Dramatists Play Service)
A Lie of the Mind by Sam Shepard (Dramatists Play Service)
A Life in the Theatre by David Mamet
The Little Foxes by Lillian Hellman (Dramatists Play Service)
Long Day's Journey into Night by Eugene O'Neill (Yale University Press)
Look Homeward, Angel by Ketti Frings (Samuel French)
Lost in Yonkers by Neil Simon (Samuel French)
Love in Vain: A Vision of Robert Johnson by Alan Greenberg
Lovers and Other Strangers by Renée Taylor and Joseph Bologna (Samuel French)

Luv by Murray Schisgal (Dramatists Play Service)
The Madman and the Nun by Stanislaw Witkiewicz
Ma Rainey's Black Bottom by August Wilson
Marvin's Room by Scott McPherson
Master Class by Terrence McNally
Master Harold and the Boys by Athol Fugard
The Matchmaker by Thornton Wilder (Samuel French)
Member of the Wedding by Carson McCullers
The Middle Ages by A. R. Gurney, Jr. (Dramatists Play Service)
The Miracle Worker by William Gibson
Moonchildren by Michael Weller (Samuel French)
A Moon for the Misbegotten by Eugene O'Neill (Samuel French)
Murder at the Howard Johnson's by Ron Clark and Sam Bobrick (Samuel French)
The Nerd by Larry Shue (Dramatists Play Service)
'Night, Mother by Marsha Norman (Dramatists Play Service)
The Night of the Iguana by Tennessee Williams (Dramatists Play Service)
No Exit by Jean Paul Sartre
No Place to Be Somebody by Charles Gordone (Samuel French)
The Odd Couple (Female Version) by Neil Simon (Samuel French)
The Odd Couple (Male Version) by Neil Simon (Samuel French)
Of Mice and Men by John Steinbeck (Dramatists Play Service)
Oh Dad, Poor Dad, Mamma's Hung You in the Closet and I'm Feelin' So Sad by Arthur Kopit
     (Samuel French)
Old Times by Harold Pinter
The Only Game in Town by Frank D. Gilroy (Samuel French)
On the Open Road by Steve Tesich (Samuel French)
The Philadelphia Story by Philip Barry (Samuel French)
Picasso at the Lapin Agile by Steve Martin
Picnic by William Inge (Dramatists Play Service)
The Prisoner of Second Avenue by Neil Simon (Samuel French)
The Rainmaker by N. Richard Nash (Samuel French)
A Raisin in the Sun by Lorraine Hansberry (Samuel French)
The Red Coat by John Patrick Shanley (Dramatists Play Service)
Scenes from American Life by A. R. Gurney, Jr. (Samuel French)
The Sea Horse by Edward J. Moore (Samuel French)
Sexual Perversity in Chicago by David Mamet (Samuel French)
The Shadow Box by Michael Cristofer (Samuel French)
The Sign in Sidney Brustein's Window by Lorraine Hansberry (Samuel French)
Six Degrees of Separation by John Guare (Dramatists Play Service)
So Sad by Arthur Kopit (Samuel French)
Speed-the-Plow by David Mamet (Samuel French)
Splendor in the Grass by William Inge (Dramatists Play Service)
Spoils of War by Michael Weller (Samuel French)
Steel Magnolias by Robert Harling (Dramatists Play Service)
Strange Snow by Stephen Metcalfe (Samuel French)
A Streetcar Named Desire by Tennessee Williams (Dramatists Play Service)
The Subject Was Roses by Frank D. Gilroy (Samuel French)
Summer and Smoke by Tennessee Williams (Dramatists Play Service)

Sweet Bird of Youth by Tennessee Williams (Dramatists Play Service)
The Tenth Man by Paddy Chayefsky (Samuel French)
That Championship Season by Jason Miller (Samuel French)
The Time of Your Life by William Saroyan (Samuel French)
To Gillian on her 37th Birthday by Michael Brady (Broadway Play Publishing)
A Touch of the Poet by Eugene O'Neill (Random House)
Toys in the Attic by Lillian Hellman (Dramatists Play Service)
Tribute by Bernard Slade (Samuel French)
True West by Sam Shepard (Samuel French)
Twice around the Park by Murray Schisgal (Samuel French)
A View from the Bridge by Arthur Miller (Dramatists Play Service)
Vikings by Stephen Metcalfe (Samuel French)
Waiting for Lefty by Clifford Odets (Grove Press)
Welcome to the Dollhouse by Todd Solondz
What I Did Last Summer by A. R. Gurney, Jr. (Dramatists Play Service)
When You Comin' Back, Red Ryder? by Mark Medoff (Dramatists Play Service)
Who's Afraid of Virginia Woolf? by Edward Albee (Dramatists Play Service)
The Women by Clare Boothe Luce (Dramatists Play Service)
The Zoo Story by Edward Albee (Dramatists Play Service)

AN ACTING CHECKLIST

Here is a checklist that summarizes the material on action we covered in Part II. These are the questions you should ask yourself in the earliest phases of your rehearsal process.

I. The Givens: What, Who, Where, When

A. *What* happens in this scene?

1. What is the *main event* of the scene? How does it move the plot of the play forward? How does it contribute to the play's meaning?
2. What *changes* in the world of the play as a result of this scene?

B. *Who* is in this scene?

1. What is the *general* relationship?
2. What is the *specific* relationship?
3. Does your relationship *change* in this scene?
4. What is discovered about your character in this scene?

C. *Where* is this scene?

1. How does the *physical* environment influence what happens?
2. How does the *social* environment influence what happens?

D. *When* is this scene?

1. How does the *historical* time influence the scene?
2. How does the *season of the year* influence the scene?
3. How does the *time of day* influence the scene?

II. Scene Structure

A. What is the *main conflict* of this scene? How does it relate to the overall conflict of the play?

B. What is the *breakdown* of the scene, beat by beat? Be specific about each beat change.

C. What is the *crisis,* the moment after which the conflict must be resolved?

D. How does this scene grow out of preceding scenes? How does this scene lead into following scenes?

III. Objectives

A. What is your *superobjective?*

B. What is your *scene* objective? How does it relate to your superobjective?

C. Break down your *beat objectives* in sequence. Do you begin to feel the logic of their sequence, the *score?*

D. Examine the sequence of your *immediate* objectives through the scene. Express each in a transitive verb as "SIP" (singular, immediate, and personally important); try to think of each as a desired change in the other character.

BIBLIOGRAPHY

Aristotle. *The Poetics,* trans. Kenneth A. Telford. Chicago: Gateway, 1961.

Artaud, Antonin. *The Theatre and Its Double.* New York: Grove Press, 1958.

Bach, George. *Aggression Lab.* Dubuque, IA: Kendall/Hunt, 1971.

Bacon, Wallace A., and Robert S. Breen. *Literature as Experience.* New York: McGraw-Hill, 1959.

Ball, David. *Backwards and Forwards: A Technical Manual for Reading Plays.* Carbondale: Southern Illinois University Press, 1983.

Barton, John. *Playing Shakespeare.* London and New York: Metheun, 1984.

Bates, Brian. *The Way of the Actor.* Boston: Shambhala, 1987.

Beck, Julian. *The Life of the Theatre.* San Francisco: City Lights Books, 1972.

Beckerman, Bernard. *Dynamics of Drama.* New York: Drama Book Publishers, 1979.

Benedetti, Robert. *Action! Acting for Film and Television.* Boston: Allyn & Bacon, 2001.

———— *The Actor in You: Sixteen Simple Steps to Understanding the Art of Acting.* Boston: Allyn & Bacon, 1999.

———— *The Director at Work.* Englewood Cliffs, NJ: Prentice-Hall, 1984.

Berne, Eric. *Games People Play.* New York: Grove Press, 1964.

Berry, Cicely. *Text in Action.* London: Virgin Publishing, 2001.

———— *Voice and the Actor.* New York: Wiley Publishing, 1973.

Birdwhistell, Raymond. *Introduction to Kinesics.* Louisville, KY: University of Louisville Press, 1957.

Boleslavsky, Richard. *Acting: The First Six Lessons.* New York: Theatre Arts Books, 1933.

Branden, Nathaniel. *The Disowned Self.* New York: Bantam, 1973.

———— *The Psychology of Self-Esteem.* New York: Bantam, 1971.

Braun, Edward, trans. and ed. *Meyerhold on Theatre.* New York: Hill & Wang, 1969.

Brockett, Oscar G. *The Theatre: An Introduction,* 4th ed. New York: Holt, Rinehart & Winston, 1979.

Brook, Peter. *The Empty Space.* New York: Atheneum, 1968.

Bullough, Edward. *Aesthetics.* Stanford, CA: Stanford University Press, 1957.

Burns, David D. *Feeling Good.* New York: Signet, 1980.

Campbell, Joseph. *The Masks of God.* New York: Viking, 1959.

Cassirer, Ernst. *The Philosophy of Symbolic Forms,* trans. Ralph Manheim. New Haven, CT: Yale University Press, 1953.

Chaikin, Joseph. *The Presence of the Actor.* New York: Atheneum, 1972.

Chekhov, Michael. *To the Actor.* New York: Harper & Row, 1953.

Cohen, Robert. *Acting Power.* Palo Alto, CA: Mayfield, 1978.

Cole, Toby, ed. *Acting: A Handbook of the Stanislavski Method.* New York: Crown, 1971.

Cole, Toby, and Helen Chinoy, eds. *Actors on Acting.* New York: Crown, 1970.

Crawford, Jerry. *Acting in Person and in Style,* 3rd ed. Dubuque, IA: Wm. C. Brown, 1983.

Dewey, John. *Experience and Nature.* La Salle, IL.: Open Court, 1925.

Ernst, Earle. *The Kabuki Theatre.* New York: Grove Press, 1956.

Esslin, Martin. *Brecht: The Man and His Work.* New York: Doubleday, 1960.

———— *The Theatre of the Absurd.* New York: Doubleday, 1961.

Feldenkrais, Moshe. *Awareness through Movement.* New York: Harper & Row, 1972.

Gielgud, John. *An Actor and His Time.* New York: Penguin, 1981.

Goffman, Erving. *The Presentation of Self in Everyday Life.* New York: Doubleday, 1959.

Gorchakov, Nikolai. *Stanislavski Directs.* New York: Funk & Wagnalls, 1954.

Green, Michael. *Downwind of Upstage.* New York: Hawthorn, 1964.

Grotowski, Jerzy. *Towards a Poor Theatre.* New York: Simon & Schuster, 1968.

Guthrie, Tyrone. *Tyrone Guthrie on Acting.* New York: Viking, 1971.

Hagen, Uta. *Respect for Acting.* New York: Macmillan, 1973.

Hall, Edward. *The Silent Language.* New York: Doubleday, 1959.

Halprin, Lawrence. *The RSVP Cycles.* New York: George Braziller, 1969.

Harrop, John, and Sabin Epstein. *Acting with Style.* Englewood Cliffs, NJ: Prentice-Hall, 1982.

Herrigel, Eugen. *Zen in the Art of Archery.* New York: Vintage, 1971.

Jacobson, Edmund. *Progressive Relaxation.* Chicago: University of Chicago Press, 1938.

Johnstone, Keith. *Impro: Improvisation and the Theatre.* New York: Theatre Arts Books, 1983.

Jones, Frank Pierce. *Body Awareness in Action.* New York: Schocken Books, 1976.

Joseph, Bertram. *Acting Shakespeare.* New York: Theatre Arts Books, 1960.

Kalter, Joanmarie. *Actors on Acting.* New York: Sterling, 1978.

Kirby, E. T., ed. *Total Theatre.* New York: Dutton, 1969.

Kuritz, Paul. *Playing.* Englewood Cliffs, NJ: Prentice-Hall, 1982.

Lang, R. D. *The Politics of Experience.* New York: Ballantine, 1967.

Lao Tsu. *Tao Te Ching,* trans. Gia Fu Feng and Jane English. New York: Vintage, 1972.

Lessac, Arthur. *Body Wisdom: The Use and Training of the Human Body.* New York: Drama Book Specialists, 1978.

———— *The Use and Training of the Human Voice.* New York: Mayfield/McGraw-Hill, 1981.

Lewis, Robert. *Advice to Players.* New York: Harper & Row, 1980.

———— *Method or Madness?* London: Heinemann, 1960.

Linklater, Kristin. *Freeing the Natural Voice.* New York: Drama Book Specialists, 1976.

Lowen, Alexander. *The Language of the Body.* New York: Collier, 1971.

Mamet, David. *Writing in Restaurants.* New York: Viking Penguin, 1986.

Maslov, Abraham. *Motivation and Personality.* New York: Harper & Row, 1954.

May, Rollo. *The Courage to Create.* New York: Norton, 1975.

O'Connor, Gary. *Ralph Richardson: An Actor's Life.* New York: Atheneum, 1982.

Olivier, Laurence. *Confessions of an Actor.* New York: Simon & Schuster, 1982.

Otto, Walter. *Dionysus.* Bloomington: Indiana University Press, 1965.

Perls, Frederick S., Ralph F. Hefferline, and Paul Goodman. *Gestalt Therapy.* New York: Julian Press, 1951.

Ram, Dass. *Be Here Now.* New Mexico: Lama Foundation, 1971.

———— *The Only Dance There Is.* New York: Doubleday/Anchor, 1974.

Redgrave, Michael. *In My Mind's I.* New York: Viking, 1983.

Richards, Mary Caroline. *Centering.* Wesleyan, CT: Wesleyan University Press, 1964.

Rodenburg, Patsy. *The Actor Speaks.* New York: Palgrave Macmillan, 2000.

Sainer, Arthur. *The Radical Theatre Notebook.* New York: Discus/Avon, 1975.

St. Denis, Michel. *Theatre: The Rediscovery of Style.* New York: Theatre Arts Books, 1960.

Sapir, Edward. *Language.* New York: Harcourt, Brace & World, 1949.

Schechner, Richard. *Environmental Theatre.* New York: Hawthorn, 1973.

Schlauch, Margaret. *The Gift of Language.* New York: Dover, 1955.

Shurtleff, Michael. *Audition.* New York: Walker & Co., 1978.

Spolin, Viola. *Improvisation for the Theatre.* Evanston, IL.: Northwestern University Press, 1963.

Stanislavski, Constantin. *An Actor Prepares,* trans. Elizabeth Reynolds Hapgood. New York: Theatre Arts Books, 1936.

―――― *An Actor's Handbook,* trans. and ed. Elizabeth Reynolds Hapgood. New York: Theatre Arts Books, 1936.

―――― *Building a Character,* trans. Elizabeth Reynolds Hapgood. New York: Theatre Arts Books, 1949.

―――― *Creating A Role,* trans. Elizabeth Reynolds Hapgood. New York: Theatre Arts Books, 1949.

―――― *My Life in Art,* trans. J. J. Robbins. New York: Theatre Arts Books, 1952.

Suzuki, D. T. *Zen Buddhism.* New York: Doubleday/Anchor, 1956.

Suzuki, Shunrya. *Zen Mind, Beginner's Mind.* New York: Weatherhill, 1970.

Trungpa, Chogyam. *Cutting through Spiritual Materialism.* Berkeley, CA: Shambhala, 1973.

Watts, Alan. *The Book: On the Taboo against Knowing Who You Are.* New York: Random House, 1972.

Wellek, Rene, and Austin Warren. *Theory of Literature.* New York: Harvest/Harcourt, Brace & Co., 1942.

Willet, John, ed. *Brecht on Theatre.* New York: Hill & Wang, 1964.

NOTES

LESSON ONE

1. Erving Goffman, *The Presentation of Self in Everyday Life* (New York: Double-day, 1959), pp. 71–74. Copyright © by Erving Goffman.
2. Brian Bates, *The Way of the Actor* (Boston: Shambhala, 1987), p. 7.
3. Bates, p. 114.
4. Bates, p. 9.
5. From an interview.
6. Constantin Stanislavski, *My Life in Art,* trans. J. J. Robbins (New York: Theatre Arts Books, 1952). Copyright © 1924 by Little, Brown & Co., and 1952 by Elizabeth Reynolds Hapgood.
7. David Mamet, *Writing in Restaurants* (New York: Viking Penguin, 1986), p. 116. Copyright © 1986 by David Mamet. All rights reserved.

LESSON TWO

1. Frederick S. Perls, Ralph F. Hefferline, and Paul Goodman, *Gestalt Therapy* (New York: Julian Press, 1951), p. 134 (Dell Paperback, 1964).
2. Mary Caroline Richards, *Centering in Pottery, Poetry, and the Person* (Wesleyan, CT: Wesleyan University Press, 1964), p. 38–39. Copyright © by Mary Caroline Richards.
3. Perls, Hefferline, and Goodman, p. 33.

LESSON THREE

1. Richards, p. 25.

LESSON FOUR

1. Raymond Birdwhistell, *Introduction to Kinesics* (Louisville, KY: University of Louisville Press, 1957), pp. 29–30.
2. Edward T. Hall, *The Silent Language* (New York: Doubleday, 1959), p. 43. Copyright © 1959 by Edward T. Hall.
3. Hall, p. 42.
4. Wallace A. Bacon and Robert S. Breen, *Literature as Experience* (New York: McGraw-Hill, 1959), p. 32.

LESSON FIVE

1. Margaret Schlauch, *The Gift of Language* (New York: Dover, 1955), p. 3.
2. Edward Sapir, *Language* (New York: Harcourt, Brace & World, 1949), pp. 8–9.
3. Sapir, p. 5.
4. Bacon and Breen, p. 286.

LESSON SIX

1. Ernst Cassirer, *The Philosophy of Symbolic Forms,* trans. Ralph Manheim (New Haven, CT: Yale University Press, 1953), p. 148.

LESSON SEVEN

1. August Strindberg, "Notes to the Members of the Intimate Theatre," trans. Everett Sprinchorn, *The Tulane Drama Review,* 6, no. 2 (November 1961), p. 157. This material is also copyrighted by The Drama Review, 1967.

LESSON NINE

1. Constantin Stanislavski, *An Actor's Handbook,* trans. and ed. Elizabeth Reynolds Hapgood (New York: Theatre Arts Books, 1936), p. 8. Copyright © 1936, 1961, 1963 by Elizabeth Reynolds Hapgood. Theatre Arts Books, 153 Waverly Place, New York, NY 10014.
2. Constantin Stanislavski, *Building a Character,* trans. Elizabeth Reynolds Hapgood (New York: Theatre Arts Books, 1949), pp. 218–36. Theatre Arts Books, 153 Waverly Place, New York, NY 10014.
3. Constantin Stanislavski, *Creating a Role,* trans. Elizabeth Reynolds Hapgood (New York: Theatre Arts Books, 1961), p. 62.
4. Stanislavski, *Actor's Handbook,* p. 9.

LESSON TEN

1. Stanislavski, *Actor's Handbook,* p. 9.
2. Mamet, pp. 26–27.

LESSON ELEVEN

1. Stanislavski, *Actor's Handbook,* p. 138.

LESSON FOURTEEN

1. Stanislavski, *Actor's Handbook,* pp. 137–38.

LESSON FIFTEEN

1. Oscar G. Brockett, *The Theatre: An Introduction,* 3rd ed. (New York: Holt, Rinehart & Winston, 1974), pp. 39–40.
2. Brockett, pp. 39–40.

LESSON SIXTEEN

1. Mamet, p. 76.
2. Jan Kott, "King Lear or Endgame," *The Evergreen Review* (August–September 1964), p. 55.
3. Moshe Feldenkrais, *Awareness through Movement* (New York: Harper & Row, 1972), pp. 45–46.

LESSON SEVENTEEN

1. Stanislavski, *Building a Character,* pp. 218–36.
2. Stanislavski, *Building a Character,* pp. 218–36.
3. Stanislavski, *Building a Character,* pp. 218–36.
4. Stanislavski, *Building a Character,* pp. 218–36.
5. Stanislavski, *Building a Character,* pp. 218–36.

LESSON EIGHTEEN

1. Alexander Lowen, *The Language of the Body* (New York: Collier, 1971), p. 32.
2. This list is adapted from Nathaniel Branden, *The Disowned Self* (New York: Bantam, 1973), pp. 111–114.

LESSON NINETEEN

1. David D. Burns, *Feeling Good* (New York: Signet, 1980), pp. 11–12.
2. Stanislavski, *Actor's Handbook,* p. 56.
3. Mamet, p. 127.
4. Stanislavski, *Building a Character,* p. 70.
5. Stanislavski, *Building a Character,* p. 70.

LESSON TWENTY-THREE

1. Strindberg, p. 157.
2. Quoted in an interview.
3. Mamet, pp. 20–21.
4. Mamet, p. 19.
5. Mamet, p. 21.
6. Stanislavski, *My Life in Art,* pp. 217–218.

AFTERWORD

1. Gorchakov, pp. 40–41.

APPENDIX A

1. From "Whodunit," by Tom Reeder, *Cheers* Episode #60593-057, 1984. Used by permission of Paramount Pictures Corporation.
2. From *Zoot Suit* by Luis Valdez. Reprinted with permission from the publisher of *Zoot Suit and Other Plays* (Houston: Arte Publico Press–University of Houston, 1992).

A GLOSSARY OF ACTING TERMS

action used in two ways: in a play or film script, the dramatic action is what happens in the story or scene in the most fundamental sense. For the actor, the action is what his or her character does to try to fulfill a need by winning some objective. Stanislavski spoke of both Spiritual (inner) and Physical (outer) action. Note that speaking is one of the most common forms of action; that is, a saying is also a doing. To be "in action" is to be totally involved in the task at hand and is the most desirable condition for the actor. Action is the most fundamental concept behind most systems of acting. *See also* Automatic Action, Choice, Indirect Action, Inner Action, Justifying, Motivation, Objective, Reacting, Score, Stimulus, Strategy, Suppression, and Verb.

ad lib to insert words of your own into a script, usually on the spur of the moment.

AFTRA American Federation of Television and Radio Artists. The union that once covered radio acting and some television shows; it has now merged with the Screen Actors Guild. *See* SAG.

agent someone who represents actors and tries to get them work. An agent normally gets 10 percent commission on everything an actor makes. In film and television, actors are usually auditioned only when submitted by a licensed agent, so getting an agent is often the first step in initiating a professional film or television career.

attitude the way your character feels about something that has happened.

automatic action Stanislavski's term for what is generally called a habit or reflex; something your character does without thinking.

beat a unit of action with its own specific conflict and crisis. In each beat, your character will have a single objective. Beats are formed of moments and flow to create the underlying structure of a scene. The term may have been created by someone with a Russian accent saying *bit* of action, though it makes sense as a unit of rhythm (as in *downbeat*) because the beats' flow is the primary rhythm of a scene.

beat change when one of the characters changes his or her strategy or objective, moving the scene in a new direction. A beat change results from either an automatic action or a deliberate choice made by one of the characters.

believability something consistent with the created reality and style of the world of the story and the personality of the character, whether it is like everyday life or not.

bio *See* Résumé.

blocking establishing the positions and movements of the characters on the stage or in relation to the camera. Good blocking should express the underlying action of the scene. *See also* Mark.

breakdown *See* Scenario.

call the time an actor is to report for work. Missing a call is a serious offense. In the theater, calls are posted on the call board; in film and television, they are announced on a call sheet distributed near the end of each day's shooting for the following day.

callback in the audition process, there are usually preliminary auditions from which a small number of actors are called back for a final decision.

casting director preliminary auditions, especially in film and television, are usually conducted by a casting director, who then selects the actors for callbacks with the director or producer. Casting directors are extremely important to actors starting out and can be more important to the establishment of a career than agents.

cheating out standing so that your face is turned slightly toward the audience or camera. More important on stage than in film.

choice When pursuing a need, your character may consider several alternative courses of action, then make a strategic choice, which appears to hold out the best chance of success. Examining your character's significant choices can give you a wealth of information about him or her.

climax the "main event" that is the resolution of the underlying conflict of a story and is therefore the end of suspense. Scenes normally do not have climaxes, since the suspense of the story must carry on into the next scene.

continuity in film and television, making sure that every detail of a shot matches the shots that may precede or follow it. The actor will have to be aware, for instance, whether the right hand was over the left, how much liquid was in a glass, and so on. Continuity is the responsibility of the script supervisor, an unsung hero who remembers details like these even days later.

costume parade in the theater, the first showing of the costumes on the set and under lights for approval by the director.

coverage In film, a scene will often be shot from a wide perspective called the "master"; the camera will then be repositioned for tighter shots called "coverage," which the editor will later insert into the master. This means that the actor's performance in coverage must match the master. It also means that the "close-ups," which are the most demanding on actors, are shot hours after the master, and actors have to be careful to "save" something for them.

crisis the event in a story after which the outcome becomes—in hindsight—inevitable. Before this point, the energy of the story rises in suspense; during the crisis, the outcome hangs in the balance; after the crisis, the energy flows toward resolution. Although a crisis (or "turning point") will lead to a climax it is not always the same thing as the climax and is often not the emotional high point of the story. A scene will have a crisis in which the main issue of that scene is decided. A beat will also have a crisis just before the beat change.

cross when the actor moves from point A to point B. Such movements need to be justified by some inner need. There are different kinds of crosses, such as the "banana," which is a slight curve so that the actor ends cheated out.

cue anything that causes something to happen. For the actor, it refers to the line or event just before his or her character speaks or moves. It can also refer to a change in the lighting or sound.

cueing the way one line follows another. In real life, we often overlap one another and begin responding slightly before the other person has finished. In film, overlapping is sometimes avoided because it limits the editor's ability to cut from take to take. (Cueing sometimes refers to helping an actor learn or remember lines by prompting him or her, as in "will you cue me?")

cue-to-cue   a frustrating form of technical rehearsal in which the actors are asked to jump from light cue to light cue. To be avoided if at all possible or conducted without the actors, since it is disruptive to the actors' experience of the rhythms of the show.

demonstration   Bertolt Brecht's idea that the actor does not "become" the character completely but, rather, "demonstrates" the character's behavior for the audience while still expressing some attitude about it. While this may sound like "indicating," the good Brechtian actor's passionate commitment to the ethical point being made gives the performance its own special kind of reality, whereas ordinary indicating feels merely empty and unreal.

denouement   French for "unraveling," that final portion of a story in which the loose ends are wrapped up.

deputy   in an Equity company, a member of the cast elected to serve as the representative of the actors to the management. *See* Equity.

downstage   At one time, stages were sloped to enhance the illusion of perspective, so moving toward the audience was literally to move "down" stage, and moving away from the audience was literally "up" stage. Even though stages today are rarely sloped (or "raked"), we still use this terminology.

dramatic   the quality of an event when the outcome is important and cannot be foretold. The essence is in wondering, "What will happen?" *See also* Suspense.

dramatic function   the job a character was created to do within the story; can be related to plot, meaning, the audience's understanding of the main character, or any combination of these.

dress rehearsal   the final rehearsals that are conducted under performance conditions.

dual consciousness   the actor's ability to be immersed in the character and the character's world while still reserving a level of awareness for artistic judgment. Different types of material make different demands on actors in this regard, with film requiring the virtual elimination of the actor's awareness in favor of the character's.

economy   doing enough to fulfill the dramatic function and believability of the character without extraneous details or effort.

emotion memory   the actor's application of some memory from the actor's real or imaginary past to enrich his or her response to the situation in the scene. While it may be useful in rehearsal, this device is never to be used in performance for fear of taking the actor out of the here and now. Also called *recall.*

empathy   actors' ability to put themselves in the place of another person, both for purposes of observation and for applying the Magic If to a role. It is possible to empathize with someone even if a person does not sympathize with him or her.

Equity   Actors Equity Association (AEA), the main theatrical union for actors. The Equity Rule Book establishes the conditions under which actors may work in the theater. When there is a grievance, it is reported to the elected Equity deputy.

exposition   providing information about what has happened before in order to help the audience understand what is going on in a story or scene. The difficulty in writing or playing exposition is to avoid interrupting the action by falling into an "informational" tone. One old piece of advice is to "make exposition ammunition"; that is, your character must have a reason for providing expository information, and it must be justified by inner need just like any other action.

extra   in film and television, a nonspeaking actor who rounds out the reality of a scene. In theater, once called *supernumerary*. Despite sometimes being called "scenery with mouths," professional extras in film are skilled workers who can repeat precise movements and blocking, and who know how to be believable without being distracting. Their union, the Screen Extras Guild (SEG), recently merged with the Screen Actors Guild (SAG).

eye line   in film, the direction in which you are looking must match the spatial relationship established by the camera in the scene. Usually, the other actor will stand in a spot that will give you the correct eye line. When your eye line is "close to the lens," the other actor may be pressed up against the camera. The DP (director of photography) or the camera operator will guide you in providing the correct eye line.

focus   the thing you are concentrating on at any given moment, usually your objective.

functional traits   those traits your character was given (or that you provide) to allow the character to believably fulfill his or her dramatic function within the story.

givens   more completely, the given circumstances: the world and situation within which your character lives, especially as it affects his or her action. The circumstances include who, when, where, and what.

going up   forgetting your lines. A terrible experience, but if you keep your action going, perhaps even resorting to paraphrase, it can sometimes provide wonderfully rich moments. Lines are learned more tenuously in film than on stage in order to guarantee the kind of freshness and authenticity the camera demands.

head shot   the glossy 8 × 10 photograph actors hand out along with their résumé. It should be attractive but not limiting in the way it portrays you—its function is merely to help someone remember which actor you were.

improvisation   performing without a script. Although most comedic improvs are based on a scenario in which the actors have some idea of the basic beats of the scene and the climax, an "open-ended" improv may be based only on a situation or relationship. In traditional theater, some directors use improvisation as a rehearsal device in which the actors explore their characters in situations beyond those contained in the script. Many good actors are terrible at improvisation, and many good improvisers are better at stand-up comedy than at characterizational acting.

indicating   showing instead of doing, that is, standing outside the reality of your character and playing the emotion or some quality of the character instead of immersing yourself in the experience of the action.

indirect action   When there is some obstacle to direct action, a character may choose an indirect strategy, saying or doing one thing while really intending another. The obstacle may be internal or external. When there is indirect action, there is also subtext. *See also* Subtext.

inner action   the inner process of reaction, attitude, need, and choice that results in outer or observable action. A believable performance integrates inner and outer action into one flow of stimulus and response. This integration is called "justifying" the external action by connecting it to an internal process.

inner monologue   the "stream of consciousness" of the character. As a training or rehearsal device, actors sometimes verbalize or at least think through their characters' inner monologues to be sure they have provided full inner justification for their external actions.

intention   *See* Objective.

justifying   the process of connecting outer (visible or audible) actions to inner needs and processes. The script provides the basis for the outer actions; as much as the script may also hint at the inner action that produces this outer action, however, it is finally the task of the actor to justify it, and in so doing the actor puts his or her personal stamp on the performance.

LORT   League of Resident Theatres, an organization that has negotiated a specific contract with Actors Equity governing the operation of regional theaters that maintain some form of a resident company. Being a member of a resident company, including the various summer festivals, is the best growth experience an actor can have and is the traditional stepping stone from training to a professional career.

Magic If   Stanislavski's technique in which you put yourself in the given circumstances of your character *as if* you lived in that world, then experience your character's needs *as if* they were your own, and choosing and pursuing your character's action *as if* it were your own. This process results in metamorphosis or transformation, whereby the actor "becomes" the character, though without losing the dual consciousness that provides artistic control. *See also* Transformation.

matching   in film, the need to match details and emotional tone from shot to shot. *See also* Coverage.

mark   in film and television, a piece of colored tape that tells the actor where to stand at a specific moment in a scene. The actor must "hit" these marks without looking down.

master   *See* Coverage.

metamorphosis   *See* Transformation.

moment   a brief period of time when something of special value is happening. We speak of "making the moment." Can also refer to one transaction between characters. Several moments work together to make up a beat.

motivation   the inner need that drives your character's action, that usually comes from something that has just happened in the scene, however much it may awaken some long-standing need in your character. It is important that the energy coming from this past motivation drives you toward some objective in the immediate future, since you can't play motivation, only the action toward which it drives you. In other words, *motivation must lead to aspiration.*

need   whatever your character needs that drives him or her to pursue an action to try to satisfy that need. We sometimes distinguish between what we "want" and what we "need"; the dancer *wants* to be able to move beautifully, but he or she *needs* to work at the barre several hours a day. For the actor, either a want or a need will successfully drive action.

objective   the thing your character pursues through action that he or she thinks will satisfy a need. An objective is best defined using a transitive verb phrase, such as "to persuade him to give me a territory in town." In practice, the most useful form of objective is *a change in the other character,* such as "to get him to look at me with compassion." The terms *intention* and *task* are sometimes used to mean *objective.*

off book   memorizing your lines so you can perform without the script. During the period immediately after going off book, it is expected that you will have to be prompted (call for lines), and you should do so without apology so that you do not lose concentration or your sense of action.

out (or in)   on stage, away from center (or toward center).

overlap   *See* Cueing.

pace   the momentum or flow of a scene. Momentum is different than tempo, which refers to the speed of the action. Regardless of tempo, a scene has good pace when the connections of cause and effect, action and reaction, are strong and real so that the action flows with integrity and purpose. Paradoxically, slowing the tempo of a scene will sometimes improve the pace because the actors are forced to experience the connections of action and reaction more fully.

paraphrase   using your own words in place of the words of the script, though with an effort to mean the same thing. Speaking in paraphrase can sometimes help you to examine the meaning of your lines and to "own" or personalize them. It can also help carry you over moments in which you "go up" on your lines. In film and television, a modest amount of paraphrase is sometimes tolerated as a way of producing a more personal performance.

personalization   the indispensable process of making the character's needs, choices, habits, and actions your own. *See* Magic If.

playable   a way of understanding an objective or action that is useful in performance and contributes to the movement of the scene. The most playable objectives are SIP: Singular, Immediate, and Personally important. The best way of defining an objective is as *a change in the other character,* as this will draw your energy outward and into the immediate future, bringing you into strong interaction with the other character.

playing through   letting the action flow with good pace by keeping your awareness moving toward the future objective and avoiding falling into internal feelings or the past. *Your energy is most useful to the scene when it is oriented outward and into the future.*

plot   the sequence of the events as the story unfolds. The actor needs to be aware of how each of his or her actions moves the plot forward, especially when a scene contains a *plot point* that needs to be solidly established.

projection   in the theater, speaking loudly enough and with enough clarity to be heard and understood throughout the auditorium. Good projection is usually more a matter of clarity than sheer volume. In film, however, any sense of projection will read as unreal.

prompt book   the copy of the script kept by the stage manager that contains the blocking, the lighting and sound cues, and all the rest of the physical aspects of a production. It is possible to re-create a production from the prompt book, and this is sometimes done in the case of great European productions. Some of Shakespeare's plays were printed from his prompt books. In film, the script supervisor keeps a book that records every shot and permits the editor to access particular takes in a scene.

prompting   giving the actor the line when he or she asks for it, usually by calling "line." This is done by the stage manager in the theater, and by the script supervisor in film.

prop   anything your character handles. In theater, it is wise to begin working with rehearsal substitutes as soon as you are off book.

public solitude   Stanislavski's concept of how the actor, through focus on the objective, can "forget" that he or she is in public and thereby avoid self-consciousness and stage fright. The concept does *not* imply that the actor neglects the discipline of producing a publicly effective performance.

reacting   allowing yourself to respond to the immediate stimulus in the scene and allowing it to make you do what your character does in response. This requires real hearing and seeing, and the courage to surrender yourself to accepting the stimulus as your partner actually provides it, rather than playing an idea of it that you have in your head. Since everything your character does is in reaction to something, we say that "acting is reacting." The ideal is to be "more moved than moving."

read-through   a rehearsal in which the entire scene or script is read aloud.

reel   a videotape containing a compilation of an actor's appearances on film. A reel may contain work in student films or classroom exercises. Although a reel may be useful in the early stages of a film career, they are rarely worth the effort expended on making them.

relationship   All characters exist in relationship to other characters, and we come to understand a character mostly by observing the way others relate to him or her. For this reason, we say that actors create each other's characters more than they create their own. It is important that you develop your character in specific relationship to the performances of the other actors in your scene.

relaxation   the key to most everything else. For the actor, relaxation is not a reduction of energy; rather, it is a freeing of energy and a readiness to react. The term *restful alertness* is the best description.

repertory   a body of plays performed by a company of actors. When a number of plays are performed on alternating days, it is called "rotating" or true repertory. The regional repertory movement in this country is an important source of entry-level jobs for young actors.

résumé   the sheet listing an actor's basic information and the roles he or she has performed, where and under whose direction, as well as his or her training and special skills.

running lines   two or more actors going over their lines together. The best way to memorize lines.

SAG   Screen Actors Guild, the main union for film and for television shot on film. A powerful union with nearly 100,000 members, 94 precent of whom are unemployed at any given moment. An aspiring actor can join the union by being hired for a union job, though this is a Catch-22 situation. Some agents will represent young actors informally even before they are members of the union, thereby giving them a chance to audition for union jobs.

scenario   a listing of the beats of a scene. Also called a breakdown, the scenario gives the actors a sense of the underlying structure of the scene; it serves them as a sort of map as they move through the journey of the scene.

scene   a section of a play with its own main conflict and crisis. A scene usually contains one of the major events of the story and makes a major change in the plot or central relationship. In film or television scripts, scenes are also determined by changes in location or lighting requirements, and each scene is given a "slug line" as in INTERIOR LIVING ROOM—NIGHT. In some older plays, scenes are marked by the entrance of major characters; these are called French scenes.

score   Stanislavski spoke of the score of a role as the sequence of a character's objectives. The actor comes to understand the logic of this sequence and eventually this flow of action carries the actor through the role, serving as a kind of total choreography for mind and body. *See also* Spine.

sense memory   the use of a memory from the actor's real or imagined past of sensations similar to those required by a scene in order to enrich the actor's response to the scene. Stanislavski believed that every cell in the body was capable of such memory, and he urged actors to develop their storehouse of such memories. Also called *recall.*

set-up   to prepare for the punch line of a joke, the entrance of a character, or some other important event. In television sitcoms, setting up a joke is called "laying pipe." In film, a set-up is one camera position.

shot   in film or television, one piece of film from one camera position, beginning when the director calls "action" and ending when he or she calls "cut."

sides   In the theater, sides are small versions of a play that contained only the speeches of individual characters; these are rarely used today. In film, sides are miniature copies of the scenes to be shot on a given day and are distributed each morning by the second assistant director.

spine   Stanislavski spoke of each beat and scene in a role fitting together like the vertebrae in a spine. When the actor experiences this connectedness, the role begins to flow as if under its own power. Also called the through-line of the role. Similar to the score of the role, in which the through-line is understood as a sequence of objectives.

spiritual action   Stanislavski's term for the inner phase of action, which produces physical or external action.

spontaneity   each moment of a performance should feel as if it were happening for the first time and yet be controllable and consistent from performance to performance. Stanislavski believed that this could be achieved by an act being so fully rehearsed that it becomes "automatic and therefore free," that is, because you don't need to think about it, you are free to experience it afresh each time you do it.

stage directions   the indications in a script about the character's gestures, tone of voice, and so on, such as (*he moves away angrily*). Some teachers and directors tell actors to ignore stage directions because in some so-called acting versions of a play these may have been inserted not by the writer but from the prompt book of an earlier production. However, many writers provide stage directions, and you should consider them for the information they contain about the behavior and emotion of your character, even if that behavior eventually takes a different form in your particular production.

stage fright   Everyone gets it. The only antidote is to be fully focused on the task at hand, and passionately committed to it.

stage right or left   Directions on a stage are given from the actor's point of view as he or she faces the audience; that is, stage right is audience left. In film, the director will say either "move to your right" or "move to camera left."

stimulus   the thing your character is reacting to at any given moment. The most useful stimuli are in the immediate present, however much they may trigger needs or feelings from your character's past.

strategy   your character's sense of how best to pursue an objective within the given circumstances. The strategic choices he or she makes express the way he or she sees the world and the other characters.

substitution   a special kind of emotional recall in which someone from the actor's real or imaginary past is substituted (in the actor's own mind) for the other character in a scene in order to enrich the actor's response to that character. This is a dangerous device because it may take the actor out of the here and now, but with caution it may be useful.

subtext   when pursuing an objective indirectly, your character may be saying or doing one thing while really meaning another. For instance, if I want to tell you I love you but am afraid you will reject me, I may approach the subject indirectly by talking about how stupid the people I work with are, and how you are the only person who understands me. In such cases, there is a difference between the surface activity (the text) and the hidden agenda (the subtext). The character may be conscious or unconscious of the subtext; in either case, it is important that the actor avoid bringing the subtext to the surface of the scene by trying to play or indicate it. (This term is sometimes carelessly used merely to refer to the character's attitude about something or someone.)

superobjective   the character's main desire in life, the life goal toward which each of his or her individual objectives is directed. Characters, like people in everyday life, are often unconscious of this life goal, but it pervades everything they do. Stanislavski also spoke of a superobjective *for the actor,* which was "to understand how every moment of the performance contributes to the reason why the play was written."

suppression   the choice *not* to act in response to a stimulus but, rather, to "hold down" the energy the stimulus has aroused. By allowing yourself to feel the urge to act, then make the effort to suppress it, you can turn a "not doing" into a playable action. A "not doing" is useful because it helps build suspense.

suspense   a condition in which something is about to happen, but the outcome is delayed and in doubt. The more important the potential event, the more doubtful the outcome, and the longer it is delayed, the greater the suspense. The essence is the question, "What will happen?" which, from the actor's point of view, usually translates into "What will he or she do?"

table reading   usually the first rehearsal of a script in which the actors literally sit at a table and read it aloud. During any reading, it is important that the actors try to play in relationship and experience the action of the scene, and not fall into a flat, "literary" tone.

take   in film, a single shot from "action" to "cut." There may be many takes of a given shot until the director is satisfied. The take intended for use will be indicated by the director saying "print it," though several takes may be printed to give the editor a choice of performances.

task   *See* Objective.

technical rehearsal   in theater, the rehearsal in which the lighting, sound, and nearly completed set are first brought together under the command of the stagemanager. At the technical rehearsal, the lighting and sound board operators have their first chance to rehearse their cues, and the designers are seeing the set and props in action. Great patience is required of the actors at a "tech" rehearsal, which is sometimes quite lengthy.

tempo   the speed at which a scene is played, not to be confused with *pace.* The actor must be able to justify the action at any tempo, and Stanislavski would sometimes have actors play a scene at various tempos as a training exercise. Within a given tempo, there are variations which produce rhythm.

temporhythm   the term used by Stanislavski to refer to the whole issue of overall tempo and the variations in tempo that produce the rhythms within a scene. He believed that the temporhythms of a scene were fundamental to the correctness of the action of the scene and could "all by themselves" move the actor to the correct emotion.

through-line   *See* Spine.

transaction   one give and take between the characters, sometimes also called a moment. Each transaction can be judged by asking two questions: First, has one character truly affected the other? Second, does this "link" in the chain of action and reaction move the scene in the proper direction?

transformation   the process by which the actor begins to "become" the character, or, more accurately, make the character his or her "own." To use the language of William James, the character becomes a new "me" to be inhabited by the actor's "I." Stanislavski used the term *metamorphosis*.

universal   the quality of an action, event, or character trait that allows anyone to recognize and respond to it as related to his or her own life.

upstage   *See* Downstage.

upstaging   in theater, literally to position yourself upstage of the other characters so they are forced to turn toward you (and away from the audience) in order to speak to you. In film or theater, this term also refers to any behavior that draws attention to you and away from the other character. To be avoided at all cost.

verb   the verb phrase that succinctly describes your action at a given moment, such as "to persuade." Only transitive verbs are used, and all forms of the verb "to be" (such as "being angry" or "being a victim") are avoided.

visualization   the actor's ability to imagine a situation, to "see" it in the mind's eye. A special and effective form of rehearsal called Visuo-Motor Behavior Rehearsal (VMBR) allows you to visualize your performance while in a relaxed state, allowing your deep muscles to respond to your mental image.

INDEX

Note: This index does not duplicate headings in the table of contents. It is recommended that readers check there for items not found below.